For
Muhsin S. Mahdi,
who taught by showing
what could be done

Alfarabi
The Political Writings,
Volume II

A VOLUME IN THE SERIES
Agora Editions

General Editor: Thomas L. Pangle
Founding Editor: Allan Bloom

A list of titles in this series is available at
www.cornellpress.cornell.edu.

ALFARABI

The Political Writings

VOLUME II

"POLITICAL REGIME" and
"SUMMARY OF PLATO'S LAWS"

TRANSLATED, ANNOTATED,
AND WITH INTRODUCTIONS BY

CHARLES E. BUTTERWORTH

Cornell University Press

ITHACA AND LONDON

First published 2015 by Cornell University Press
First paperback printing 2019
ISBN 978-1-5017-4679-6 (pbk.)

The first volume of *Alfarabi, The Political Writings* is cataloged as follows:

Library of Congress Cataloging-in-Publication Data

Farabi.
[Selections. English. 2001]
Alfarabi, the political writings : *Selected Aphorisms* and other texts / translated and annotated by Charles E. Butterworth.
p. cm.—(Agora editions)
Includes bibliographical references and index.
ISBN 0-8014-3857-8
1. Philosophy, Islamic—Early works to 1800. I. Butterworth, Charles E. II. Title. III. Agora editions (Cornell University Press)
B753.F43 E5 2001
181'.6—dc21

00-012887

The paperback edition was published in 2004 with the ISBN 978-0-8014-8913-6 (pbk.).

This volume has the ISBN 978-0-8014-5380-9 (cloth).

Contents

Preface

Uncertainty about Alfarabi's place of birth and the early years of his life notwithstanding, it is generally agreed that he was born in about 870/256[1] beyond the Oxus River—either in Farab, Kazakhstan, or Faryab, Turkestan. In the course of his life, Abū Naṣr Muḥammad Ibn Muḥammad Ibn Tarkhān Ibn Awzalagh al-Fārābī moved often and thus resided in Bukhara, Marv, Haran, Baghdad, Constantinople, Aleppo, Cairo, and Damascus. The son of an army officer in the service of the Samanids, Alfarabi studied Islamic jurisprudence and music in Bukhara. He then journeyed to Marv where he studied Aristotelian logic with Nestorian Christian monks, most notably, Yūḥannā Ibn Ḥaylān.

While in his early twenties, he left Marv for Baghdad, where he continued to study logic with Ibn Ḥaylān. It is said that he began to study philosophy there by following the courses of the famous Nestorian Christian translator and student of Aristotle, Mattā Ibn Yūnus. At the same time, he improved his grasp of Arabic by studying with the prominent philologist Ibn al-Sarrāj.

Around 905/293 or 910/298, Alfarabi traveled from Baghdad to Byzantium (perhaps reaching Constantinople) to study Greek sciences and philosophy. He remained there for about eight years and then returned to Baghdad where he busied himself with teaching and writing. In about 942/330, political upheavals prompted him to leave Baghdad for Damascus. While in Damascus, he visited Aleppo. A few years later, political

1. That is, 870 of the Common Era and 256 of the Anno Hejirae (the year 622 CE, when Muhammad and his followers fled from Mecca to Medina, which marks the beginning of the Muslim calendar).

turmoil drove him to Egypt, where he stayed until returning to Damascus in 948/337 or 949/338. A little over a year later, in 950/339, he died in Damascus.[2]

Alfarabi's learning was such that he came to be widely acclaimed as "the second teacher," that is, second after Aristotle. Surely the most important philosopher within the Arabic-Islamic tradition, Alfarabi writes in a charming yet deceptively subtle style and couches his observations in simple language and straightforward declarative sentences. Most often, he sets forth an apparently unobjectionable story about natural and conventional things. As the exposition unfolds, it becomes apparent that Alfarabi has accounted for the natural world, political leadership, prophecy, moral virtue, civic order, the organization of the sciences, even the philosophic pursuits of Plato or Aristotle—in short, all the major subjects of interest to humans. He enumerates the reasons for which human beings associate, how civic life can best be arranged to meet the highest human needs, the ways most actual regimes differ from this best order, and why philosophy and religion nonetheless deem it best. These writings, extraordinary in their breadth and deep learning, extend through all the sciences and embrace every part of philosophy.

Alfarabi qualifies as the founder of Arabic-Islamic political philosophy because he is the first to explore the challenge to traditional philosophy presented by revealed religion, especially in its claims that the Creator provides for human well-being by means of an inspired prophet-legislator. This is especially evident in his two accounts of the old political science in the last chapter of the explicitly popular *Enumeration of the Sciences*. Both presuppose the validity of the traditional separation between practical and theoretical science, but neither is adequate for the radically new situation created by the appearance of revealed religion. The two accounts explain in detail the actions and ways of life needed for sound political rule to flourish, but are silent about opinions—especially the kind of theoretical opinions set forth in religion—and thus unable to point to the kind of rulership needed now that religion holds sway. Nor can either speak about the opinions or actions addressed by the jurisprudence and theology of revealed religion. These tasks require a political science that

2. For the preceding biographical observations, see Muhsin S. Mahdi, "Al-Fārābī," in *Dictionary of Scientific Biography*, ed. C. C. Gillispie (New York: Charles Scribner's, 1971), 4:523–526; and "al-Fārābī's Imperfect State," *Journal of the American Oriental Society* 110, no. 4 (1990): 712–713.

combines theoretical and practical science along with prudence and shows how they are to be ordered in the soul of the ruler.

In his *Book of Religion*, Alfarabi outlines this broader political science. He speaks of religious beliefs as opinions and of acts of worship as actions, noting that both are prescribed for a community by a supreme ruler or prophet. His new political science views religion as centered in a political community whose supreme ruler seems identical with the founder of a religion. Indeed, the goals and prescriptions of the supreme ruler are those of the prophet-lawgiver. All that is said or done by this supreme ruler finds justification in philosophy, and religion thus depends on philosophy—theoretical as well as practical. Similarly, by presenting the art of jurisprudence as a means to identify particular details the supreme ruler failed to regulate before his death, Alfarabi makes it depend on practical philosophy and thus to be part of this broader political science. In sum, his new political science offers a comprehensive view of the universe and identifies the practical acumen that permits the one possessing this understanding, either the supreme ruler or a successor endowed with his qualities, to rule wisely. Able to explain the various ranks of all the beings, this political science also stresses the importance of religion for uniting the citizens and for helping them attain the virtues that prolong decent political life. In the *Political Regime* and *Principles of the Opinions of the Inhabitants of the Virtuous City*, Alfarabi further illustrates the new opinions. Their core argument is best stated in the *Attainment of Happiness*—the first part of his famous trilogy, the *Philosophy of Plato and Aristotle*—by his declaration that "the idea of the philosopher, supreme ruler, prince, lawgiver, and imam is but a single idea."[3]

In all these writings, the exposition is seamless. However unusual or at variance with common assumptions the account may seem, it is presented as though it were unobjectionable. Only in two writings—*Selected Aphorisms* and *Summary of Plato's Laws*—does Alfarabi provide a glimpse into differences of opinions with respect to these various teachings. That is to say, Alfarabi's public teaching respects the conventional opinions of his time and place. He also has another teaching at variance with this public teaching—what might be called a private teaching—that points

3. See Alfarabi, *Attainment of Happiness*, sec. 58, in *Alfarabi, Philosophy of Plato and Aristotle*, trans. Muhsin Mahdi (Ithaca, NY: Cornell University Press, 2001).

to the shortcomings in the accepted opinions. Although he never explicitly admits to such a teaching, his rich explanation of Plato's indirectness prompts the suspicion that he follows a similar procedure in his own writing. To grasp its contours, one must make sense of each of these writings and discern how they relate to one another.

It is therefore a special pleasure to present this translation of the *Political Regime* along with the *Summary of Plato's Laws* as a complement to Muhsin Mahdi's translation of the *Philosophy of Plato and Aristotle*, already noted, as well as the recent translation of the *Selected Aphorisms*, chapter 5 of the *Enumeration of the Sciences*, and *Book of Religion*, plus the ever enigmatic *Harmonization of the Two Opinions of the Two Sages, Plato the Divine and Aristotle.*[4] Moreover, it is now possible to announce that these three volumes will soon be followed by two others, one providing a complete translation of the *Book of Letters* and the other a new translation of the *Virtuous City*—the former accompanied by the critical new Arabic edition that Muhsin Mahdi prepared before his death, but never saw into print. Desirable as it might seem to pair the translation of the *Political Regime* with that of the *Virtuous City*, given their many parallels and similarities, the juxtaposition of the former with the *Summary of Plato's Laws* in the present volume permits thoughtful readers to consider Alfarabi's transition from a discussion of what might be to what can be, much as Plato did in the *Republic* and the *Laws*. With the appearance of this volume, then, all who are desirous of learning about Alfarabi's political teaching—able to read Arabic or not—will have accurate presentations of his basic political texts at their disposal.

One of the joys of bringing a work like this to fruition is being able to acknowledge formally all those who have helped in that process. Any mention of Alfarabi's name immediately brings to mind that of Muhsin Mahdi, who has surely done more than any other scholar in recent years to advance our scholarly awareness, knowledge, and understanding of the "second teacher" and his writings. Indeed, Fauzi Najjar readily noted how much his own excellent edition of the *Political Regime* was dependent on Mahdi's discovery of a manuscript that offered a more complete and correct reading of the text than all of the others then known. Likewise, Mahdi drew Thérèse-Anne Druart's attention to one otherwise unknown

4. See Alfarabi, *The Political Writings: "Selected Aphorisms" and Other Texts*, trans. Charles E. Butterworth (Ithaca, NY: Cornell University Press, 2001).

manuscript of the *Summary of Plato's Laws* and then shared a microfilm of yet another with her. His working translation of that text served as the starting point for the one presented here. It is therefore all the sadder that he did not live long enough to see this testimony of his labors come to light. To credit him with having laid the foundations for the study of Arabic and Islamic political philosophy is only to state the obvious, and it is acknowledgment he richly deserves.

The translations of the first part of the *Political Regime* by Miriam Galston, of the second part by Fauzi Najjar, and of the whole text by Thérèse-Anne Druart have been extraordinarily helpful as I have tried to make my way through the text. I can only hope that this new version reflects how very much I have profited from their endeavors to capture the elusive prose of the "second teacher." Special thanks are also due Thérèse-Anne Druart for always giving such ready and gracious access to her astounding collection of recently published articles and books. Joshua Parens has been a most careful and thoughtful reader of this translation of the *Political Regime*, and George Saliba has patiently helped me understand some of the finer points of medieval Arabic astronomy as it relates to this elusive text. Ghada Almadbouh, Gregory McBrayer, and Alexander Orwin have assisted me by their thoughtful reading and critique of the translation of the *Political Regime*, as have numerous students at the University of Maryland and Georgetown University. Similarly, the contributions of Cecilia Martini Bonadeo and Philippe Vallat to the June 2014 Marquette University Abrahamic Workshop in Medieval Philosophy, along with the questions and criticisms of Richard Taylor and the other participants concerning my own presentation of the *Political Regime*, prompted me to reconsider many passages in the introduction and translation. Equally helpful were the contributions from the participants in the NEH Summer Institute for College and University Teachers, "Medieval Political Philosophy: Islamic, Jewish, and Christian," held at Gonzaga University in June 2014.

In translating the *Summary of Plato's Laws*, I profited from the version prepared by Muhsin Mahdi and circulated among his students as well as other interested readers over several decades. Hopefully, my additions and alterations assist our understanding and appreciation of a very elusive text. Comments from colleagues, Paul Rahe in particular, have been most helpful. For encouragement in the difficult task of composing the introduction to this all too enigmatic writing, and constant willingness to hear me out as I essayed one approach or another, I am deeply grateful to Primrose Tishman.

Most helpful in this whole endeavor has been Thomas Pangle. His thoughtful reading of the whole manuscript and pointed questions about translations as well as interpretations assisted me greatly in my efforts to present clear, cogent introductions and translations. In much the same manner, I have benefited from the judicious, thoughtful, critical reading Miriam Galston and Thérèse-Anne Druart have accorded the *Political Regime* and *Summary of Plato's Laws,* respectively. Their generosity of spirit and gifts of sagacious counsel are deeply appreciated. I am also very grateful to Morgan Davis and Brigham Young University Press for graciously permitting me to use the material from Averroës, *The Book of the Decisive Treatise: Determining the Connection between the Law and Wisdom, and Epistle Dedicatory,* translation, with introduction and notes, by Charles E. Butterworth (Provo, UT: Brigham Young University Press, 2001) that appears in appendix B. Finally, it is a great pleasure to acknowledge the support of the Earhart Foundation.

My hope is that all will find some pleasure in seeing the finished product to which their efforts have contributed so much. The faults that remain are my own.

Alfarabi
The Political Writings,
Volume II

Political Regime, Nicknamed Principles of the Existents

Introduction

The Translation

This translation is based on Fauzi Najjar's excellent edition of the Arabic text.[1] Although he indicates the page numbers of the older Hyderabad version[2] in the margins of his text, his edition is so much more reliable and readable that it renders the former one obsolete. For that reason, I indicate the pages of his edition within square brackets in this translation. While I usually follow Najjar's division of the text into major paragraphs or sections, there are occasions when I depart from it. The numbering of the sections is my own, as is their further division into unnumbered paragraphs. Moreover, while accepting Najjar's division of the text into two major parts, I have further divided it into subparts and divisions of subparts—placing them between square brackets—in an attempt to make sense of Alfarabi's larger exposition. To provide an overview of these different divisions of the text, I have placed a summary outline of it before the translation.

In my quest to make sense of this often recondite text and render it into readable English, I have been fortunate to have access to two unpublished working translations—namely, that of the whole work by Thérèse-Anne

1. See Fauzi M. Najjar, ed., *Abū Naṣr al-Fārābī, Kitāb al-Siyāsa al-Madaniyya, al-Mulaqqab bi-Mabādi' al-Mawjūdāt* (Beirut: al-Maṭba'a al-Kāthūlīkiyya, 1964).

2. *Kitāb al-Siyāsa al-Madaniyya* (Ḥaidar Ābād al-Dukn: Maṭba'a Majlis Dā'irat al-Ma'ārif al-'Ūthmāniyya, 1346 AH [1927]).

Druart and also the one Miriam Galston did of part 1—as well as to Najjar's published translation of part 2.[3] Generally speaking, the present translation falls between that of Druart on the one hand and those of Galston and Najjar on the other. That is, it seeks to steer a middle course between the literalness of Druart—one that sometimes makes it difficult to seize the sense of the text—and the more readable, but at times less accurate, renderings of Galston and Najjar. By no means is such a description of these three translations to be taken as a criticism. On the contrary, in the course of seeking to find my own way through this text, I have repeatedly marveled at the wisdom and depth of understanding shown by my predecessors. If I have succeeded in any measure, it is because I have had such excellent guides.

The 2007 translation of *Political Regime*, part 1 by Jon McGinnis and David Reisman[4]—of which I learned only after having finished my own translation—reads more smoothly than the versions of Druart and Galston, but is nowhere near as helpful or trustworthy. In part, that is due to McGinnis and Reisman allowing their sense of how the text should read to guide the way they present what it actually does say. Thus, their lack of interest in the practical—or ethical and political—aspect of Alfarabi's teaching (what they call "value theory"[5]) and predilection for considering Alfarabi as primarily a thinker interested in physics and metaphysics lead them to ignore central terms in Alfarabi's vocabulary. When Alfarabi speaks of the fair or beautiful with respect to human action—what is generally understood as "noble" (Arabic, *jamīl*; Greek, *kalos*)—McGinnis and Reisman translate that as "virtuous." They then translate the term Alfarabi uses for "virtue" (*faḍīla*) as "excellence" and thereby obscure how his use of such terminology allows him to bring his own thinking into line with that of Plato and Aristotle precisely with respect to these issues concerning human action.

Moreover, they render technical terms inconsistently and flout grammatical rules. For example, the title by which the work has been

3. The second draft of Druart's translation dates from 1981 and is available from the Translation Clearing House at the Department of Philosophy, Oklahoma State University, ref. no. A-30-50d. Galston's text was distributed privately for use by students. For Najjar's translation, see "Alfarabi: The Political Regime," in *Medieval Political Philosophy: A Sourcebook*, ed. Ralph Lerner and Muhsin Mahdi, 1st ed. (New York: Free Press of Glencoe, 1963), 31–57.

4. *The Principles of Existing Things* in *Classical Arabic Philosophy: An Anthology of Sources*, trans. Jon McGinnis and David C. Reisman (Indianapolis: Hackett 2007), 81–104.

5. Ibid., xxvii–xxviii.

traditionally known—*Political Regime*—is transformed by them into *Governance of Cities*. They arrive at that formulation by translating a single noun modified by a corresponding adjective (*siyāsa* modified by *madaniyya*) as though it were a single noun in a genitive construction with a plural noun, that is, as though the title were *siyāsat al-mudun*, and by misconstruing the familiar term *siyāsa* as a synonym for *tadbīr*. Similarly, without explanation of any sort, they present the subtitle of this work as its title, while making the title appear to be the subtitle. While this highlights what they deem to be the basic characteristic of Alfarabi's text, it does so by distorting the way the text has been traditionally known and cited.[6] Additional examples could be adduced, but these suffice to indicate that their translation—smoothness notwithstanding—is unreliable.

An excellent way to apprehend the differences between the version of the text they offer and the one I set forth here is to compare our respective translations of sections 4 and 55, below (secs. 4–7 and 57 of their text, pp. 82–83 and 101). In both instances, it is patent that McGinnis and Reisman are more intent on providing an image of what they think Alfarabi should be saying than on putting into English the equivalent of what he has actually said in Arabic. Explanation of what an author says, even interpretation of it, is important and highly desirable as a means of approaching a particular text. But it is not the same as a translation of what the author has composed, for it does not allow the author to express himself in his own voice—difficult as it may be for a translator to decipher that voice at times.

Their procedure apparently stems from conviction that they understand Alfarabi better than he understood himself—an opinion linked to a questionable interpretation of the history of ideas—and that what he actually has to say is not all that important. That disposition likewise guides their introduction to the collection and casts doubt on what might otherwise have proved to be a helpful, lucid summary account of Aristotelian and Neoplatonic doctrines familiar to Alfarabi and other authors in the medieval Arabic-Islamic tradition. It is highly regrettable that blemishes such as these detract from their undertaking, for the texts they present could offer interested readers a fine overview of the writings characterizing philosophy within that general tradition.

The French translations of the *Political Regime* by Philippe Vallat and Amor Cherni have proved useful for making sense of some of the more

6. Ibid., xii.

recondite passages in the text. Solid grounding in the writings of Aristotle, evident in the annotations of both, permits them to identify and propose persuasive solutions to elusive problems. However, Vallat's conjectures about Alfarabi and his teaching, as well as about the text itself, tend to distract more than they help. By contrast, Rafael Guerrero's Spanish translation is commendable and appealing because of its directness even though it has not influenced my own reading of Alfarabi's text.[7]

Part 1 of the *Political Regime* is especially difficult to put into clear English, because it is so laden with terminology evoking a Neoplatonic metaphysical perspective used by Alfarabi to demonstrate its limits, even while presenting a detailed and apparently sympathetic exposition of it. In part 2, he speaks more directly and much more simply about things familiar to most readers. Yet he prefaces that exposition by following the earlier Neoplatonic presentation through to its consequences in human action and thus preserves the unfamiliar terminology of part 1. Moreover, throughout the work as a whole, Alfarabi unduly tries the patience of his reader by using pronouns whose antecedents fade into the mists. Though these antecedents can usually be located, one must wonder why he refers to them by pronouns rather than by their proper names. Still, so as not to prejudge Alfarabi's explanation, I refrain—insofar as is possible in keeping with clear English usage—from replacing the pronouns by their antecedents. For the same reason, I have not capitalized terms like "the first," "the first cause," or "the active intellect." After much hesitation, I also decided to let the text at times read in as stilted and artificial a manner in English as it does in Arabic: while desiring to do nothing that would keep a dedicated reader from following Alfarabi's argument, I also wish in no way to lull that reader into thinking the text is somehow patently clear and simple. The larger goal of this translation, then, is to reflect, as accurately as possible, both Alfarabi's terminology and his repetitive use of it as he painstakingly explains the parameters of the physical and even metaphysical setting in which human associations are formed.

As with the other texts presented in this series of translations, the overriding goal here is to render Alfarabi's prose faithfully in intelligible and readable English. Thus, to the extent possible, a single English word

7. See *Abū Naṣr al-Fārābī: Le régime politique*, trans. Philippe Vallat (Paris: Les Belles Lettres, 2012); *Abû Nasr al-Fârâbî: La politique civile ou les principes des existants*, trans. Amor Cherni (Paris: al-Bouraq, 2012); *"El libro de la política."* in *Al-Fārābī, Obras filosóficas y políticas*, trans. Rafael Ramón Guerrero (Madrid: Debate, CSIC, 1992), 17–70.

is used to render a single Arabic word. Yet because this text is so opaque, and because Alfarabi frequently uses terms in multiple senses, it has at times been necessary to render a single Arabic term by different English terms. When it seemed important to alert the reader to this change in terminology, that has been done via the notes. Moreover, readers are warmly encouraged to consult the Arabic-English and English-Arabic glossaries at the end of the volume for particular questions about Alfarabi's vocabulary and how it is rendered here.

The Teaching of the Text

The *Political Regime* begins abruptly with a detailed account of the universe from something like a Neoplatonic perspective. There is no introduction, nor any attempt to explain what the book is about. The detailed account of the universe reveals it to be thoroughly ordered, with everything that occurs in it forming part of the larger order. There follows an explanation of how human beings fit into that order, of the way political life allows them to fulfill their purpose, and a taxonomy of imperfect cities. Cities are imperfect because their inhabitants misapprehend that order and turn away from conduct that would allow them to achieve human perfection and thus be in accord with the order so thoroughly detailed in the earlier parts of the treatise.

Yet simple reflection reveals that no regime adheres to that order. If all existing political regimes are thus flawed, what can be done to transform them into something admirable? Or, as the subtitle[8] suggests, is the work better understood as a treatise on metaphysics rather than on politics?

Major Themes

The treatise clearly consists of two parts. One focuses on nature and natural existing things as well as the principles beyond nature that guide the existing things. Of concern in the other are human beings, their development and fulfillment or ultimate happiness, and their forms of political association. There are no formal divisions in any of the manuscripts that have come down to us—not even of these two major parts. Thus,

8. As noted, the full title is *Book of the Political Regime, Nicknamed Principles of the Existents.*

the division of the text into two parts, each part into sixty-three sections, and the sections into paragraphs and sentences is my doing. It should be noted, nonetheless, that there are roughly as many pages devoted to the exposition of what is termed here part 1 as to that of part 2. Moreover, almost half of the second part of the text (sections 64–91) continues to elaborate the Neoplatonic perspective that characterizes the discussion in the first part. In the second part, the exposition centers on human beings and their place in the larger cosmic whole, as well as on how a proper organization of human life in political association provides the conditions whereby human beings might achieve their purpose. Only in what is roughly the last fourth of the text does Alfarabi consider political life as it usually is, this perhaps as an indirect indication of why so few human beings attain the ultimate perfection that is their purpose or end.

THE WORLD AROUND US

Six sorts of principles, ranked so that each has precedence over the next, account for the bodies and accidents constituting the world. The first three—namely, the first principle or first cause, the secondary causes (the spiritual existing things that bring about the heavens and the planets), and the active intellect—are in no way corporeal. They are neither bodies nor in bodies. Although the latter three—that is, soul, form, and material—are in bodies, they are not bodies. Not only are there six sorts of principles that comprise six rankings, but there are also six kinds of bodies: heavenly, rational animal, nonrational animal, plant, mineral, and elemental (earth, water, fire, and air).[9]

Such is the world—the cosmos or the universe, the whole. But is it always such? That is, does the world always exist with all of these principles, rankings, and bodies? Or do some come into existence after others, some having been derived from others? If not, are bodies alone subject to temporal constraints? And what about the whole itself? Has it always been such? Questions such as these are not addressed directly in our text, but the numerous allusions to them suggest that coming into existence does not apply to the world—that it has always been as it is described here. Occasional exceptions to this generalization—references to the way

9. *Political Regime,* sec. 1; Arabic text, 31:2–11. See also Aristotle, *On the Heavens* 1.1.268a1–3.6.305a32; *On the Soul* 3.5.430a10–27.

things are "from the outset," to the passage from potential to actual existence, or to forms being created—underline its tenuous character.[10]

What we can infer from this description is that these sorts of principles, these rankings, and these bodies account for all that exists, starting from the most remote cause and coming down through all of the different strata of the heavens to our human sphere of existence—to the sphere beneath the moon. Of the first cause, we are told that it is perfect in all respects and without defect of any kind; that there is nothing prior to it; and that it is distinct, complete, and one. Consequently, it is without material and exists as intellect. Indeed, "it is an intelligible insofar as it is intellect"; that is, "it intellects its essence itself" and "through what it intellects of its essence, it becomes something that intellects and, in that its essence intellects it, an intelligible." In a manner similar to this, it is possible to explain how the first cause may be said to have knowledge and wisdom or how they may be attributed to it.[11] Only when it is so described does Alfarabi's declaration that "the first [cause] is what ought to be believed to be the deity"[12] make sense. Note, moreover, that he does not say the first cause is the deity, but only that it is "what ought to be believed" to be the deity.

There is more. Precisely because the first is first, all else comes from it. Yet there is nothing in the first, which has already been described as complete in and of itself, that needs to give rise to other existing things. Rather, its existence is such that a flowing or emanating of existence from it brings about another thing. Alfarabi explains that because the first "exists for its own sake," then "attached to, and following from, its substance is that something else exists from it." In other words, "its existing such that existence emanates from it to something else is in its substance." This is the way it is. And "its existing such that it becomes substantiated in its essence is the very existence by which something else attains existence from it." Consequently, there is no reason to think of prior and posterior

10. Consider also Alfarabi's comparison of our intellectual apprehension and knowledge to those of the first cause, *Political Regime*, sec. 26; Arabic text, 47:2–4: "There is no link between our own apprehension and its apprehension, nor between our knowledge and its knowledge. And if there is a link, it is a trifling link. Therefore, there is no link between our pleasure, gladness, and delight in ourselves and what the first has of that. Or if there is a link, it is a very trifling link."

11. *Political Regime*, secs. 20–25; Arabic text, 42:14–46:3, esp. 45:5 and 7–8.

12. Ibid., sec. 2; Arabic text, 31:12. Here, as elsewhere, Alfarabi refers to this entity simply as "the first" (*al-awwal*), inviting the perspicacious reader to complete the thought.

when considering the way existence comes about from the first cause: "the existence of what exists from it does not become subsequent to it in time at all; rather, it is subsequent to it only in all the rest of the modes of being subsequent." In other words, the world is eternal.[13]

It is also providential, that is, ordered in such a manner that it is normal or natural for humans to find their fulfillment in the world as do the other existing things. This comes about through the intermediary of the active intellect or, more precisely, by means of its activity. Whereas existence alone suffices for the first cause and the secondary causes, a new mode of existence is introduced with the active intellect. It acts upon human beings by drawing them toward it, but in such a manner that they eventually lose their corporeal attributes in order to become one with it and then to remain in that state of unity. Alfarabi offers no reason for humans needing to shed their bodies. Nor need he do so. Reflection shows how much the body is in tension with thought. But in alerting the reader that "of the active intellect it ought to be said that it is the trustworthy spirit and the holy spirit," he points to a broader context that sheds some light on the stipulation.[14]

Alfarabi's explanation of the universe in terms that take human well-being into account necessarily comes close to opinions expressed in religious discourse and generally accepted by those adhering to the major religious traditions of his day. Indeed, his description of the first cause and the way it works is highly evocative of speech used to describe the deity and its actions. Insofar as the planets move independently of the earth and—although subordinate to the first cause—according to their own principles, it is as reasonable to call such principles secondary causes as to consider them noncorporeal or spiritual existing things. Alfarabi's ready acknowledgment of such parallels or similarities, their superficiality notwithstanding, indirectly suggests that the agreement may be deeper.

To be sure, the fragility, even the questionableness, of his procedure becomes especially evident when he turns to the issue of providence

13. Ibid., secs. 27–28; Arabic text, 47:11–48:17, esp. 48:10–11, 11–13, and 16–17.

14. Ibid., sec. 3; Arabic text, 32:6–12, esp. 32:11. For the Quranic references to these terms, especially that of Quran 16:102 for "holy spirit," see below, n. 3 to sec. 3. See also the reference to "holy spirit" in Alfarabi, *Book of Religion*, sec. 26, in Alfarabi, *The Political Writings: "Selected Aphorisms" and Other Texts*, trans. Charles E. Butterworth (Ithaca, NY: Cornell University Press, 2001); Arabic text, *Abū Naṣr al-Fārābī, Kitāb al-Milla wa Nuṣūṣ Ukhrā*, ed. Muhsin Mahdi (Beirut: Dār al-Mashriq, 1968).

deriving from the active intellect or holy spirit. Or does it? Here, nothing is to be found that resembles Plato's depiction of how inquiries about human concerns pursued by variously gifted speakers invariably leads to confusion or Aristotle's cautious weighing of the pros and cons in the way different thinkers have addressed the same kinds of opinions. By setting forth a single view as the sole account of the whole, expressing no doubts about what he affirms, insisting that what he says fully explains the way things are, and pointing to the way it conforms with generally accepted opinions, Alfarabi forestalls the reader's uncertainty and forces him to figure out for himself just how accurate the portrait is. Still, however necessary, such reflections lead away from the major task of examining that portrait more closely. So let us return to it.

While there are at least as many secondary causes as there are heavenly bodies, the multiplicity of existing things first comes to light with the explanation of the soul. It encompasses not only the souls of the heavenly bodies, but those of rational and nonrational animals as well. The highest manifestation of the soul is reason, the kind of reason that apprehends other entities intellectually. It is highest because intelligence—full rational knowledge of self or essence and thus of existence—is most characteristic of the first cause and thus of the effect it has on all other entities. That is to say, the universe is intelligible. It is such as to be intellectually apprehended. Therefore, whatever is or exists fully and completely has knowledge of itself as it is. In this sense, it is actual and thus substantial.

Now the souls of the heavenly bodies differ from those of the rational and nonrational animals in that they are always actual and thus always intellectually apprehending and in that their souls are less complex. The souls of rational animals—human beings—move from being potential to becoming actual as they intellect more. Those of nonrational animals remain potential because they have no means of intellectually apprehending anything. The rational faculty proper to human beings allows them to intellect, to distinguish between noble and base actions and moral habits, to deliberate about the course of action that ought to be pursued in a particular instance, and to grasp what is pleasurable and painful as well as useful and harmful. Other faculties of the human soul—the appetitive, imaginative, and sense-perceptive—contribute to the functioning of the rational. Thus, the appetitive faculty prompts pursuit and desire, flight and aversion, and gives rise to the various passions. By the imaginative faculty, both the useful and harmful and the pleasurable and painful are apprehended; while the sense-perceptive apprehends only the pleasurable and painful.[15]

It seems, then, that in human beings the appetitive faculty works most closely with the rational and the sense-perceptive least closely. Moreover, while they can apprehend what is useful and harmful as well as what is pleasurable and painful by nonrational faculties, they can apprehend what is noble and base—whether with respect to actions or moral habits—by the rational faculty alone. Thus, nonrational animals endowed with the appetitive, imaginative, and sense-perceptive faculties are able to apprehend both the useful and harmful and the pleasurable and painful. Those not having the imaginative faculty act in response only to apprehensions of pleasure and pain. Simply put, human beings alone can act in accordance with what is noble and base.

The active intellect stands as a demarcation of sorts in the chain of existence. As noted, the secondary causes—that is, the souls of the heavenly bodies—are above it in rank. They attain to an intellectual apprehension of their own existence, then look up to the first cause and seek to apprehend it intellectually. Only on itself does the first cause look. In apprehending its own self or essence intellectually, it apprehends all other existing things. That is evident insofar as it is the first cause. This singular focus on self and on what is higher comes to an end only with the active intellect. Although it forms an intellectual apprehension of the secondary causes, the first cause, and its own self or essence, it also assists the rational intellect of human beings to gain an intellectual apprehension of their own selves or essences. In a manner of speaking, then, the active intellect looks down as well as up.

When human beings gain such an intellectual apprehension, their soul passes from being a potential intellect to being one in actuality. The human being becomes complete, and "his happiness is perfected." To express this transition, Alfarabi has recourse to a simile.

> The status of the active intellect with respect to the human being is that of the sun with respect to vision. For the sun gives light to vision so that,

15. *Political Regime*, secs. 4–6; Arabic text, 32:13–34:10. See also Alfarabi, *Philosophy of Aristotle*, sec. 99, 132:7–10 in *Alfarabi, Philosophy of Plato and Aristotle*, trans. Muhsin Mahdi (Ithaca, NY: Cornell University Press, 2001); Arabic text, *Falsafat Arisṭūṭālīs*, ed. Muhsin Mahdi (Beirut: Dār Majallat Shi'r, 1961): "It has become evident that that necessary [cognizance] is for the sake of this [human cognizance] and that the one we previously supposed to be superfluous is not, but is the one necessary for a human being to become substantial or to arrive at his final perfection."

> through the light procured from the sun, vision becomes actual viewing after having been potential viewing. By that light, it views the sun itself, which is the cause for it having vision in actuality. Moreover, the colors that were potentially seen become seen in actuality, and the vision that was potential becomes actual vision. Similarly, the active intellect provides a human being with something it traces upon his rational faculty, the status of that thing with respect to the rational soul being the status of light with respect to vision.

Even more important than the simile is the explanation Alfarabi provides of what has taken place.

> By means of that thing, the rational soul intellects the active intellect; and by means of it, things that are potentially intellected become intellected in actuality. By means of it, a human being, who is potentially an intellect, becomes an intellect in actuality and in perfection until he comes to be in proximity to the rank of the active intellect. So he becomes an intellect in his essence after having not been like that and an intelligible in his essence after having not been like that.

Finally, Alfarabi notes, the human being thereby "becomes divine after having become material."[16] What this final judgment means, given the context, is that the human being comes to be fully complete or fully substantial by becoming fully intellectual. That is because the divine is intricately linked to the intelligible in this whole exposition.

The looking down put in motion by the active intellect continues with human beings. But their looking down does not result in the elevation of other existing things. Their looking down allows them to explain the role of the nonrational existing things, even those like plants and rocks that admit of being intellectually apprehended yet cannot apprehend anything intellectually in turn, and thus to understand the order among the existing things beneath them as well as those above them.[17] According to what has been posited thus far, it is evident that the first cause as well as

16. *Political Regime*, secs. 7–9; Arabic text, 34:11–36:5. The passages cited are sec. 9; Arabic text, 35:12–17 and 35:17–36:4. See also ibid., sec. 38; Arabic text, 55:7–10 where Alfarabi explains that when "potential intelligibles become actual intelligibles and an intellect that was a potential intellect . . . gets to be an actual intellect," something that "is not possible for anything other than a human being . . . this is the ultimate happiness which is the most excellent perfection it is possible for a human being to obtain."

17. See ibid., secs. 53–63; Arabic text, 62:11–69:14.

the secondary causes and the active intellect are now just as they always have been or that those aspects of the universe above our own—above the sphere of the moon to paraphrase Alfarabi[18]—are eternal. It is only in our domain that change, coming into being and passing away, is to be found. More important, whereas we can affect those higher causes or rankings in no way, we can and must act upon the causes within our sphere. From reflection on the order of the whole, then, we must now focus on how we can turn to our advantage the consideration or providential concern offered us by the active intellect.

HAPPINESS OR ULTIMATE PERFECTION

Just as part 1 of the *Political Regime* may be divided into three subdivisions—one providing an overview of the general principles constituting the universe, another explaining the way the highest principles function, and a final one detailing the operation of the lower principles and their relationship to the higher ones—so part 2 may be divided into three similar sorts of subdivisions. Here, the overview enumerates the different kinds of political or civic associations formed by human beings and how they are affected by natural phenomena, the explanation of the higher principles is an account of the virtuous city, and the one parallel to the lower principles and their functioning is a taxonomy of the nonvirtuous cities.[19] Lest a hurried reader fail to notice the parallel between the two parts, Alfarabi points directly at the end of the first to the continuation of the theme in the second. The very first sentence of the final section in the first part affirms that "some species of animals and plants are able to gain their necessary affairs only by individual members coming together with one another in an association." He continues and explains how different species of animals and plants provide for their well-being with respect to the issue of associating with others in the species or remaining isolated from one another. The reason for such attention to this question becomes patent with the declaration, at the very beginning of part 2, that "human beings are of the species that cannot complete its necessary affairs nor

18. See ibid., sec. 2; Arabic text, 32:3.

19. For part 1, see ibid., secs. 1–14, 15–35, and 26–63; Arabic text, 31:2–39:13, 39:14–53:10, and 53:11–69:14. For part 2, see secs. 64–67, 68–91, and 92–126; Arabic text, 69:16–71:13, 71:14–87:4, and 87:5–107:19. The outline at the beginning of the translation also indicates the divisions of the work.

gain its most excellent state except by coming together as many associations in a single dwelling-place."[20]

These human associations may be classified as perfect and imperfect, with the perfect divided into city, nation, and association of nations. The city stands forth as first among the perfect associations, but not necessarily as most perfect. There is cause to wonder, not only because of the way Alfarabi presents the city with all of its defects in the taxonomy that closes the treatise, but also because of his assertion at the beginning of this second part that "the unqualifiedly perfect human association is divided into nations."[21] If this is his final word, it is one by which he distances himself dramatically from Plato and Aristotle. But it is not certain that this is all he has to say about cities and nations. In the sequel, he tacitly turns his gaze away from nations to speak primarily—albeit not exclusively—about cities. At the very least, Alfarabi raises here a new question about the proper size for sound human association.

For the rest, the political teaching set forth in part 2 is perfectly consonant with the teaching about the universe presented in part 1. Because individual human beings do not have all the virtues needed for human perfection, they work together so that all may obtain what is needed and a few succeed in reaching ultimate perfection. In this, there is no more reason to hope for exceptional aid from the heavenly bodies than to fear interference from them. Good and evil arise from human volition, not from extraordinary intervention on the part of the universal order or anything superseding it. So human beings must learn to choose responsibly, use their volition wisely, and pursue praiseworthy and noble actions rather than blameworthy or base ones. To this end, the primary sciences and primary intellectual apprehensions acquired by the rational part of the soul guide them.

Different natural climates and soils coming about from the interaction between the heavenly bodies and the earth account for the variety in flora and fauna, physical distinctions among human beings, and even diversity in speech—nothing more.[22] Whereas the heavenly bodies thereby play a minor role in human affairs, there is no clearly discernible one on the part of the first cause. Human well-being thus results solely from human effort and striving. Provision for it or providence derives from the active intellect being knowable.

20. Ibid., secs. 63–64; Arabic text, 69:5–17, esp. 5–6 and 16–17.
21. Ibid., sec. 64; Arabic text, 70:5.
22. Ibid., secs. 65–67; Arabic text, 70:5–71:13.

Beginning with a sentient longing to know that functions as will, human beings acquire an imaginative longing as another will and, later, a third will generated from reason. Unique to human beings, it enables them to discern what is worthy of praise or blame as well as what is noble or base and choose between them. Voluntary good and evil become identical to the noble and base as what foster or hinder the intellectual apprehension that is happiness. Due to ignorance or error, it may be misapprehended as pleasure, wealth, honor, domination, or yet other things. Again, having correctly discerned what happiness is, individuals may fail to strive with all their might for it.[23] To do either is to fall short of good action and bring about evil, as Alfarabi explains when discussing the nonvirtuous cities.

Yet simple observation reveals that some humans grasp things intellectually more easily and readily than others, just as some are more attentive to the voice of reason and less lured by passion. Moreover, all too few are those who receive an education teaching them to understand how the things they first discern through the senses fit into the larger whole or how knowledge of some things permits others to be inferred. Even fewer are those fortunate enough to encounter and be able to profit from the instruction of a teacher or guide cognizant of the way things interact. Because such intellectual strengths or weaknesses derive from natural dispositions—the material of which humans are constituted—and are not due to any intention on the part of the heavenly bodies, the role of human volition remains paramount. Though Alfarabi is silent about chance, the absence of intention on the part of the heavenly bodies or first cause must allow it to exist along with the variety arising from material.[24]

In sum, the goal for human beings is to become aware of true happiness, distinguish it from what only appears to be happiness, and use deliberation and other faculties to strive toward its attainment. Those unable to accomplish these actions on their own need teachers and guides. Some may even need to be prodded or compelled by a ruler. There are also gradations among rulers so that some follow the lead of others or discern how to achieve certain kinds of good things, but not all, and thus fall short of bringing their subjects to happiness. The one who can achieve

23. See ibid., secs. 68–69 with sec. 4; Arabic text, 71:14–72:14 and 32:13–33:15.

24. Ibid., secs. 70–77; Arabic text, 72:15–77:17. See also Alfarabi, *Selected Aphorisms*, aphs. 74–75, in *Alfarabi, The Political Writings: "Selected Aphorisms" and Other Texts*; Arabic text, *Abū Naṣr al-Fārābī, Fuṣūl Muntazaʿa*, ed. Fauzi M. Najjar (Beirut: Dār al-Mashriq, 1971).

this stands out as a supreme or first ruler—a king in truth according to the ancients and one of whom, Alfarabi notes, "it ought to be said that he receives revelation."[25] His existence, exceedingly rare, but surely providential, results from his own endeavor and is in accord with the order of the universe. It is not due to the first cause or active intellect singling out a particular human being. Revelation consists in the human being starting from things that are first known and learning about the way the whole functions.[26]

Thus, here, as in what he says earlier about the first cause and the active intellect, Alfarabi intimates how philosophic doctrines sustain and enrich the generally received opinions of his day. He thereby buttresses the popular view, even while indirectly correcting it. Not only does he give new meaning to terms like "God," "holy spirit," and "revelation"; he also uses others familiar to religious discourse, such as *sharīʿa* and *sunna*, in novel ways to indicate their applicability to wider horizons. Lest the occurrence of overly technical or recondite terminology here arouse suspicion that the explanation is not quite orthodox, he brings it all back to the first cause in a reassuring manner:

> This emanation proceeding from the active intellect to the passive intellect by the intermediary of the acquired intellect is revelation. Because the active intellect is an emanation from the existence of the first cause, it is possible due to this to say that the first cause is what brings revelation to this human being by the intermediary of the active intellect. The rulership of this human being is the first rulership, and the rest of the human rulerships are subsequent to this one and proceed from it. And that is evident.[27]

Even the admission that some virtuous few who have profited from the rulership of this remarkable individual may happen to live in separate cities and be governed by other rulers does not detract from the seemliness of the argument. It is as possible for the revelation of that supreme ruler not to hold sway in all places as it is for philosophers to spring up in cities not supportive of its teachings. Both appear strange to the inhabitants of these other cities.[28]

25. See *Political Regime*, secs. 78–82, esp. sec. 80; Arabic text, 78:1–81:4, esp. 79:12–13. See also Alfarabi, *Selected Aphorisms*, aphs. 30–32.

26. See *Political Regime*, secs. 68 and 70; Arabic text, 71:14–72:4 and 72:15–73:8. See also Alfarabi, *Book of Religion*, secs. 1 and 16.

27. *Political Regime*, sec. 80; Arabic text, 79:17–80:4.

28. See ibid., sec. 81; Arabic text, 80:7–11.

As noted, the individual soul that successfully discerns the ultimate principles unites with the active intellect. It attains happiness insofar as it frees itself from body or material. Hence, the virtuous city is one in which the best citizens move on to a noncorporeal existence; only those who have not yet filled their soul with good and rid it of evil remain as citizens. The first ruler, somehow still tied to material, strives to assist these laggards to advance to true happiness. His task, one in keeping with the subtitle of the work, is quite unambiguous:

> Each of the inhabitants of the virtuous city needs to be cognizant of the principles of the ultimate existents, their rankings, happiness, the first rulership that belongs to the virtuous city, and the rankings of its rulership. Then, after that, [each needs to be cognizant of] the defined actions by which happiness is gained when they are performed. These actions are not to be restricted to being known without being done and the inhabitants of the city being brought to do them.[29]

It is not clear when or even how those fortunate enough to attain happiness divest themselves of their material forms. But it is patent that those who do inhabit a city where the citizens are primarily intent on improving their intellectual and moral faculties so as to grasp fully the way things are, thereby attaining happiness, will benefit mightily from the goodwill and gracious conduct of their fellow citizens whatever their own rank in this hierarchical chain marking the pursuit of happiness.

Still, not all human beings can form a concept of the order of things or become cognizant of the principles of the ultimate existing things. Lack of ability or having no experience in such endeavors makes them dependent on images or representations. Happily, that does not matter. The "meanings and essences are one and immutable," even though the language and images used to represent them vary. Differently stated, the type of speech used is less important than what is said. Despite his use of scientific or philosophic language here, Alfarabi readily acknowledges the merit of a presentation that imitates what he has said—one set forth in language appealing more readily to most people and approximating the way things are, the language of religion.[30]

29. Ibid., sec. 88; Arabic text, 84:17–85:2. See also ibid., secs. 83–88; Arabic text, 81:5–84:16.
30. See ibid., sec. 90; Arabic text, 85:14. See also secs. 89–91; Arabic text, 85:3–87:4.

Even so, it all too frequently happens that people are not persuaded by such imitations and persist in pursuing what they imagine to be happiness. Distinct from the best or virtuous city governed by a ruler who strives to lead citizens to what they can achieve of true happiness are ignorant, immoral, and errant cities as well as individuals within the best city who refuse opinions and actions that would ensure their happiness. There are also individuals who see beyond the dominant images in all cities and point to their insufficiency, apparently without success. Their recalcitrance stems from their discernment that the city might aim higher, and they are thus exceptions to the larger exposition.[31] Apart from the passing reference to them, Alfarabi's analysis of these different kinds of cities and the recalcitrant citizens whom he calls "weeds" focuses on ignorant cities, those in which the citizens aim at goods they mistakenly believe will lead them to happiness. The goods in question range from what is needful to preserve their bodies, to wealth, pleasure, honor, domination, and, finally, freedom.[32]

Three things stand out in Alfarabi's account of the ignorant cities and the weeds. First is the fulsome detail lavished upon them, especially in the description of the timocratic and democratic cities, the city of domination, and the weeds. The second is his recourse to unusually strong language when labeling the city intent on wealth as depraved and the one that pursues pleasure as vile. No such terminology occurs in Alfarabi's lengthy account of the city of domination, but there is little doubt he deems it simply the worst. Third is his ambiguous judgment about the necessary, timocratic, and democratic cities—one contrasting starkly with the lack of nuance in his account of the immoral and errant cities. Attributing the rise of the one to the flawed character of the citizens and that of the other to the faulty instruction they received, he voices no hope for reform with respect to either one. Lack of resolve to pursue the actions they recognize as leading to happiness prompts the citizens of immoral cities to succumb to their desires and substitute one of the goals pursued in the ignorant cities, whereas the citizens of errant cities are prevented from achieving happiness due to their receiving a representation of the universe and the existing things different from the one set forth in this treatise.[33]

31. See ibid., sec. 123; Arabic text, 104:17–105:6.

32. Ibid., secs. 94–119; Arabic text, 88:4–103:13. For the immoral and errant cities and the weeds, see ibid., secs. 120, 121, and 122–126; Arabic text, 103:14–104:2, 104:3–6, and 104:7–107:19.

33. See ibid., secs. 120–121; Arabic text, 103:14–104:6.

Because the timocratic city introduces a hierarchical order among the citizens and obliges them to be useful to one another, Alfarabi calls it "similar to the virtuous city" and deems it "the best among the ignorant cities." Subsequently, he revises that judgment and urges that "it is more possible and easier for the virtuous cities and the rulership of the virtuous to emerge from the necessary and democratic cities than from the other [ignorant] cities."[34] Although he offers no reason for the new opinion, perhaps it is prompted by concern that the wrong things might come to be honored in the timocratic city or excessive love of honor lead it to become tyrannic. What sets the necessary city apart, despite its focus on the most basic of human goods—self-preservation—is that it promotes an orderly and successful pursuit of this goal.[35]

That the democratic city—the city or association of freedom—offers promise of such radical transformation arises from the great variety in pursuits permitted in it.

> The democratic city is the city in which every one of its inhabitants is unrestrained and left to himself to do what he likes. Its inhabitants are equal to one another, and their traditional law is that no human being is superior to another in anything at all. Its inhabitants are free to do what they like. One [inhabitant] has authority over another or over someone else only insofar as he does what removes that person's freedom.
>
> Thus there arises among them many moral habits, many endeavors, many desires, and taking pleasure in countless things. Its inhabitants consist of countless similar and dissimilar groups. In this city are brought together those [associations] that were kept separate in all those [other] cities—the vile and the venerable ones. Rulerships come about through any chance one of the rest of those things we have mentioned. The public, which does not have what the rulers have, has authority over those who are said to be their rulers. The one who rules them does so only by the will of the ruled, and their rulers are subject to the passions of the ruled. If their situation is examined closely, it turns out that in truth there is no ruler among them and no ruled.[36]

Freedom and lack of ordered hierarchy, characteristics that seem at first glance to be great flaws, are precisely what allow it to be so malleable:

34. See ibid., sec. 117; Arabic text, 102:3–4. See also sec. 103; Arabic text, 93:13–94:4.
35. See ibid., sec. 94; Arabic text, 88:4–13.
36. Ibid., sec. 113; Arabic text, 99:7–17.

> Of [all] their cities, this is the marvelous and happy city. On the surface, it is like an embroidered garment replete with colored figures and dyes. Everyone loves it and loves to dwell in it, because every human being who has a passion or desire for anything is able to gain it in this city. . . .
>
> Thus this city comes to be many cities, not distinguished from one another but interwoven with one another, the parts of one interspersed among the parts of another. Nor is the foreigner distinguished from the native resident. All of the passions and ways of life come together in it. Therefore, it is not impossible as time draws on that virtuous people emerge in it. There may chance to exist in it wise men, rhetoricians, and poets concerned with every type of object. It is possible to glean from it parts of the virtuous city, and this is the best that emerges in this city. Thus, of the ignorant cities this city has both the most good and the most evil. The bigger, more prosperous, more populous, more fertile, and more perfect it becomes for people, the more prevalent and greater are these two.[37]

As long as doubt about the highest human good prevails or to the extent that it appears to be beyond reach, there is need for a city that permits variety of this sort. Such circumstances make freedom and the association that promotes it—the democratic city—worthy of praise.

Implications

In sum, we learn from Alfarabi's exposition that it is not certain what the universe—and in particular the sphere beneath the moon inhabited by human beings—is like. However, it looks very much as though it is ordered and also as though its order is beneficent with respect to them. Differently stated, it looks to be intelligible or such as to be figured out and that human beings become complete or more fully human to the extent that they do make sense of it. Many signs point to things being like this. But they are no more than signs. That guarded observation is even more warranted with respect to the spheres beyond the moon—the spheres of the heavenly bodies—and with respect to whatever it is that brings all of this into existence.

Yet the more we reflect on these things, the more evident it becomes that such a conclusion is more tenable than one that denies order, intelligibility, or fulfillment of existence. In addition, a conclusion of this sort allows us to make sense of the ephemeral incidents that occur in life and

37. Ibid., sec. 115; Arabic text, 100:11–14 and 100:16–101:5.

of the traditional ways people have tried to make sense of things. It provides a means of understanding better the wisdom of generally accepted opinions and, more important perhaps, of what they try to help us fathom. Still, precisely because we have the fortune of taking such an excellent teacher as Alfarabi for our guide, we must not fail to recognize that what is more tenable is by no means the same as what is more certain.

From him, we have now learned that what occurs in political life mirrors what occurs in the universe—or at least it should mirror it. Just as there is an order in the universe, such that some existing things are subordinated to others according to their functions, so should there be an order in the political realm. Some human beings do perform better actions of concern to all than others, just as some human beings are clearly better at ruling than others. In order that what is established by reason reflect what exists by nature, political arrangements should take into account that human beings are not equal. Even more, those setting down political arrangements should observe the natural differences or inequality of talents that exist among human beings when legislating what human beings do.

Such a lesson raises three questions, each pointing to an important political consequence. First, what is theoretical knowledge really, that is, what is actually known about the universe and its parts or even about human beings? Second, are the differences in ability that can be pointed to among human beings, that is, the inequalities, so important as to be respected politically? Third, what is the significance of those differences not being respected now? Differently stated, but coming back to the same point, does democracy fly in the face of natural order?

All that has preceded in the exposition points to the way our theoretical understanding of the universe and its parts can guide practice, but falls short of showing whether we can realistically claim to possess theoretical knowledge. The account presented here, like any account, is no more than a likely story. If we are to be perfectly honest with ourselves, we must admit that we do not have sufficient theoretical understanding on which to base practice. At best, we have only inferences based on what appears to us—unless this is what theoretical understanding is all about. According to Alfarabi, wisdom—which is one element or aspect of theoretical knowledge or understanding—allows us to discern the unity in all things and eventually to see the one.[38] Even if we do not actually have

38. See Alfarabi, *Selected Aphorisms*, aph. 37.

wisdom, we have some inkling of what it aims at and thus can base our practice on that inkling.

Moreover, reflection about the whole and about the order of the existing things in it, especially our species, gives us some idea of what we can and should strive for in order to reach our end or perfection. Though it is difficult to lay out all the steps for achieving that end in political association, we can point to what is wrong with political associations that do not strive for ultimate happiness. Still, if we are to be perfectly honest about this line of reasoning, we must admit that we discern the error about ends only by analyzing our usual actions and seeking to understand why we perform various activities—what we do them for. Such reasoning falls short of the standards for theoretical knowledge.

Observation of political life today—observation guided by these broader considerations, but clearly not by theoretical knowledge or certainty about the way things are—shows it to be based not on citizens sharing in common goods, but on selfish acquisition. That is, we strive to obtain wealth, honor, or pleasure for ourselves; at most, we show some concern not to harm others while engaged in this pursuit. If we knew what justice were in itself, we could say that such conduct is not just. But even given our present ignorance, we can be sure that it does not build a sense of association.[39] In sum, it is possible to argue persuasively that the pursuit of such ends, especially in this selfish manner, is not the highest goal for human beings. It is likewise possible to make some inferences about what a better human life would entail. Greater certainty is not available.

Another way out of our ignorance is to examine how people interact and to think about how greater unity can be achieved among them. The premise here is that it is good to have unity among those who live together and cooperate for a common enterprise, whether that enterprise be the advancement of a household's welfare, that of a city, a nation, or even—on the off chance that we could come to discern how important it is to respect our common humanity—an association of nations. Were love or friendship to prevail among the citizens of a polity and, even more, were they all to hold the same opinions—opinions, not facts or knowledge—about the beginning, the end, and what falls between the two, there would be great unity among them; and it would have a positive force.[40]

39. See ibid., aph. 62.
40. See ibid., aph. 61.

Now, however, at least two reasons prompt us no longer to consider striving for such unity appropriate—at least not on this level. Although both are based on the practical awareness we have about human beings, neither reaches to the heart of the matter—that is, to determining whether a particular set of opinions is true. First, despite being aware of different opinions among human beings about all of these issues, we can detect no way to reconcile the differences. Nor do they, in fact, admit of being reconciled. The most it is possible to do today is accept them as different and thus refrain from critiquing and criticizing them or arguing against them in order to promote our own. Differently stated, it is possible only to strive to be tolerant of the opinions held by others and to search for a new ground that might promote unity among human beings. (This is, in some respects, what respect for human rights is all about.) Second, what we have learned about the many intolerant attempts over time to force citizens to hold the same opinions prompts us to conclude that endeavors to promote unity must lead to irreparable loss of freedom. We fear such a danger more than the promised benefit unity of opinion might promote.

But this merely leads back to the need to think constantly about the ends of our actions. We rightly fear the intolerant consequences of enforcing unified opinions. These consequences are known. But we fail to consider the yet unknown ones likely to result from people thinking and then doing what they please. Alfarabi does draw our attention to them, however. He first does so somewhat obliquely when, in his discussion of the immoral cities, he passes over the love people have for freedom in silence. Shortly afterward, he points more directly to them in his account of the opinions that characterize one faction of weeds.[41]

With respect to the second question, difference of ability has always been taken into account when there is a focus on practice. That is, no one has compunctions about demanding that a physician, ship pilot, or military leader have precise knowledge of the art in question. Possession of such skills leads to these individuals being distinguished from others in honor or financial reward. Political life differs in part because there is no clarity about what skill or ability is needed for political leadership. Leaders become such only insofar as others agree to follow them. But the art of

41. *Political Regime,* secs. 122 and 125; Arabic text, 104:7–16 and 105:13–107:17, esp. 106:15–107:17.

forming political leaders remains as remote and opaque today as it was during the days of Socrates.

Here, citizens are all too willing to let their ignorance dominate. No one has conclusively shown that there is no such thing as an art of politics. Nor has it been proved that differences among human beings are politically irrelevant. Rather, paying attention to such differences has been ruled undemocratic and thus out of order.

Finally, from the perspective of natural hierarchy, the problem with democracy is that it aims at freedom and equality rather than human perfection. Insofar as those are the ends, calls for democratic or popular rule contribute nothing to human well-being. Hence, the original question returns: Is human perfection, as identified in the natural hierarchy, truly the human end? Should attention to, and focus on, it dominate political practice to the extent that all other considerations become subordinate? At this point, Alfarabi's indirect praise of democracy becomes most relevant. As he suggests, abundant human experience shows that more human goods are fostered in democratic than in monarchic regimes. That observation holds true whether the discussion is focused on Athens as distinct from Sparta or one malevolent and ignorant caliph as distinct from a benevolent and enlightened one.

Important as these political lessons are, additional implications result from the admission of fundamental ignorance that this treatise forces on us. Thus, obvious as Alfarabi's insistence on the need for the soul to separate from the body seems when presented in both the first and second parts of the exposition and as much in keeping as it is with our awareness of human mortality, it is a doctrine fraught with difficulties. At the very least, it turns citizens away from civic engagement and unduly prompts them to pursue private theoretical activities—perhaps even activities tending away from the civic or political and more to the mystical or irrational. Closely examined, then, it appears to be a doctrine more deserving of criticism and rejection. Alfarabi's adoption of precisely that stance in the *Selected Aphorisms* shows that his ready endorsement of it here must be more closely examined.[42]

42. See Alfarabi, *Selected Aphorisms*, aph. 81.

Nor is Alfarabi's teaching in this treatise about the existence of natural evil in addition to voluntary evil as what keeps people from attaining happiness consonant with what he says in other writings, most notably the *Selected Aphorisms* and *Book of Religion*.[43] More important, it compromises his own teaching here about providence. If evil exists by nature, even as a flaw due to material and a means to distinguish individual achievement within species, providence is severely restricted if not simply eliminated. The labored explanation in the first part of the treatise of vipers existing so as to facilitate the dissolution of material has a political parallel of sorts in the second part with the existence of weeds, despite resembling philosophers who attain human excellence. Just as dissonant is the suggestion that natural disasters and other chance events sometimes oblige excellent human beings to live separately in nonvirtuous cities and perhaps forego the attainment of happiness. Such anomalies reveal that the account of the whole presented here, painstaking details notwithstanding, is not as seamless as first appears. In one respect, that may be due to it allowing for no dialectical examination of contrasting opinions. Or it may be Alfarabi's way of pointing to its inadequacy.

That issues like these come to the fore as problematic, even as not admitting of resolution, is in keeping with Alfarabi's allusions here and there to how the treatise buttresses opinions set forth in religion. The subtitle of the treatise, presented as an alternative or substitute title, is "the principles of the existents." Alfarabi explains here not only how concepts developed in philosophy resonate with those presented in religion, but also insists on accepting the different means used to bring citizens to awareness of the principles of existing things. He thus acknowledges that some people can understand these existing things and the way they come about only by forming imaginative representations of them. Coincidentally, if it is reasonable to speak of coincidence with respect to the writing of this "second teacher," the first mention of religion in the treatise occurs in the context of this admission.[44] The explicit sense of the argument is that religion explains the universe and its constituent elements—the existing things, if you will—in the same manner as philosophy, albeit in terms and images easier to grasp. A caveat is in order, all the same: imaginative speech presents the existing things not as they are, but in language that allows people to become aware of them. Reason alone perceives and presents them and their principles fully and accurately.

43. See ibid., aph. 74; and Alfarabi, *Book of Religion*, sec. 27.
44. See *Political Regime*, sec. 90; Arabic text, 85:12–86:10, esp. 85:18–86:2.

The Text

Summary Outline

I. THE WORLD AROUND US (¶¶ 1–63)
  A. GENERAL PRINCIPLES (1–14)
    1. The six principles and their six rankings (¶ 1)
    2. The first cause and the secondary causes(¶ 2)
    3. The active intellect (¶ 3)
    4. The ranking of the soul (¶¶ 4–9)
    5. Form and material (¶¶ 10–14)
  B. PARTICULARS CONCERNING THE INCORPOREAL SUBSTANCES (¶¶ 15–35)
    1. Incorporeal substances other than the first cause (¶¶ 15–19)
    2. The first cause (¶¶ 20–33)
    3. The relation between the secondary causes, the active intellect, and the first cause (¶¶ 34–35)
  C. PARTICULARS CONCERNING THE CORPOREAL SUBSTANCES AND EXISTENCE IN GENERAL (¶¶ 36–63)
    1. Basic difference between the heavenly bodies and the nonheavenly bodies (¶¶ 36–38)
    2. How accidental contraries arise among the heavenly bodies (¶¶ 39–40)
    3. Possible existence (¶¶ 41–43)
    4. The role of form and material in possible existence (¶¶ 44–52)
    5. How the different realms of existence come into existence and assist one another (¶¶ 53–63)

II. THE POLITICAL WORLD (¶¶ 64–126)
  A. THE DIVISIONS OF HUMAN ASSOCIATIONS (¶¶ 64–67)
    1. Perfect and defective associations (¶ 64)
    2. How nations are distinguished from one another (¶¶ 65–67)
  B. THE VIRTUOUS CITY (¶¶ 68–91)
    1. The active intellect and human happiness (¶¶ 68–77)
      a. The active intellect, the heavenly bodies, and will (¶ 68)
      b. Will and choice (¶ 69)
      c. Happiness (¶ 70)
      d. Voluntary good and evil (¶¶ 71–72)
      e. On attaining human happiness (¶¶ 73–77)
    2. Different kinds of rulers or guides to happiness (¶¶ 78–82)
      a. The need for a ruler and qualification for rulership (¶ 78)
      b. The first ruler (¶¶ 79–80)
      c. Those governed by such a person (¶ 81)
      d. The differences in subordinate rulers (¶ 82)
    3. Attaining happiness (¶¶ 83–91)
      a. True happiness occurring in a city (¶¶ 83–85)
      b. What happens when bad actions are established in a city (¶ 86)
      c. The resemblance between the ranks and orders of the city and of the universe (¶ 87)
      d. The need to remove natural and voluntary evils to attain happiness (¶¶ 88–91)
  C. THE DIFFERENT KINDS OF NONVIRTUOUS CITIES (¶¶ 92–126)
    1. The cities contrary to the virtuous city (¶ 92)
    2. The different categories of the ignorant city (¶¶ 93–119)
      a. The necessary city (¶ 94)
      b. The plutocratic city (¶ 95)
      c. The hedonistic city (¶ 96)
      d. The timocratic city (¶¶ 97–103)
      e. The city of domination (¶¶ 104–112)
      f. The democratic city (¶¶ 113–117)
      g. Summary (¶¶ 118–119)
    3. The immoral cities (¶ 120)
    4. The errant cities (¶ 121)
    5. The weeds in the virtuous cities (¶¶ 122–126)

[Part 1: The World around Us]

[A. General Principles]

[1. THE SIX PRINCIPLES AND THEIR SIX RANKINGS]

[31] 1. Abū Naṣr said: The principles that constitute bodies and their accidents—which are of six sorts—are of six major rankings, and each ranking embraces one of the sorts. The first cause is in the first ranking; the secondary causes are in the second ranking; the active intellect is in the third ranking; the soul is in the fourth ranking; form is in the fifth ranking; material is in the sixth ranking. What is in the first ranking cannot be many; rather, it is only one, unique. What is in each of the rest of the rankings is many. Three of them are neither bodies nor in bodies—namely, the first cause, the secondary ones, and the active intellect. And three are in bodies even though they are not themselves bodies—namely, soul, form, and material. There are six kinds of bodies: the heavenly body, the rational animal, nonrational animals, plants, minerals, and the four elements. The whole brought together from these six kinds of bodies is the world.

[2. THE FIRST CAUSE AND THE SECONDARY CAUSES]

2. The first [cause] is what ought to be believed to be the deity. It is the proximate cause for the existence of the secondary [causes] and for the existence of the active intellect. The secondary ones are the causes for the existence of the heavenly bodies; from them, [32] these bodies attain their substances; and from each of the secondary ones results the existence of every one of the heavenly bodies. From the highest of the secondary [causes] in rank results the existence of the first heavens, and from the lowest of them results the existence of the sphere of the moon. From each of the intermediate ones results the existence of each of the planets that are between these two.[1] The secondary [causes] are as numerous as the heavenly bodies; and the secondary [causes] ought to be said to be spiritual existents, angels, and the like.

1. Omitting *al-falakain* ("two planets") with Feyzullah 1279. The idea is that the planets belong between the first heavens and the sphere of the moon.

[3. THE ACTIVE INTELLECT]

3. The activity of the active intellect is looking out for[2] the rational animal and seeking for it to obtain the ultimate ranking of perfection that a human being can obtain, namely, ultimate happiness—which is for a human being to reach the ranking of the active intellect. Now that comes about only by attaining separation from bodies, not having need of anything lesser—not body, material, nor accident—for subsistence, and by always remaining at that perfection.

While the active intellect is one in essence, its rank also embraces those rational animals who have become transcendent and achieved happiness. Of the active intellect, it ought to be said that it is the trustworthy spirit and the holy spirit.[3] It is called by names resembling these two, while its ranking is called kingship and names resembling that.

[4. THE RANKING OF THE SOUL]

4. The principles in the ranking of the soul are many. Among them are the souls of the heavenly bodies, the souls of the rational animal, and the souls of the nonrational animals. Those belonging to the rational animal are the rational faculty, the appetitive faculty, the imaginative faculty, and the sense-perceptive faculty.

It is by the rational faculty that [33] a human being embraces the sciences and the arts; distinguishes between noble and base actions and moral habits; deliberates about what ought to be done or not done; and, in addition, apprehends the useful and the harmful, the pleasurable and the painful. Of the rational, some is theoretical and some practical. Of the practical, some involves skill and some deliberation. By the theoretical, a human being embraces knowledge of what is not such as to be carried out at all; and by the practical, a human being becomes cognizant of[4] what

2. The term is *ʿināya,* which also means "providence."

3. The terms are *al-rūḥ al-amīn* and *rūḥ al-qudus* and are usually taken as epithets of Gabriel. The first could also be rendered as "faithful spirit" or even "trusted spirit." It occurs once in the Quran (26:193), whereas *rūḥ al-qudus* occurs four times. In the first three (2:87, 2:253, and 5:113), it is used in reference to Jesus and is said to have strengthened him. At 16:102, it refers to the agent by whom the Quran was revealed.

4. The verb translated as "becomes cognizant of" is *yaʿrif,* the present of *ʿarafa.* To distinguish *ʿarafa* and its derivatives from *ʿalima* and its derivatives, the former is translated as "to be cognizant of" and so forth, while the latter is translated as "to know" and *ʿilm* as "science" or "knowledge." The goal of such a distinction is to preserve the difference between *gignōskein* and *epistasthai* reflected by these terms.

is such as to be carried out by means of his volition. By the skillful, the arts and crafts are embraced; and by the deliberative, there comes about thought and deliberation concerning each thing that ought to be carried out or not.

By the appetitive [faculty], there comes about the human appetite for seeking or fleeing something, longing for or loathing it, and preferring or avoiding it. By it, come about hatred and love, friendship and enmity, fear and trust, anger and contentedness, harshness and compassion, and the rest of the affections of the soul.

The imaginative [faculty] is what preserves the traces of sense-perceptions after they have been absent from sense and, in waking and sleep, combines some with others and separates some from others in combinations or separations, some of which are accurate and some false. In addition, among the actions and moral habits, it apprehends those that are useful and harmful, pleasurable and painful, but not those that are noble and base.

What pertains to the sense-perceptive [faculty] is evident. It is the one that apprehends sense-perceptible things by means of the five senses of which everyone is cognizant. It apprehends the pleasurable and the painful, but does not distinguish the harmful and the useful, nor the noble and the base.

5. Some nonrational animals are found to have the three remaining faculties apart from the rational one. For them, the imaginative faculty takes the place of the rational faculty in the rational animal. And some are found to have only the sense-perceptive faculty and the appetitive faculty.

6. The souls of the heavenly bodies are of a species different from these souls [34] and are distinct from them with respect to their substances. By them,[5] the heavenly bodies become substantial; and through them, they move in a circle. They are of a more venerable, perfect, and excellent existence than the souls of the species of animals around us. That is because they are in no way potential, not at any moment. Rather, they are always actual because their intelligibles have been continuously attained in them from the outset and because they are always intellecting them.

5. Reading *bi-hā* for sense and in keeping with the parallel *'an-hā* of the next clause, rather than *bi-hādhā* with Najjar and all the mss.

Now our own souls are potential at first, then become actual. That is, at first they are receptive traits disposed so as to intellect the intelligibles. Then, afterward, they attain the intelligibles; and at that point, they become actual.

The heavenly bodies have neither the sense-perceptive nor the imaginative soul. Rather, they have only the soul that intellects. In this respect, they are somewhat comparable to the rational soul. What the heavenly souls intellect are things that are intelligible in their substances, namely, the substances separate from material. Each of these souls intellects the first [cause], its [own] essence, and the secondary [cause] that gave it its substance.

7. Most of the intelligibles a human being intellects pertaining to things in material are not intellected by the heavenly souls because by their substances they are of too high a rank to intellect the intelligibles beneath them. Now the first [cause] intellects its essence, even though its essence is, in some respect, all of the existents. Indeed, when it intellects its essence, it has already intellected all of the existents in some respect because each of the rest of the existents secures existence only from its existence. Each of the secondary [causes] intellects its [own] essence and intellects the first [cause].

8. The active intellect intellects the first [cause] and all the secondary [causes], and it intellects its essence. It also makes things that are not intelligibles in their essences intelligibles. Things that are intelligibles in their essences are things separate from bodies that are not constituted by material in any way, and these are intelligibles in their substances. For the substances of these [intelligibles] only intellect and are intellected; indeed, they are intellected insofar as they intellect, and what is intellected of them is what intellects.

The rest of the intelligibles are not like that. That is, whereas rocks and plants, for example, are intellected, [35] what is intellected of them does not also intellect. Those that are bodies or in bodies are not intellected by their substances, nor is anything pertaining to them that has the rank of substance an intellect in actuality. Rather, it is the active intellect that makes them intelligibles in actuality. It makes some of them intellects in actuality and raises them from the level of existence they are in to a rank of existence higher than what they were given by nature.

Consequently, the rational intellect by which a human being is a human being is not in its substance an intellect in actuality. It is not endowed by nature to be an intellect in actuality, but the active intellect causes it to become an intellect in actuality and makes the rest of the things intelligible in actuality for the rational faculty. When the rational faculty attains to being an intellect in actuality, that intellect it now is in actuality also becomes similar to the separate things and it intellects its essence that is [now] intellect in actuality. And what is intellected of it becomes what intellects. At that point, it comes to be a substance that is intellected in that it is an intelligible insofar as it intellects. And, at that point, what intellects, what is intellected, and intellect come to be a single thing itself in it. Through this, it becomes such as to be in the rank of the active intellect. And when a human being obtains this rank, his happiness is perfected.

Sun allows you to see, active intellect fulfills potential

9. The status of the active intellect with respect to the human being is that *to reason* of the sun with respect to vision. For the sun gives light to vision so that, through the light procured from the sun, vision becomes actual viewing after having been potential viewing. By that light, it views the sun itself, which is the cause for it having vision in actuality. Moreover, the colors that were potentially seen become seen in actuality, and the vision that was potential becomes actual vision. Similarly, the active intellect provides a human being with something it traces on his rational faculty, the status of that thing with respect to the rational soul being the status of light with respect to vision.

By means of that thing, the rational soul intellects [36] the active intellect; and by means of it, things that are potentially intellected become intellected in actuality. By means of it, a human being, who is potentially an intellect, becomes an intellect in actuality and in perfection until he comes to be in proximity to the rank of the active intellect. So he becomes an intellect in his essence after having not been like that and an intelligible in his essence after having not been like that. And he becomes divine after having been material.[6] This is the function of the active intellect, and for this it is called the active intellect.

knowledge of God?

[5. FORM AND MATERIAL]

10. Form is the bodily substance in a body, like the shape of a bed in a bed. And material is like the wood of a bed. So form is that by which embodied substance becomes actual substance, and material is that by which it comes to be potential substance. For a bed is a potential bed insofar as it

6. Or, literally, "hylic," the term being *hayūlānī* ("primordial material").

is wood, and it becomes an actual bed when its shape is attained in the wood. Form is constituted in material, and material is a subject to carry forms. For forms are not constituted in themselves, but need to exist in a subject; and material is their subject. The existence of material is only for the sake of the forms.

It is as though the first purpose were only that forms come to exist. Since they are constituted only in a particular subject, material is established as a subject to carry forms. Therefore, when forms do not exist, the existence of material is in vain. And nothing in natural existents is in vain. Therefore, it is not possible for primary material[7] to exist devoid of a particular form. For material is merely a principle and cause in the manner of a subject for carrying a form. It is not an agent or an end, nor does it have existence by itself without a form. Both material and form are called [37] "nature," except that this name is more fitting for form.

An example of that is vision. For it is a substance. The body of the eye is its material, and the faculty by which it views is its form. By the two of them coming together, vision comes to be vision in actuality. And the rest of the natural bodies are like that.

11. As long as souls are not perfected and do not perform their actions, they are merely faculties and traits disposed to accept the traces of things: like vision before it views and before the traces of things viewed are attained in it, the imaginative [faculty] before the traces of things imagined are attained in it, and the rational [faculty] before the traces of the intelligibles are attained in it and they [all] become forms. For when the traces are actually attained—I mean, the traces of sense-perceptions in the sense-perceptive faculty, imagined things in the imaginative faculty, and the traces of intelligibles in the rational faculty—they then become different from the forms, even though these traces attained in the previous traits are similar to forms in material. They are called forms only due to similarity.

Those most remote from being forms are the traces of the intelligibles attained in the rational faculty. They are almost separate from material, and their existence in the rational faculty is very dissimilar from the existence of form in material. When the intellect actually reaches the point of

7. The term is *al-mādda al-ūlā* and is thus to be understood as different from hylic material; see preceding note.

being similar to the active intellect, it is not then a form nor similar to a form even though one faction homonymously also calls all disembodied substances forms. They establish some forms as separate from material, [that is,] not needing it and being rid of it; and others as not [38] separate from material, namely, the forms we have mentioned. This is one of the divisions of the homonymous noun.

12. There are rankings of the forms needing material. The lowest in ranking are the forms of the four elements. And these four are in four materials. The four materials are of one and the same species. For the one that is material for fire can itself be established as material for air and for the rest of the elements. The remaining forms are the forms of bodies arising from the mixing and blending of the elements, and some are higher than others. For the forms of minerals are of a higher ranking than the forms of the elements; the forms of plants—their variance from one another notwithstanding—are of a higher ranking than the forms of minerals; and the forms of the species of nonrational animals—their variance from one another notwithstanding—are higher than the forms of plants. Next, the forms of the rational animal—namely, the natural traits it has insofar as it is rational—are higher than the forms of nonrational animals.

13. Both form and primary material are the most defective of these principles in existence. That is because each of them requires the other for its existence and constitution. For form cannot be constituted except in material. In its substance and nature, material exists for the sake of the form, and its indeedness[8] is for it to carry the form. When form does not exist, material does not exist—since this material truly has no form at all in its essence. Therefore, its existence devoid of form is a vain existence; and with natural affairs, it is not at all possible for something to exist in vain.

8. The term is *inniyyatuhā*. At the very beginning of his *Book of Letters*, Alfarabi explains "the meaning of 'indeed' [*inna*] is firmness, permanence, perfection, and sureness in existence and in knowledge of a thing. . . . Therefore, the philosophers call perfect existence the 'indeedness' [*inniyya*] of the thing—namely, its very whatness—and they say 'and what is the indeedness of the thing,' meaning what is its most perfect existence, namely, its whatness"; see Alfarabi, *Book of Letters*, trans. Charles E. Butterworth (forthcoming), part 1, chap. 1, sec. 1; for the Arabic text, see *Abū Naṣr al-Fārābī, Kitāb al-Ḥurūf*, ed. Muhsin Mahdi (Beirut: Dār al-Mashriq, 1969). A revised edition of the Arabic, based on new manuscript evidence, will accompany the forthcoming English translation. See also *Abū Naṣr al-Fārābī, Kitāb al-Alfāẓ al-Mustaʿmala fī al-Manṭiq*, ed. Muhsin Mahdi (Beirut: Dār al-Mashriq, 1968), sec. 7/1, 45:4–11; R. Dozy, *Supplément aux dictionnaires arabes* (Beirut: Librairie du Liban, 1968), 1:39b.

Similarly, when material does not exist, [39] form does not exist inasmuch as form needs a subject in order to be constituted.

14. Next, each of the two has a particularly characteristic defect and a particularly characteristic perfection that the other does not have. For by means of form, a body has the more perfect of its dual existence—namely, its actual existence. And by means of material, a body has the more defective of its dual existence—namely, its potential existence. Now form does not exist so that material may exist by means of it nor because it was created for the sake of material. Yet material exists for the sake of form—I mean, so that form will be constituted by it. So, in this, form surpasses material. And material surpasses form in that it does not need to be in a subject to exist, whereas form does need that. Material has no contrary, nor is it opposed by privation. Yet form has privation or a contrary. And it is not possible for what has privation or a contrary to be always existent.

Forms are similar to accidents, since forms are constituted in a subject; and accidents are also constituted in a subject. Forms are distinct[9] from accidents in that the subjects of accidents are not established so that the accidents may exist nor to carry the accidents. Yet the subjects of forms—namely, materials—are established only to carry forms. Now material is a subject for contrary forms and thus receives a form and the contrary of that form or its privation. So it continuously transfers from form to form without interruption and is not more appropriate for a [given] form than for its contrary. Rather, it is equally receptive to the contraries.

form cannot exist w/o material but also material has no meaning w/o form

[B. Particulars Concerning the Incorporeal Substances]

[1. INCORPOREAL SUBSTANCES OTHER THAN THE FIRST CAUSE]

15. None of the defects that particularly characterize form and material attaches to the incorporeal substances. For none of them is constituted in a subject; nor is the existence of any of them for the sake of anything else—not as material, as an instrument for something else, or as serving anything else—nor does any of them need an existence that it procures in the future by acting on something else or by something else acting on it in order to increase. Moreover, there is no contrary to any of them nor any

---

9. Literally, "are separate from" (*tufāriq*).   *form/material have no specific purpose*

opposing privation. And these are more appropriately substances than [40] are form and material.

16. The secondary [causes] and the active intellect are beneath the first [cause]. Even if these ways of being defective do not attach to them, they are not exempt from other defects. That is because their substances are procured from something else, their existence follows upon the existence of something else, and their substances do not obtain perfection such that they suffice unto themselves without procuring existence from something else. Rather, their existence emanates to them from what is more perfect in existence. This is a defect common to every existence other than the first [cause]. *defect = 2nd comes from 1st cause*

17. Moreover, not one of the secondary [causes] nor the active intellect is so sufficient that, by limiting itself to intellecting its essence alone, it attains a splendid and radiant existence or delight, pleasure, and beauty. Rather, for that, it needs to intellect the essence of another more perfect and more splendid being in addition to its [own] essence. So in the essence of each of them there is, in this respect, some kind of multiplicity. For in some respect the essence of what intellects a particular thing becomes that thing, even though it nonetheless has an essence particularly characteristic of it. It is as though the virtue of its essence does not become complete except by some kind of multiplicity assisting it. Therefore, multiplicity in what makes something be a substance becomes a defect in the existence of that thing. *think about something higher to be happy*

Yet it is not in their natures to have a splendid, beautiful, and radiant existence by intellecting what is beneath them in existence, what exists from each of them, or what follows the existence of any one of the existents. For none of these is bound to or inherent in any of them. Nor in order for something else to exist from any of them does the essence of any of them require an instrument or [41] another state apart from its [own] essence and substance. Rather, simply by itself, its essence suffices for it not to have recourse to an instrument or a state other than its substance for bringing something else into existence.

18. The souls that are in the heavenly bodies are free from the modes of defect that are in form and in material. Yet they are in subjects, and in this respect they resemble forms. Still, their subjects are not material. Rather, each of them has a particularly characteristic subject that cannot

be a subject for anything other than it; and in this respect it is separate from form.

All the modes of defect that exist for the secondary [causes] exist for them,[10] and they exceed in defectiveness in that the multiplicity giving them substance exceeds what gives substances to the secondary [causes]. For they attain beauty and delight only by intellecting their essence, intellecting the secondary [causes], and intellecting the first [cause]. Then, in addition, it follows from the existence giving them substance that they give existence to other existents external to their substances. Moreover, they do not suffice so that existence emanates from them to something else without an instrument and without another state coming about. So in each of the two respects, they require other things external to their essences. By "the two respects," I mean their being constituted and that they give existence to something else.

The secondary [causes] are free from whatever is external to their essence, and that holds for each of the two respects. They do not, however, procure splendor and beauty by intellecting the existents that are beneath them nor by their existence being limited to them without existence emanating from it to something else. [42]

19. When the sense-perceptive and imaginative souls that are in animals are perfected by attaining the traces of sense-perceived and imagined things, they become similar to the separate things. This similarity does not, however, draw them beyond the nature of material[11] existence and the nature of the forms.

When the rational part of the soul is perfected and becomes an intellect in actuality, it closely resembles the separate things. Yet it procures the perfection of existence, becoming actual, splendor, radiance, and beauty not just by intellecting the things above it in rank, but by intellecting the things that are beneath it in rank as well and by greatly magnifying the multiplicity in what is made substantial by means of it. When it becomes completely separated from all the parts of the soul apart from it, its existence also comes to be limited to itself alone and does not emanate to anything apart from it.[12]

→ think about 1st cause but also below!

10. That is, the souls of the heavenly bodies.
11. Literally, "hylic" (*al-hayūlānī*); see above, sec. 9, n. 6.
12. Here and in the next paragraph the antecedent is "the rational part of the soul" (*al-juzʾ al-nāṭiq min al-nafs*).

When it becomes separated from the appetitive, imaginative, and sense-perceptive [souls], it is given existence by something apart from it. It is likely that what is attained from it for something else is only so that it increases in more perfect existence by what it does. When it is separated from its instrument, it can have no effect on anything else and remains limited to its own existence. For it is likely that its substance is not such that existence would emanate from it to anything else. Rather, its dose of existence is for it to continue to preserve existence by means of its substance. And with respect to the causes, it comes to be a cause in that it is an end, not in that it is an agent.

[2. THE FIRST CAUSE]

20. There is no defect at all in the first [cause], not in any way. Nor is it possible for there to be an existence more perfect and more excellent than its existence. Nor is it possible for there to be an existence prior to it or in the same rank [43] as its existence that it does not surpass. Therefore it is not possible it would have procured its existence from something other than it that is prior to it; and it is even more remote that it would have procured that from what is more defective than it. Therefore, it is in its substance likewise completely distinct from anything else.

It is not possible for its existence to belong to more than one. For, with anything having this existence, it is not possible that there be any distinction between it and another also having this very same existence. If there were a distinction between the two, what makes them distinct from one another would be something other than what they both share in. Thus the thing by which each is made distinct from the other would be a part constituting the existence of both, and the existence of each of them would be divisible in speech. So each of its two parts would be a cause for its essence being constituted, and it would not be first. Rather, there would then be an existent prior to it by which it is constituted. And that is absurd, since it is first. As long as there is no distinction between the two of them, it is not possible for them to be many—not as two nor as more [than two].

21. Moreover, if it were possible for there to be something else that has this very existence, it would be possible for there to be an existence external to its existence that it does not surpass and that is in the same rank. Therefore, its existence would be beneath the existence of what brings the two existences together, and its existence would then have a defect. For

when something is complete, nothing exists external to it that it can have. Therefore, it is not possible that its existence be external to its essence for anything whatever. Thus, it is not at all possible for it to have a contrary, because the contrary of a thing exists in the same rank as it does. Nor is it possible for there to be any existence at all in its same rank that it does not surpass, lest its existence be a defective existence. [44]

22. Moreover, the existence of whatever has a contrary becomes perfect by its contrary ceasing to exist. That is because a thing having a contrary exists along with its contrary in that they are preserved by external things—things external to their essence and substance. For the substance of neither one of the two contraries suffices to preserve its essence from its contrary. Therefore, it would result that the first must have some other cause for its existence. Thus it is not possible for there to be a contrary in its ranking. Rather, it is alone, unique. So it is one in this respect.

23. Moreover, in its essence it is not divisible in speech; I mean, it is not divided into things that make it substantial. That is because it is not possible for each of the parts of the statement explaining its essence to denote a part of what makes it substantial. Were it so, the parts making it substantial would be causes of its existence in the way the meanings referred to by the parts of the definition are causes of the defined thing's existence and in the way material and form are causes of the existence of what is constituted by them. That is not possible for it, since it is first. If it does not admit of this kind of division, then its being divided according to quantity or the rest of the modes of division is [even] more remote. So in this other respect as well, it is one.

Therefore, it is also not possible that the existence by which it is set apart from the rest of the existents be other than that by which it exists in its essence. So its being set apart from all else by unity is, therefore, its essence. For one of the meanings of unity is [45] the particularly characteristic existence by which every existent is set apart from all else. It is that by which each existent is said to be "one" insofar as it is particularly characterized as being so. So the first is one in this way also and is more deserving of the name "one" and its meaning than any one other than it.

Because it has no material, not in any way, it is an intellect by its substance. For it is material that prevents a thing from being an intellect and from intellecting in actuality. And it is an intelligible insofar as it is an intellect. For that of it which is intellect is an intelligible for that of it which is intellect.[13] To be an intelligible, it does not need another external essence to intellect it. Rather, it intellects its essence itself. Through what it intellects of its essence, it becomes something that intellects and, in that its essence intellects it, an intelligible. Likewise, to be an intellect and something that intellects, it does not need to procure another essence and another thing from outside. Rather, it comes to be an intellect and something that intellects by intellecting its essence. For the essence that intellects is the one that is intellected.

24. The case is similar with respect to it knowing. To know, it does not need another essence through knowledge of which it procures a virtue external to its essence; nor, to be known, [does it need] another essence that knows it. Rather, in its substance it suffices for knowing and being known. Its knowledge of its essence is nothing other than its substance. That it knows, is known, and is knowledge are one essence and one substance.

1st cause simply can & know & intellect itself

25. It is similar with respect to it being wise. Wisdom is to intellect the most excellent things by the most excellent knowledge. By what [46] it intellects and knows of its essence, it knows the most excellent things by the most excellent knowledge. The most excellent knowledge is complete knowledge that does not cease when it concerns what always is without ceasing. Therefore, it is wise not due to a wisdom it procures through knowledge of something else external to its essence; rather, for it to become wise, it suffices that it knows its essence.

26. Beauty, splendor, and radiance in each existent is for its existence to be most excellent and to reach its final perfection. Since the most excellent existence is that of the first, its beauty thus surpasses the beauty of every beautiful thing. Similarly, its radiance, splendor, and beauty belong to it due to its substance and essence—that is, in itself and due to what it intellects of its essence. More pleasure, joy, gladness, and delight follow and are attained by what is most beautiful being apprehended by the most certain

Beauty belongs to 1st b/c at its very essence

13. This apparently circular statement reiterates the point made above in sec. 8, end. As Najjar suggests by his editing, no greater clarity is gained by replacing the clause *alladhī huwa minh 'aql* ("that of it which is intellect") with the clause *alladhī huwiyyatuh 'aql* ("that whose identity is intellect"), from the nearly identical passage in Alfarabi's *Mabādi' Ārā' Ahl al-Madīna al-Fāḍila* (*Principles of the Opinions of the Inhabitants of the Virtuous City*) per Richard Walzer's edition and translation, *Al-Farabi on the Perfect State* (Oxford: Clarendon Press, 1985), 70:6–7.

apprehension. And it is unqualifiedly the most beautiful, most splendid, and most radiant; and its apprehension of its essence is the most certain apprehension and the most excellent knowledge. Thus, the pleasure the first [cause] has is a pleasure whose core we ourselves do not understand and whose great extent we do not recognize except by analogy and in relation to the trifling pleasure we ourselves find when we presume that we have apprehended what for us is more beautiful and more splendid by means of a more certain apprehension—either by sense-perception, imagination, or intellectual knowledge. If in this state we ourselves have attained a pleasure we presume surpasses every pleasure in greatness and we are ourselves in utter delight by what we gain of that, then the analogy between its knowledge and apprehension of what is more excellent and more beautiful and our own knowledge and apprehension of what is more beautiful and more splendid is the analogy between its gladness, [47] pleasure, and delight in itself and what we ourselves gain from that of pleasure, gladness, and delight in ourselves.

There is no link between our own apprehension and its apprehension, nor between our knowledge and its knowledge. And if there is a link, it is a trifling link. Therefore, there is no link between our pleasure, gladness, and delight in ourselves and what the first has of that. Or if there is a link, it is a very trifling link. How is there to be a link between what is a trifling part and what has an extent in time that is unlimited or between what has many defects and what is utterly perfect? If what takes more pleasure in its essence, is gladdened by it, and delights in it with a greater delight, loves its essence, and is more passionate about it, then it is evident that the first [cause] is necessarily passionate about its essence, loves it, and marvels at it with a passion and marvel whose link to our passion in being pleased with the virtue of our essence is like the link of its own virtue and perfection of its essence to our own virtue and perfection at which we ourselves marvel. That of it that loves is itself the beloved, and that of it that marvels is itself the marveled at; for it is the primary beloved and the primary object of passion.

27. When the existence belonging to the first [cause] exists, it necessarily results that the rest of the natural existents not dependent on human choice exist from it according to the way they exist—that is, some observed by means of sense-perception and some known by means of demonstration. What exists from the first cause is in the manner of an emanation of its existence to the existence of another thing and as the existence of

something else emanating from its existence. In this way, the existence of what exists from it [48] is not in any way a cause of it, not as being the end for its existence nor as providing it a particular perfection—as occurs with most of the things that come about from us. For we are disposed so that many of those things come about from us. Those things are the ends for the sake of which we exist, and many of those ends provide us with a perfection we did not have.

28. The purpose of the existence of the first [cause] is not the existence of the rest of the things so that they are the ends of its existence and there is for its existence another cause external to it. Nor in its giving existence does it gain another perfection external to what it has or gain the perfection of its essence the way that is gained by someone who is generous with his money or something else and procures pleasure, honor, rulership, or some other thing from among the goods and perfections by what he spends so that the existence of something else comes to be the cause of his attaining a good and an existence he did not have. All of these things are absurd with respect to the first [cause], because they would eliminate its primacy and necessitate something other than it being prior and being a cause of its existence. Rather, it exists for its own sake;[14] that something else exists from it attaches to, and follows from, its substance.

Therefore, that existence emanates from its existence to something else is in its substance; and the existence by which it becomes substantiated in its essence is the very existence by which something else attains existence from it. It is not divided into two things so that by one of them its essence becomes substantiated and by the other something else is attained from it. Nor does it need something other than its essence and substance for the existence of something else to emanate from its existence, the way we and many other of the existents that act [on others] need that. Nor is its existence by which existence emanates from it to something else more perfect than its existence by which it becomes substantial. Therefore the existence of what exists from it does not become subsequent to it in time at all; rather, it is subsequent to it only in all the rest of the modes of being subsequent. [49]

14. Or "for the sake of its essence" (*li-ajl dhātih*).

29. The names by which it ought to be called are the names that signify perfection and excellence of existence for the existents around us. Yet nothing in those names should signify that it is of the perfection and excellence those names customarily signify with respect to the existents around us, but rather of the perfection that particularly characterizes it in its substance. Moreover, the kinds of perfections that are customarily signified by the many names are many. And it ought not to be presumed that the kinds of its perfections signified by its many names are many kinds into which it is divided and by all of which it is made substantial. Rather, those many names ought to signify a single substance and a single existence that is not at all divided. Moreover, when it chances to happen that, with respect to one [of the existents] around us, one of those names signifies an excellence and perfection external to its substance, what that name signifies with respect to the first ought to be established as a perfection and excellence in its substance. An example is "beautiful," which, with respect to many of the existents, signifies a perfection in color, shape, or position, not in the substance of that thing.

30. Of the names that signify perfection and excellence in the things around us, some signify what it is in its essence and not insofar as it is related to another thing—like being, oneness, and what is similar to that. Others signify what it is in relation to something else external to it—like justice and generosity. With respect to what is around us, these latter names signify only an excellence and a perfection of a part of its essence—that is, the relation it has to something external—whereby that relation comes to be a part of the sum of what [50] that name signifies, and excellence and perfection come to be constituted insofar as they are related to something else. When examples of these names are transferred and the first is called by them and it is intended that they signify the relation it has to something else due to the existence emanating from it, the relation ought not to be established as a part of its perfection signified by that name nor its perfection as constituted by that relation. Rather, that name ought to be established as signifying its substance and its perfection. Let the relation be established as following upon and attached to that perfection and that relation as constituted by its substance and by that perfection it has. And let that relation be established as necessarily following upon and attached to that whose substance was mentioned.

31. Of the names the first shares with other things, some are common to all of the existents and some are shared with some of the existents. From

many of the names it shares with something else, it becomes evident that that name signifies its own perfection first, then that of something else second—according to its ranking in existence with respect to the first, like the name "existent" and the name "one." For these two first of all signify only what makes the first substantial; then they signify the rest of the things insofar as they are made substantial from the first and are secured and procured from it.

32. When many of the shared names that signify the substance of the first and its existence also signify [51] something else, they signify only the similarity—great or trifling—imagined with respect to the existence of the first.[15] Now these names are said with respect to the first in the most prior and most deserving ways and are said with respect to something else in subsequent ways. It is not impossible for our calling the first by these names to be subsequent in time to our calling something else by them. For it is evident that we call the first by many of them as a way of relating it to something else and after our having called something else by it for a particular time. Now it is not impossible for what is prior by nature and in existence to be subsequent in time without any defect attaching to that priority.

33. We have many names to signify generally accepted perfections around us. And we use many of them only to signify those perfections insofar as they are perfections, not insofar as they are those kinds of perfections. So it is evident that for the most excellent of the perfections, than which there is no more excellent perfection, that name is necessarily more appropriate. Whenever we ourselves notice a more complete perfection among the existents, we establish it as more deserving of that name until we ascend to knowledge of[16] what is at the terminal point of perfection and establish it as that name by which the first [cause] is naturally called.

Then we establish the rest of the existents whose state with respect to that name is that of their rankings with respect to the first [cause]—like "existent," for example, and "one." Some of them signify one kind of perfection and not another. Among these kinds is what, with respect to the substance of the first [cause], pertains to the most excellent modes that kind can have raised in fancy up to the most lofty levels of that kind's

15. Reading *fī wujūd al-awwal* for sense, rather than *fī al-wujūd al-awwal* ("in the first existence") with Najjar and all the mss.
16. Adding *ilā* with Feyzullah 1265.

perfection until there remains no manner of defect at all—like "knowledge," for example, "intellect," [52] and "wisdom." With examples like these, it necessarily results that the name of that kind is most appropriate and most deserved.

When a kind of perfection connected to a particular defect and vileness in existence is then isolated from what it is connected to, its substance passes away completely. So it [the first cause] ought not to be called by that kind of perfection. If that is so, then it is even more removed from being called by names that signify vileness of existence.

[3. THE RELATION BETWEEN THE SECONDARY CAUSES, THE ACTIVE INTELLECT, AND THE FIRST CAUSE]

34. Then, after the first [cause], there exist the secondary [causes] and the active intellect. The secondary [causes] have rankings in existence. However, each of them also has a particular existence by which it is made substantial in its essence. And the existence that is particularly characteristic of it is the very existence from which existence emanates to something else. For something else to come to exist from them and for existence to emanate to something else from their existence, they do not need things external to their essences. They all secure existence from the first [cause].

Each of them intellects the first [cause] and intellects its [own] essence. Yet none of them suffices in its essence for being delighted with its essence alone. Rather, it comes to be delighted in itself through intellecting the first [cause] in addition to intellecting its essence. The superiority of the first [cause] over the excellence of its [the secondary cause's] essence is proportionate to the superiority of its delight in itself through intellecting the first [cause] over its delight in itself through intellecting its essence. Similarly, the analogy between its [the secondary cause's] pleasure in its essence through intellecting the first [cause] and its pleasure in its essence through intellecting its essence is proportionate to the increased excellence of the first [cause] over the excellence of its [the secondary cause's] essence. The same holds for its marveling at its essence and its passion for its essence. So what is first beloved and first marveled at in its soul is what it intellects of the first [cause] and, second, what it intellects of its essence. The first [cause], then, according to its relation to these as well, is the primary beloved and the primary object of passion. [53]

35. Therefore, all of these are divided in various ways. The perfection and defect in each of them and what each ought to be called are easy [to discern] according to this example—namely, by our comparing it[17] with what is said of the first [cause]. Each of these secondary [causes] was completely accorded its full existence at the outset; and there remained no existence that it might become in the future lest it strive toward something other than what it was given at the outset. Therefore they neither move nor strive toward anything at all, but from the existence of each of them the existence of each single heaven emanates. From the first of them there results the existence of the first heaven [and so on] until it terminates at the last heaven in which is the moon. The substance of each of the heavens is composed of two things: a subject and a soul. While the soul that is in each of them exists in a subject, it is also the parts of the soul that is actual intellect in that it intellects its essence, intellects the secondary [cause] from which it has its existence, and intellects the first [cause].

[C. Particulars Concerning the Corporeal Substances and Existence in General]

[1. BASIC DIFFERENCE BETWEEN THE HEAVENLY BODIES AND THE NONHEAVENLY BODIES]

36. The substances of the heavenly bodies are divided into many things insofar as they are substances. With respect to the rankings of the existents, they are in the first rankings of defectiveness due to the thing that makes them substantial in actuality needing a particular subject.[18] Therefore, they resemble the substances composed of material and form. In addition, their substances do not suffice for bringing about another thing. And no action upon something else manages to emanate from their perfection and excellence unless it gets them another existence external to their substances and to the things that make them substantial.

External to what makes an existing thing substantial is quantity, quality, [54] or some other category. Therefore every one of these substances

17. Reading *bi-iqtiyāsinā lah* for sense, rather than *bi-iqtibāsinā lah* ("by our acquiring it") with Najjar and all the mss.

18. Namely, the soul; see above, secs. 4 and 6. In saying that "the substances of the heavenly bodies . . . are in the first rankings of defectiveness," Alfarabi means they are the least defective as the subsequent exposition makes clear.

possesses defined magnitudes and shapes, other defined qualities, and the rest of the categories that necessarily follow these.

However, each comes to have only what is most excellent of all that. And it follows that they come to be in the most excellent place, since it necessarily results that each defined body is in a defined place. Moreover, these substances were completely accorded most of their existence; and there remained something trifling not such as to be fully accorded them all at once from the outset, but only such that it exists as theirs in the future gradually and continuously. Therefore, they strive to gain it and do gain it only by continuous motion. Thus, they move continuously and do not interrupt their motion. They move and strive so as to [reach] their finest existence. What is most venerable in their existence and closest to what is most venerable was accorded them from the outset. And the subject of each of them is able to accept no form other than the form it attained at the outset. In addition, their substances have no contraries.

37. The existents beneath the heavenly bodies are at the terminal point of defectiveness with respect to existence. That is because at the outset they were not given everything by which they are made completely substantial. Rather, they were given only their substances in remote potentiality, not in actuality. For they were given only their primary material. Therefore, they are always striving toward the form by which they are made substantial. And primary material is potentially all of the substances that are beneath the heavens. Insofar as they are potentially substances, they move so as to attain substance in actuality. Then—due to their posteriority, backwardness, and vile existence—it obtains that they are unable in and of themselves to be aroused and to strive toward becoming perfected except by an external mover. Their external mover is the [55] heavenly body and its parts, then the active intellect. For both of these perfect the existence of the things that are beneath the heavenly body.

38. Such is the substance, nature, and action of the heavenly body that from it results first of all the existence of primary material. Then, after that, it gives primary material all that is in its nature, possibility, and disposition to accept from the forms, whatever they may be.

By its nature and substance, the active intellect is prepared to look into everything the heavenly body makes ready and gives. Thus it wants to make whatever accepts transcendence and separation from material in some particular way transcend material and privation so that it will come to be in a ranking closer to it. That is, so that potential intelligibles become actual intelligibles and an intellect that was a potential intellect thereby gets to be an actual intellect. It is not possible for anything other than a human being to come to be like that. So this is the ultimate happiness that is the most excellent perfection it is possible for a human being to obtain.

Through these two[19] is perfected the existence of the things that remain subsequent and that—to be drawn out into existence—need the modes such as to draw them out into existence and the modes such as to continue their existence.

[2. HOW ACCIDENTAL CONTRARIES ARISE AMONG THE HEAVENLY BODIES]

39. The heavenly bodies are many, and they move in many sorts of circular motions around the earth. The power[20] of the first heaven, which is one, attaches to all of them. Therefore, they all move with the motion of the first heaven. And they have other powers that make them distinct and in which their motions are different. So, from the power in which the whole of the heavenly body shares, there results the existence of primary material common to everything beneath the heavens. And from the things that make them distinct, there results the existence of the many different forms in primary material.

Then, attached to the heavenly bodies, due to some having different positions from others and different positions from the earth, is that [56] they are close to a thing at times and far from it at times, they come together at times and separate at times, they appear at times and are veiled at times, and they happen to accelerate at times and to slow down at times. These are contraries that are not in their substances, but in the relations of some to others, in their relations to the earth, or in their relations to both.

40. From these contraries that necessarily attach to their relations, contrary forms arise in primary material and contrary accidents and contrary changes in the bodies beneath the heavenly body. So this is the first cause for the contraries existing in primary material and in the bodies that are beneath the heavens. That is because contrary things exist in material either from contrary things or from a single thing that has no contrary

19. Namely, the heavenly body and the active intellect.
20. This is the same term, *quwwa*, that has been translated heretofore as "faculty" and "potential."

in its essence and substance, yet—due to material—has contrary states and links. In their essences, the heavenly bodies are not contrary; but their links to primary material are contrary links and, due to it, they have contrary states. So it is through primary material and the contrary forms inevitably existing in it that possibly existent things are joined together.

[3. POSSIBLE EXISTENCE]

41. Possible existents are the subsequent existents that are most defective in existence and are a mixture of existence and nonexistence. That is because between what cannot not exist and what cannot exist, these two being extremes very remote from one another, there is something to which the contradictory of each of these two extremes applies—namely, what can exist and can not exist. This is a mixture of existence and nonexistence, and it is the existence to which privation is opposed and also connected. For privation is the nonexistence of what can exist. [57]

42. Since the existence of the possible is one of the two modes of the existent, and possible existence is one of the two modes of existence, the first cause—whose existence is in its substance—does not emanate existence only to what cannot not exist; rather, it emanates existence to what can not exist, so that there remains no mode of existence it has not given.

It is not in the nature of the possible for it to have a definite single existence; rather, it is possible for it to exist thus and for it not to exist, and it is possible for it to exist as one thing and for it to exist as its opposite. Its state with respect to the two opposite existences is the same. It is not more appropriate for it to exist as this existence than for it to exist as its opposite.

And opposite here is either privation, contrary, or both. Thus it results that opposite existents exist. Indeed, it is possible for opposite existents to exist in one of three ways: either at two moments [of time]; at one moment, but in two different ways; or as being two things, each of which exists as an opposite of the other. Yet for a single thing to have two opposed existences is possible only in two ways: either at two moments or in two different ways.

43. Opposite existents come to be only through contrary forms. When something attains one of the two contraries, that is its definite existence. What makes it possible for it to exist according to two contrary existences is material. So through material the existence it comes to have is indefinite,

whereas through form its existence comes to be definite. Thus, it has two existences: a definite existence through one thing and an indefinite existence through another thing. Therefore, its existence by dint of[21] its material is at one time to be like this and at another time like that; whereas by dint of its form, it exists like this, alone, without its opposite. Thus, it necessarily results that both existences are given—that is, at one moment according to this and at another moment according to its opposite. [58]

[4. THE ROLE OF FORM AND MATERIAL IN POSSIBLE EXISTENCE]

44. The possible is in two ways: one is what can possibly exist as a particular thing and not exist as that thing, and this is material. The second is what can possibly exist and not exist as it is in its essence, and this is what is composed of material and form.

Possible existents have rankings. The lowest in ranking is what has no definite existence, not in either one of the two contraries—and that is primary material. The ones in the second ranking are what attain existence through the contraries they attain in primary material—namely, the elements. When these come to be an existent through particular forms, through attaining the forms they attain the possibility that other opposite existents[22] also come to exist. They thus become material for other forms so that when they also attain those forms, there arises for them through the secondary forms the possibility that other opposite existents also come to exist through other contrary forms. Thus those also become material for other forms so that when they also attain those [forms], there arises for them through those forms the possibility that other opposite existents also come to exist. They thus become material for [yet] other forms. And they go on like this until they terminate at forms such that the existents attained through them cannot be material for other forms. Thus, the forms of those existents are forms for every form preceding them. These final ones are the most venerable of the possible existents. And primary material is the vilest of the possible existents.

45. The ones intermediate between these two are also in rankings; and whatever is closer to primary material is more vile, while whatever is

21. Or, more literally here and in the next clause, "by right of" (*bi-ḥaqq*). See sec. 46, below.

22. Reading *mawjūdāt* here and in the next two sentences for sense, rather than *wujūdāt* ("existences") with Najjar and all the mss.

closer to the form of forms is more venerable. So the existence of primary material is [such] that it is [59] always for something else and has no existence at all for its own sake. Therefore, if that for whose sake it is created were not to exist, it would not exist either. Thus if one of these forms were not to exist, it would not exist either. Therefore, it is not possible for primary material to exist separate from a form at any moment at all. Now the existents whose form is the form of forms are always for their own sake. It is not possible that through their forms they be created for the sake of something else—I mean, that through them something else be made substantial and that they be materials for something else.

46. The ones that are intermediate may be created for their own sake, and they may be created for the sake of something else. Again, each of them has a right and a merit through its material and a right and merit through its form. The right it has through its material is to exist as another thing opposite the existence it has, and the right it has through its form is to remain existing as it is unceasingly. Now since there are two contrary merits, justice is that each be accorded its portion. So it exists as a particular thing for a moment, then perishes. And it exists as something contrary to the first existence; then that, too, survives for a moment, then perishes. And another thing contrary to the first exists, and so on perpetually.[23]

47. Moreover, the material of each of these contrary existents is the material of its opposite. So each of them has something the other one has, and the other one has something it has. For their primary materials are shared. So it is as though in this respect each has a particular right with respect to each other one that ought to come to each [60] one from each other one. Justice regarding that is evident, namely, that what exists for each ought to be for the other one and they both be accorded it.

48. Possible existents do not of themselves suffice for striving on their own for the existences that remain, for they were given only primary material. Nor, when they attain an existence, do they suffice to preserve their existence by themselves. Nor, moreover, when they have a portion of existence belonging to their contrary, is it possible for them to strive by themselves to exhaust it thoroughly. Thus it results necessarily that each of them has

23. See Aristotle, *Meteorology* 4.1.378b10–379b9; unlike Aristotle, Alfarabi utilizes political terminology here and in the sequel—"right," "merit," and "justice"—to talk about the natural processes of coming into being and passing away.

an external agent that moves and arouses it toward what is its own and to what preserves for it what it has attained of existence. The first agent that moves them toward their forms and preserves these for them when they attain them is the heavenly body and its parts.

49. It does that in [various] ways. One is to move some one of them, without an intermediate or instrument, to the form by which it has existence. Another is to give material a faculty by which it arouses itself on its own and moves toward the form by which it has existence. Another is that it gives a particular thing a faculty by which that thing moves some other thing to the form by which that other thing has existence. And another is that it gives a particular thing a faculty by which that thing gives another thing a faculty by which that other [thing] moves a particular material to the form that is such as to exist in material. In this [case], it will have moved material by the intermediary of two things. Likewise, its moving of material will have been by the intermediary of three or more things according to this ranking.

50. Similarly, it also gives each one what preserves its existence, either by establishing with the form by which it [61] has its existence another faculty or by establishing in another, external body what preserves its existence such that it preserves its existence by preserving for it that other body established for it. That other [body] is the servant of this one in preserving its existence. It preserves its existence either through the service one body gives it or by the mutual assistance of many bodies so disposed as to preserve its existence. In addition, to many of the bodies are connected other faculties by which they act upon similar [kinds of] materials by giving them forms similar to the forms they have.

51. Sometimes when the agent encounters these materials, they have contraries of the forms toward which its wont is to move them. Then it needs another faculty by which to make those contrary forms cease. Since it is likewise not impossible for something else to act upon it in the same way as it acts upon something else and to seek to nullify it just as it seeks to nullify something else, it results that these materials will have another faculty to combat the contrary that seeks to nullify its existence.

That by which it nullifies something else and strips it of the form by which it has its existence may be a faculty in its essence connected to the form by which it has its existence. And sometimes that faculty is in another body external to its essence. So the latter is either an instrument or something serving it for extracting the material disposed to it from the contraries of that body. An example of that is vipers. For this species is an instrument of the elements or their servant in that it extracts the materials of the elements from the rest of the animals. Similarly, the faculty by which it [the agent] makes something similar to itself in species from materials may be connected with its form in a single body, and it may be in another body external to its essence—like sperm in the male animal, for it is an instrument for it.

These faculties are also forms in the bodies that have these faculties. Things like these are for other things—I mean, they are created so as to be [62] instruments or things serving other things. When these instruments are connected to forms in a single body, they are nonseparated instruments. And when they are in other bodies, they are separated instruments.

52. Each of these [possible] existents has a merit by dint of[24] its material and a merit by dint of its form. What it merits through its material is that it exist contrary to the way it does. What it merits through its form is that it exist as it does either [a] for itself alone, or [b] that its existence by dint of its form be for the sake of something else, or [c] that its merit by dint of its form be that something else come to be for it—I mean, that there be another thing created for its sake—or [d] that it have one species in which both objects are brought together—that is, that it be for itself and that it be for something else. So in it there would be something existing for itself and something used for the sake of something else. What is for the sake of something else by dint of its form is either material for it, an instrument, or something serving it. When something else is created for its sake, what is created for its sake is either to be a material for it, an instrument, or something serving it.

[5. HOW THE DIFFERENT REALMS OF BEING COME INTO EXISTENCE AND ASSIST ONE ANOTHER]

53. From the heavenly bodies and the difference in their movements, the elements are first attained, then the stony bodies, then plants, then the nonrational animals, then the rational animal. Individuals of each species

24. Here and in the rest of this section, "by dint of" would be more literally translated as "by right of" (*bi-ḥaqq*).

with innumerable kinds of faculties arise. Then the faculties established in each species no longer suffice for effecting or preserving their existence without the heavenly bodies also coming to assist some of them against others and to impede the action of some upon others by their [different] sorts of motions—changing with one another or succeeding one another. So when they assist this one against its contrary at a particular moment, they impede it at another moment and assist its contrary [63] against it. That is, for example, by increasing heat or cold or decreasing it for those [bodies] such as to act and be acted upon by heat or cold; for they increase it at times and decrease it at times.

Due to their sharing in primary material and in many of the proximate materials and because some of their forms are similar and some forms contrary, there are [other heavenly] bodies below them. Some of them assist others and some impede others—either frequently, rarely, or usually, according to how similar or contrary their forms are. For what is contrary impedes and what is similar assists.

These actions are interwoven in the possible existents and made consonant so that many mixes are attained from them. However, in coming together, they proceed in keeping with a consonance, balance, and measure by which every one of the existents attains the portion of existence allotted to it by nature either according to its material, form, or both.

54. What is according to its form is either for itself, for something else, or for both of them. So according to its form, the rational animal is not for the sake of any other species at all—not by way of material, nor by way of being an instrument or of serving. Every one of them beneath it,[25] by dint of its form, is either only for something else or brings both of them together: existing for itself and existing for something else. Justice is for both its portions to be accorded by nature. Now all of these things happen usually, frequently, or rarely. For a thing to come about rarely is a necessary consequence of its possible nature, and there is nothing [64] strange in it. In this respect and in this way, the possible existents are controlled and governed, and justice proceeds with respect to them so that each possible [existent] attains its portion of existence according to its merit.

25. Reading *dūnah* with Feyzullah 1279, rather than *dūnahā* ("beneath them") with Najjar and the other mss. The "by dint of" immediately following would be more literally translated as "by right of" (*bi-ḥaqq*).

Sometimes, after the things having faculties that effect or preserve [their own existence] have attained these faculties, the heavenly bodies act upon them in ways contrary to their faculties; and they are unable to receive them. Similarly, they are unable to receive the effect of one on another and are too weak for one or the other. The possible things having effective faculties may not be able to be effective, either because of their weakness, because of their contraries making it impossible for them, because of the power of their contraries, because their contraries are assisted by external things similar to them, or because another impediment, contrary in some other respect, impedes the agent from having an effect.

55. Thus it may be possible that the heavenly bodies do not act and do not have an effect on the subjects beneath them. [That is] due not to a weariness within them, but to their subjects not being able to receive their actions or there being another agent from among the possible things that assists their subjects and strengthens them.[26] For since possible things were given their faculties at the outset and left free to act upon one another, it is possible for them to counter the actions of the heavenly bodies or to produce similar ones. And, after giving them those faculties, the heavenly bodies come to aid or impede them.

56. Some of these possible bodies existing by nature exist for their own sake and are not used for another thing nor so that a particular action originates from them. Some are disposed so that a particular action originates from them, either with respect to themselves or with respect to something else. And some are disposed to accept the action of something else.

With what is created for its own sake and not at all for the sake of another [65] thing, a particular action may originate from it in the manner of an emanation of its existence to the existence of something else.

With all of these, when they are in a state of existence such that something tending to come forth from them does come forth without any impediment from them, that state of their existence is their final perfection. That is like the state of vision when it is viewing. When they are in a state of existence such that of itself there does not come forth what tends to come forth from them without their being transferred to a better

26. That is, strengthens the subjects so that they resist these actions and thus do not receive them.

existence than they now have, that state is their first perfection. That is like the link, with respect to writing, between the state of the sleeping scribe and his state when he is alert or like his state with respect to it when he is wearied and resting from weariness and his state when he is writing. When something is in its final perfection and what tends to originate from it is an action, that action will not be postponed and will be attained forthwith in no time. The action of what is at its final perfection will be postponed only by an impediment external to itself. That is like the light of the sun being impeded [from shining] on something covered by a wall.

Things separated from material are in their final perfections from the outset through their substances. None of them is divided into two states: a state in which it is in its first perfection and a state in which it is in its final perfection. Because neither they nor their subjects have any contraries, there is nothing to impede them in any way at all. Therefore, their actions are not postponed.

57. The heavenly bodies are in their final perfections through their substances. The action first coming forth from them is the attainment of their magnitudes, dimensions, shapes, and the rest of what they have that is immutable. The action coming forth from them second is their movements, and this is an action [coming] from their final perfections. There is nothing contrary in them, nor do they have contraries from outside. Therefore, their movement is not interrupted, not at any moment at all. [66]

58. Possible bodies are at times in their first perfection and at times in their final perfection. Because each of them has a contrary, their actions come to be postponed due to both of these causes or due to one of them. For an act [of writing] does not originate from the scribe because he is either sleeping or occupied with another thing, because the parts of writing are not ready to mind at that moment, or because all of these are complete but he has some external impediment. What is intended by the existence of all of these is that they be for the final perfections. A thing comes to have its first perfection by nature and not by coercion only so as to attain its final perfection—either because first perfection is a way to final perfection or because first perfection is something assisting final perfection,[27] as sleep and rest for an animal weary from action give it back strength for action.

27. Literally, "because it is a way to it or because it is something assisting it" (*li-annah ṭarīq ilaih wa immā li-annah muʿīn ʿalaih*).

59. Then, due to their defect, the substances of these [possible bodies] also end up becoming insufficient for attaining their perfections without there existing other existences external to their substances from among the rest of the other categories. That is, by their [the possible bodies] having magnitudes, shapes, positions, and the rest of the categories like hardness, softness, heat, cold, and other things from among the rest of the categories. With many of the species of these bodies, the individuals within each species are constituted from similar parts. And their shapes are unlimited, like the elements and minerals. Yet their shapes are according only to the chance action of their agent or to the shapes of the things surrounding them.

Similarly, the dimensions of their magnitudes are unlimited, except that they are not infinite in magnitude. At times their parts come together, and at times they separate. With some of them, when they are together in a single place, they are joined. And with some, when they are together, they only touch and are not joined. Their disjunction and conjunction is not according to a limited arrangement, but occurs by chance depending on the agent bringing them together and separating them. Therefore, the individuals beneath each of their species are not necessarily isolated from one another. Rather, that occurs with them by [67] chance, because they attain perfection even if these accidents occur in them in any chance way. So these things occur in them as what is equally possible.

60. The individuals beneath each species of plants and animals are naturally isolated from one another and are made unique by an existence that belongs to no other. Therefore, their individuals have a number by nature. Each of them is composed of dissimilar parts limited in number, and each of its parts is limited in magnitude, shape, quality, position, and ranking. The genera of possible things have rankings in existence as we have said.

So the lowest among them assists the highest in [bringing] possible existence to each of them. The elements assist the rest of them in all of their parts by the three means: material, service, and instruments. Minerals assist, but not every one of the remaining species nor by every manner of help. They assist one species by material, another species by service—as do mountains in bringing forth water gushing from springs—and another species by being an instrument. The species of plants may assist animals by these three means. Similarly, the nonrational animals assist the rational animal by these three ways. For some assist it by material, some by service, and some by being an instrument.

61. Since there is no other genus from among the possible [bodies] more excellent than the rational animal, it does not [68] assist anything more excellent than it by any of the means. That is, by means of reason it is not material for anything at all—not for what is above it nor for what is below it. Nor is it an instrument for any other thing at all; nor does it by nature serve anything else at all.

The assistance it offers some possible [bodies] other than it insofar as it is rational is by reason and will, not by nature. We will put off mentioning it now. For sometimes, by means of reason, it carries out actions that are accidentally of service to many of the natural things—like channeling water, planting trees, sowing seeds, breeding and herding animals, and similar things.

By nature, it serves no species other than its own in any way. Moreover, it has nothing by which to serve any other species nor anything at all by which to be an instrument for another species. The assistance the most venerable genus offers the lower genera of possible things is as we have said. So no rational animal serves or assists any of the lower species at all, and that is due to its form.

This ought to be understood as what we hold with respect to the assistance some species offer others.

62. Nonrational animals, insofar as they are animals, are not at all material for anything more defective than they. For none of them is by its form material for the plants. Yet in the way of service or of [being] an instrument, it is not impossible. Indeed, some animals are created by nature to serve the elements by dissolving things distant from them into the elements. For example, poisonous animals naturally hostile to the rest of the species of animals that act hostilely to the rest of the species of animals: vipers, for example, serve the elements by means of their poison by dissolving the species of animals into them. The poisons in plants are like that, yet these are sometimes poisons relatively. For that species serves two things. It ought to be known that predatory animals are not like vipers. Vipers do not have poison in order to improve their nutrition by means of the rest of the animals. Rather, they act hostilely [69] by nature toward all species of animals and are intent on nullifying them. Predators ravish not out of natural hostility, but in searching for nutrition. Vipers are not like that. Minerals as minerals are not material for the elements, but assist them by way of [being] an instrument—like the mountains in bringing forth water.

63. Some species of animals and plants are able to gain their necessary affairs only by a group of individual members coming together with one another in an association. With others, each one obtains what is necessary even if isolated from one another. But it obtains its most excellent state only by individual members coming together with one another. With others, each of the individuals has completed all of its necessary and most excellent affairs, even when isolated from one another; yet, when they do come together, one does not impede another with respect to anything belonging to the other. With others, when they come together, one impedes another with respect to the necessary or most excellent affairs. Therefore, the individuals of some species always isolate themselves from one another with respect to all of their affairs, even procreation, as with many of the sea animals. And some of them do not isolate themselves from one another except for procreation. Others do not isolate themselves from one another for most of what goes on—like the ant and the bee and many others besides these two, such as birds that feed and fly in flocks.

[Part 2: The Political World]

[A. The Divisions of Human Associations]

[1. PERFECT AND DEFECTIVE ASSOCIATIONS]

64. Human beings are [one] of the species that cannot complete their necessary affairs nor gain their most excellent state except by coming together as many associations in a single dwelling-place. Some human associations are large, some medium, and some small. The large association is an association of many nations coming together and helping one another. The medium is the nation. And the small are those the city embraces. These three are the perfect associations.

Thus the city is first in the rankings of perfections. Associations in villages, quarters, streets, and houses are defective associations. Of these, one is very defective, namely, the household association. It is part [70] of the association in the street, and the association in the street is part of the association in the quarter. And this latter association is part of the civic association.[28] The associations in quarters and the associations in villages

28. Or, with equal right, "part of the political association" (*juz' li-al-ijtimā' al-madanī*). As the exposition has developed thus far in this section, Alfarabi is pointing to the size of the association. Thus, while the Arabic word *madanī* ("civic" or "political") derives from *madīna* ("city") and thus reflects the Greek word for city (*polis*), "civic" seems to convey the sense of the argument better than "political."

are both for the sake of the city. However, the difference between them is that quarters are parts of the city, while villages serve the city. The civic association is part of the nation, and the nation is divided into cities. The unqualifiedly perfect human association is divided into nations.

[2. HOW NATIONS ARE DISTINGUISHED FROM ONE ANOTHER]

65. One nation is distinguished from another by two natural things—natural temperaments and natural states of character—and by a third, conventional, thing having some basis in natural things, namely, the tongue—I mean, the language through which expression comes about. And among nations, some are large and some small.

The first natural cause for the difference in nations with respect to these objects are [various] things. One of them is the difference in the parts of the heavenly bodies that face them with respect to the first sphere, then with respect to the sphere of the fixed stars. Then, there is the difference in the positions of the inclined spheres from parts of the earth and what occurs in those parts because of the spheres' proximity or distance.[29] Following that is the difference in the parts of the earth that are the dwelling-places of the nations. For, from the outset, this difference follows from the difference in the parts of the first sphere facing them, then the difference in the fixed stars facing them, and then the difference in the positions of the inclined spheres with respect to them.

66. From the difference in the parts of the earth follows the difference in the vapors that arise from the earth. Because every vapor is generated from a soil, it resembles that soil. Following from the difference in the vapors is the difference in air and the difference in water, due to the water in every country coming into being from the vapors that are beneath the soil of that country. And the air in each country is mixed with the vapor that rises up to it from the soil. [71] Likewise, from the difference in the sphere of the fixed stars facing it, in the first sphere, and in the positions of the inclined spheres follows the difference in air and in water.

From these follow the difference in plants and the difference in the species of nonrational animals; thus, the nutriments of the nations differ. Following from the difference in their nutriments is the difference in the materials and crops from which come to be the people who succeed those

29. The reference is to the spheres within the ecliptic circle and their inclination toward or away from the equator; see Aristotle, *On Coming To Be and Passing Away* 2.10.336a31–336b11.

who pass away. Following from that is the difference in temperaments and in natural states of character. Moreover, the difference in the parts of the heavens that face their heads is also a cause for the difference in temperaments and states of character in a way other than what was mentioned. Likewise, the difference in air is also a cause for the difference in temperaments and states of character in a way other than what was mentioned.

67. Then from the mutual help of these differences and their being mixed arise different minglings according to which the temperaments of nations and their states of character differ. In this way and according to this manner there is a consonance of these natures, a tying of some to others, and rankings of them. And this is the extent reached by the heavenly bodies in perfecting them. Now it is not up to the heavenly bodies to give the other perfections that remain; rather, that is up to the active intellect. To no species other than the human being is it possible for the active intellect to give the remaining perfections.

[B. The Virtuous City]

[1. THE ACTIVE INTELLECT AND HUMAN HAPPINESS]

68. In what the active intellect gives the human being, it proceeds in the way the heavenly bodies do. For it first gives the human being a faculty and a principle by which to strive, or by which the human being is able to strive on his own for the rest of the perfections that remain for him. That principle is the primary sciences and the primary intelligibles [72] attained in the rational part of the soul. It gives him those cognitions and those intelligibles only after the human being first proceeds and attains the sense-perceptive and the appetitive parts of the soul through which there come about the longing and loathing following upon sense-perception, as well as the instruments of these two from the parts of the body. Through these two, will is attained.

69. Will is at first only a longing [that comes] from sensation. Longing comes about through the appetitive part and sensation through the sense-perceptive part.

Then, by attaining the imaginative part of the soul and the longing that follows upon it after that, a second will is attained after the first. So this will is a longing [that comes] from imagination. After these two are attained, it is possible to attain in the rational part the primary cognitions from the active intellect.

At this point, a third kind of will is generated in the human being, namely, the longing [that comes] from reason. This is what is particularly characterized by the name "choice." This is what is in the human being in particular, apart from the rest of the animals. Through this, a human being is able to do what is praiseworthy or blameworthy, noble or base. And because of this, there is reward and punishment. Now the first two wills may come about in nonrational animals. When this [third will] is attained by the human being, it enables him to strive toward happiness or not to do so. Through it he is able to do good or to do bad, the noble or the base.

70. Happiness is unqualified good. Whatever is useful for obtaining happiness and gaining it is also good, not for its own sake but for the sake of its usefulness with respect to happiness. Whatever impedes from happiness in any way is unqualified evil. The good useful for obtaining happiness may be something existing by nature, and that may come about by will. The evil that impedes from happiness may be something [73] that exists by nature, and it may come about by will.

That which is by nature is given only by the heavenly bodies, but not from an intention on their part to help the active intellect toward its purpose nor as an intention to hamper it. For the things useful for the active intellect's purpose, as given by the heavenly bodies, come not from an intention on their part to help the active intellect in that; nor are the natural things that impede it from its purpose due to the heavenly bodies having an intention contrary to the active intellect with respect to that. Rather it is in the substance of the heavenly bodies to give whatever is in the nature of material to receive without their caring about what is useful or harmful to the purpose of the active intellect. Therefore, it is not impossible that in the sum of what is attained from the heavenly bodies there at times be what is suitable to the purpose of the active intellect and at times what is contrary to it.

71. Voluntary good and voluntary evil—namely, the noble and the base—are both generated by the human being in particular. Voluntary good is generated in only one way. That is because the faculties of the human soul are five: the theoretical-rational, the practical-rational, the appetitive, the imaginative, and the sense-perceptive. Happiness, which only the human being can intellect and be conscious of, is [cognized] by

means of the theoretical-rational faculty—not by any other of the rest of the faculties—and that is when he uses the principles and the first cognitions that the active intellect gave him.

For when he is cognizant of it,[30] he then longs for it by means of the appetitive faculty. He deliberates by means of the practical-rational [faculty] about what he ought to do so as to gain it. By means of the instruments of the appetitive [faculty], he does the actions he infers by means of deliberation. The imaginative and the sense-perceptive [faculties] contribute to and are led by the rational [faculty]. They assist it in arousing the human being to the actions by which he gains happiness. Then, everything that a human being generates is good. In this way alone is voluntary good generated. [74]

72. Voluntary evil is generated in the way I will state. Now neither the imaginative nor the sense-perceptive [faculty] is conscious of happiness. Nor is the rational [faculty] conscious of happiness in every state. Rather, the rational [faculty] is conscious of happiness only when it strives to apprehend it. There are many things here that make it possible for the human being to imagine that they are what ought to be the aim and the end in life—like the pleasant and the useful, honor, and similar things.

When a human being slackens in perfecting the theoretical-rational part, he is not conscious of happiness so as to have an appetite for it. He sets up as the goal he is intent on in his life something other than happiness—such as what is useful, what is pleasant, domination, or honor. He longs for it with the appetitive [faculty]. By means of the practical-rational [faculty], he deliberates so as to infer what will gain that end. By means of the instruments of the appetitive faculty, he does those things he has inferred. And the imaginative and the sense-perceptive [faculties] contribute to that. Then, everything that he generates is evil.

Likewise, a human being may have apprehended happiness and become cognizant of it. Yet he does not set it down as his aim and end. He does not long for it or has only a weak longing for it. He sets down as the end he longs for in life another thing other than happiness. And he uses all the rest of his faculties to gain that end. Everything that he generates is evil.

30. That is, happiness.

73. Since what is intended by the existence of the human being is that he obtain happiness, that being the ultimate perfection remaining to be given to the possible existents able to receive it, the way by which it is possible for a human being to come to this happiness ought to be stated. Now that is possible only by the active intellect having first given the primary intelligibles, which are the primary cognitions. Not every human being is created so as to be disposed to receive the first intelligibles, because individual human beings are by nature generated with varied faculties and divergent preparations. So some of them do not by nature receive any of the primary intelligibles. [75] Others receive them, but not as they are—like mad persons. And others receive them as they are. These are the ones whose human innate character is sound. These, in particular, and not the others, are able to gain happiness.

74. People whose innate character is sound share in an innate character that disposes them to receive the intelligibles in which they all share and by which they strive toward objects and actions common to all of them. Then, afterward, they diverge and differ, thereby coming to an innate character that is particular to each one [of them] and to each group. So one among them is disposed to receive certain other intelligibles that are not shared, but are particular [to him], by which he strives toward another genus. Another is disposed to receive other intelligibles that are fitting to be used in a certain other genus without one [person] sharing with his companion in any of what is particular to him. One [person] is disposed to receive many intelligibles that are fitting for one thing in a certain genus, and another is disposed to receive many intelligibles that are fitting for everything in that genus.

Similarly, they may also differ and vary concerning the faculties by which they infer the objects that, concerning a certain genus, are such as to be apprehended by inference. Thus it is not impossible for there to be two [human beings] who are given the very same intelligibles that are fitting for a certain genus, while one of the two naturally infers fewer things with respect to that genus by means of those intelligibles and the other naturally has the ability to infer everything in that genus. Similarly, two [human beings] may have an equal ability to infer the very same things, while one of the two is quicker at inferring and the other slower, or one of the two is quicker at inferring what is most excellent with respect to that genus and the other what is most vile with respect to that genus. There also may be two [human beings] who have an equal ability for inference and for speed, while one of the two has in addition an ability to guide someone else and to instruct in what he has [76] already inferred, and the other has no ability for guidance or instruction. Similarly, they may be equal with respect to ability for bodily actions.

75. The innate characters that come about by nature do not force anyone or make it necessary for anyone to do that. Rather, it is only that due to these innate characters it comes to be easier for them to do that thing toward which they are disposed by nature. And when an individual is left to his passion and nothing external moves him to its contrary, he is aroused to [do] that thing to which he was said to be disposed. When some external mover moves him to the contrary of that, he is also aroused to its contrary—but with adversity, distress, and hardship, whereas that to which he is accustomed is easy. Those for whom a certain thing is natural may happen to be very adverse to change from what they were created for; indeed, for many of them it may not be possible. That is because their brains were struck at birth by a disease and a natural chronic illness.

76. In addition to what was made natural for them, all of these innate characters need to have the will trained and be educated in the things toward which they are disposed in order that through those things they come to their final perfections or [come] close to the final ones. In a certain genus there may be extraordinary, superb innate characters that are neglected and not trained or educated in the things toward which they are disposed. So as time is drawn out in that way, their strength becomes nullified. And some among them may be educated in the vile things in that genus. Thus they emerge as extraordinary in doing and inferring the vile things from that genus. [77]

77. By nature, people vary with respect to rankings in accordance with the variation in the rankings of the kinds[31] of arts and sciences toward which they are naturally disposed. Then, those who are disposed by nature toward a certain kind [of art and science] vary in accordance with the variation in the parts of that kind. For those who are disposed to a

31. The term is "genera" (*ajnās*). Here and in what follows in this section, Alfarabi uses this term or the singular "genus" (*jins*) when speaking of the different sorts of arts and sciences.

viler part of that kind [of art and science] are beneath those who are disposed to a more excellent part. Then, those who are naturally disposed to a certain kind [of art and science] or to a part of that kind also vary in accordance with the perfection or defectiveness of [their] being disposed.

Then, afterward, inhabitants of equal natures vary with respect to the way they are educated in the things toward which they are disposed. Those who are equally educated vary according to their ability with respect to inference. For the one who has an ability to infer with respect to a certain kind [of art and science] is the ruler over one having no ability to infer what is in that kind. And one having the ability to infer more things is the ruler over one having the ability to infer only fewer things.

Then, the latter vary with respect to the faculties they have procured from education for good or bad guidance and instruction. For the one who has the ability for good guidance and instruction is the ruler over one having no faculty for guidance.[32] Moreover, when those possessing natures more defective with respect to a particular kind [of art and science] than the extraordinary natures are educated in that kind, they become more excellent [in it] than one of the inhabitants with extraordinary natures not educated in anything. Those educated in what is most excellent with respect to that kind [of art and science] are rulers over those educated in what is most vile with respect to that kind.

So one having an extraordinary nature with respect to a certain kind [of art and science], who is educated in everything he is disposed to by nature, is a ruler not only over one not having an extraordinary nature with respect to that kind [of art and science], but also over one having an extraordinary nature with respect to that kind [of art and science], who is not educated or is educated only in some trifling thing of what is in that kind [of art and science]. [78]

[2. DIFFERENT KINDS OF RULERS OR GUIDES TO HAPPINESS]

78. Since what is intended by the existence of the human being is that he obtain ultimate happiness, to obtain it he needs to know happiness and to set it before his eyes as his end. Then, after that, he needs to know the things that ought to be done so as to gain happiness by means of them, then to perform those deeds.

32. Reading *al-irshād* with Feyzullah 1279, rather than *al-istinbāṭ* ("inference") with Najjar and the other mss.

Because of what was said with respect to the difference in innate characters in individual human beings, the innate character of every human being does not on its own know happiness or the things that ought to be done; rather, for that, there is need for an instructor and a guide. Some need slight guidance and some much guidance. Nor, when he is guided to these two,[33] does he inevitably do what he has been instructed and guided to do without an external spur and being aroused toward it. Most people are like this. Therefore, they need someone who acquaints them with all of that and arouses them to do it.

It is not within the power of every human being to guide someone else. Nor is it within the power of every human being to prompt someone else to do these things. One having no ability at all to arouse someone else to do one of the things or to use him in it, having instead only the ability to do always what he is guided to, is in no way a ruler—not with respect to anything. Rather, he is always ruled in everything. One who has the power to guide someone else to a particular thing, to prompt him to do it, or to use him in it, is—with respect to that thing—a ruler over the one who is not able to do that thing by himself, but is able to when guided toward it and instructed in doing it. Then, one having the ability to arouse someone else toward that thing he was instructed in and guided toward and use him in it is a ruler over one human being and ruled by another human being.

The ruler may be a first[34] ruler, and he may be a secondary ruler. The secondary ruler is the one who is ruled by one human being while he rules another human being. [79] These two rulerships may be about a particular kind [of art and science], like farming, and like commerce and medicine. And they may be in relation to all the human kinds [of art and science].

79. The first ruler without qualification is the one who does not need—not in anything at all—to be ruled by another human being. Rather, he has already attained the sciences and cognitions in actuality and has no need of a human being to guide him in anything. He has the ability for excellent apprehension of each and every particular thing that ought to be done and the faculty for excellently guiding everyone other than himself to all that he has instructed them in; the ability to use everyone as a means

33. That is, to happiness and the things that ought to be done in order to achieve it.
34. Or "primary" or even "supreme" (*awwal*).

to do a particular thing pertaining to that action he is intent on; and the ability to determine, define, and direct the activities toward happiness.

That comes about only in an inhabitant having a great, extraordinary nature[35] when his soul has joined with the active intellect. He obtains that only by having first attained the passive intellect, then, after that, having attained the intellect called "acquired."[36] Through attaining the acquired [intellect] there comes about the conjunction with the active intellect that was mentioned in the book *On the Soul*.

80. This human being is the king in truth according to the ancients, and he is the one of whom it ought to be said that he receives revelation. For a human being receives revelation only when he obtains this rank, and that is when there remains no intermediary between him and the active intellect. Now the passive intellect is similar to material and a subject for the acquired intellect. And the acquired intellect is similar to material and a subject for the active intellect.

Then, there emanates from the active intellect to the passive intellect the faculty by which he is able to seize on the definition of things and actions and direct them toward happiness. This emanation proceeding from the active intellect to the passive intellect by the intermediary [80] of the acquired intellect is revelation. Because the active intellect is an emanation from the existence of the first cause, it is possible due to this to say that the first cause is what brings revelation to this human being by the intermediary of the active intellect. The rulership of this human being is the first rulership, and the rest of the human rulerships are subsequent to this one and proceed from it. And that is evident.

81. The people who are governed by the rulership of this ruler are the virtuous, good, and happy people. If they are a nation, then that is the virtuous nation. If they are people who have come together in a single dwelling-place, then the dwelling-place that brings all these together under this rulership is the virtuous city. If they have not come together in

35. Literally, "inhabitants having great, extraordinary natures" (*ahl al-ṭibāʾiʿ al-ʿaẓīma al-fāʾiqa*); but the context, as well as the following "his soul" (*nafsuh*), point to the singular.

36. Literally, "procured" (*al-mustafād*); so, too, in the next sentence and throughout the rest of this discussion. Though the discussion centers on Aristotle's *On the Soul* 3.5.430a10–25 and 3.7.431a1–431b19, the term "acquired intellect" comes not from Aristotle, but from Alexander of Aphrodisias in his own *On the Soul*.

a single dwelling-place, but are in separate dwelling-places whose inhabitants are governed by rulerships other than this one, then they are virtuous people who are strangers in those dwelling-places. They happen to be separate either because they have not yet chanced upon a city in which it is possible for them to come together or because they already were in a city but disasters happened to them—such as enemy aggression, epidemic, drought, or something else—forcing them to separate.

82. If there happens to be an association of these kings at a single moment in a single city, a single nation, or many nations, then their whole association is like a single king due to the agreement in their endeavors, purposes, opinions,[37] and ways of life. If they succeed one another in time, their souls will be as a single soul. The second will proceed according to the way of life of the first, and the one now present according to the way of life of the one who has passed away. Just as it is permissible for one of them to change a Law[38] he legislated at one moment if he is of the opinion that it is more fitting to change it at another moment, [81] so may the one now present who succeeds the one who has passed away change what the one who has passed away has already legislated. For the one who has passed away would change [it] himself, were he to observe the [new] condition. When there does not happen to be a human being of this condition, the Laws that the former [kings] prescribed or ordained are to be adopted, then written down and preserved, and the city is to be governed by means of them. So the ruler who governs the city by means of written Laws adopted from past leaders is the king of traditional law.[39]

[3. ATTAINING HAPPINESS]

83. When each of the inhabitants of the city does what is such as to be entrusted to him—having either learned that on his own or the ruler having guided and prompted him to it—those actions of his make him acquire good traits of the soul. So, too, does persistence in the good

37. Reading *wa ārā'ihim* with Feyzullah 1279 rather than *wa irādātihim* ("and their wills") with Najjar and the rest of the mss.

38. The Arabic term is *sharī'a,* and the verb translated in what follows as "legislate" is *sharra'a.* Similarly, the Arabic word translated as "Laws" is *sharā'i',* the plural of *sharī'a.* The term *nāmūs* ("nomos" or "convention") does not occur in this work.

39. The term is *sunna* and is usually used to refer to the sayings and deeds of the Prophet.

actions of writing make a human being acquire goodness in the art of writing—which is a trait of the soul. The more he persists in them, the more powerful goodness in writing becomes in him. His pleasure in the trait he attains in his soul is greater, and the delight of his soul in that trait is stronger. Similarly, the actions that are determined and directed toward happiness empower the part of the soul disposed by innate character toward happiness and make it become actual and perfect. So, from the power attained in becoming perfect, it manages to dispense with material and gets to be free from it. Yet it does not perish when material perishes, since in its constitution and its existence it has come not to need material. Then it attains happiness.

84. It is evident that the types of happiness attained by the inhabitants of the city vary in quantity and quality in accordance with the variation in the perfections they procure through civic[40] actions. And in accordance with that, the pleasures they gain vary. For when the soul attains separation from material and becomes incorporeal, the accidents that affect [82] bodies insofar as they are bodies are removed from it. So it cannot be said of it that it moves or that it rests. Then the sayings that are proper for what is not corporeal ought to be said of it. Everything befalling the human soul that describes body insofar as it is body ought to be negated of separated souls. To understand and to form a concept of this condition is difficult and not customary, in the way it is difficult to form a concept of substances that are not bodies nor in bodies.

85. When a group passes away, and their bodies are nullified, and their souls are delivered and made happy, then other people follow after them, take their place in the city, and perform their activities; the souls of these [people], too, are delivered. When their bodies are nullified, they come to the rankings of those in this group who have passed away. They are neighborly to them in the way that what is not corporeal is neighborly. And they join with the similar souls of the people of the single group,[41] some with others. Whenever the similar separate souls multiply and some join with others, the pleasure of each one increases. Whenever one of those who came after attaches to them, the pleasure of the one now attaching increases due to his encountering those who passed away. And

40. Or "political" (*al-madaniyya*); see above, sec. 64, n. 28.
41. That is, the group whose members have passed away.

the pleasures of those who passed away increase through joining with those who attach to them because each one intellects his essence and intellects the same as his essence many times. What is thereby intellected increases as the ones now present attach to them in future time. So there will be a boundless increase of pleasures for each one with the passing of time. That is the condition of each group.

This, then, is the true ultimate happiness that is the purpose of the active intellect.

86. When the actions of the inhabitants of a particular city are not directed toward happiness, they make them acquire traits [83] of the soul that are bad just as when the actions of writing are bad, they produce bad writing. Similarly, when the actions of any art are bad, they provide the soul bad traits with respect to that genus of those arts. And their souls become sick. Thus, they are pleased by the traits they earn through their actions just as, due to the corruption of their sense-perception, those with sick bodies—like those with fevers—take pleasure in bitter things, find them sweet, and are pained by sweet things, which appear bitter to their palates. Similarly, due to the corruption of their imagination, those with sick souls take pleasure in bad traits.

Just as among the sick there is someone who is not conscious of his disease and someone who, in addition, presumes that he is healthy—and someone among the sick who is such as this does not at all heed what a physician says—so, too, is there among those with sick souls someone who is not conscious of his sickness and who, in addition, presumes that he is virtuous and has a sound soul. So he does not at all heed what a guide, instructor, or reformer says. Thus the souls of these people remain material[42] and do not come to a perfection such that they are separate from material; so when their material is nullified, they also are nullified.

87. The rankings of the inhabitants of the city vary with respect to rulership and service in accordance with their innate characters and in accordance with the way they have been educated. The first ruler is the one who ranks the groups and each human being in each group according to the ranking it or he merits—that is, either in a ranking of service or a ranking of rulership. Thus, there will be rankings close to his [own] ranking, rankings slightly distant from it, and rankings greatly distant from it.

42. Literally, "hylic" (*hayūlāniyya*); see above, sec. 9 and n. 6.

Those are the rankings of rulership, and they descend little by little from the highest rank until they come to be the rankings of service in which there is no rulership and beneath which there is no other ranking.

When the ruler, after making these rankings, then wants to define a command about an object that he wants to prompt the inhabitants of the city or a group among the inhabitants of the city to do [84] and wants to arouse them toward it, he intimates that to the rankings closest to him; and they intimate it to whoever comes after them. Then it goes on like that until it arrives at the one who is ranked as serving that affair. Thus the parts of the city are then tied to one another, in consonance with one another, and ranked with some having precedence and others being subordinate. It comes to resemble the natural existents, and its rankings also resemble the rankings of the existents that begin at the first [cause] and terminate at primary material and the elements. The way it is tied together and its consonance are similar to the way the different existents are tied to one another and to their consonance. And the governor of that city is similar to the first cause through which the rest of the existents exist.

Then the rankings of the existents go on descending little by little, each of them coming to be ruler and ruled, until they terminate at the possible existents that have no rulership at all but only serve and exist for the sake of something else—namely, primary material and the elements.

88. Happiness is obtained only by removing evils from cities and from nations—not just the voluntary ones, but also the natural ones—and by their attaining all the goods—the natural ones and the voluntary ones. Now the function of the city's governor—that is, the king—is to govern cities so as to tie the parts of the city to one another and to give it consonance and make a ranking such that the inhabitants assist one another in removing evils and attaining goods. And [his function is] to look into everything given by the heavenly bodies. Whatever suitably assists or is useful in a particular way for obtaining happiness, he retains and increases. Whatever is harmful, he struggles to render useful. And what he is unable to do that with, he nullifies or decreases. In general, he seeks to nullify both of the evils and to bring into existence[43] both of the goods.

43. Reading *wa ījād* with Feyzullah 1279 instead of *wa ījāb* ("and to affirm") with Najjar and the rest of the mss. The two evils and goods in question are the voluntary and natural ones.

Each of the inhabitants of the virtuous city needs to be cognizant of the ultimate principles of the existents, their rankings, happiness, the first rulership that belongs to the virtuous city, and the rankings of its rulership. Then, after that, [85] [each needs to be cognizant of] the defined actions by which happiness is gained when they are performed. These actions are not to be restricted to being known without being done and the inhabitants of the city being brought to do them.

89. Now a human being either forms a concept of the principles of the existents, their rankings, happiness, and the rulership of the virtuous cities and intellects them or imagines them. To form a concept of them is to have their essences sketched in the human soul as they exist in truth. To imagine them is to have their images, their likenesses, and the objects representing them sketched in the human soul. That is similar to what is possible with objects that are seen—for example, a human being. Either we see him himself, we see a statue of him, we see an image of him in water, or we see an image of his statue in water or in other mirrors. Now our seeing him resembles the intellect's forming a concept of the principles of the existents, happiness, and the rest. And our seeing a human being in water or our seeing a statue of him resembles imagination. For our seeing a statue of him or our seeing him in a mirror is our seeing what represents him. Similarly, our imagining those things is in truth our forming a concept of what represents them, not our forming a concept of them in themselves.

90. Most people have no ability, either by innate character or by custom, to understand and form a concept of those things. For those people, an image ought to be made, by means of things that represent them, of how the principles, their rankings, the active intellect, and the first ruler come about.

While their meanings and essences are one and immutable, the things by which they are represented are many and different. Some are closer to what is represented and others more distant. That is just as it is with visible things. For the image of a human being seen in water is closer to the human being in truth than the image of the statue of a human being seen in water. Therefore it is possible to represent these things to one group and one nation by objects other than those by which they are represented to another group and another nation.

Thus it may be possible [86] for the religions of virtuous nations and virtuous cities to differ even if they all pursue the very same happiness. For religion is a sketch of these things or of their images in the soul. Since it is difficult for the public to understand these things in themselves and the way they exist, instructing them about these things is sought by other ways—and those are the ways of representation. So these things are represented to each group or nation by things of which they are more cognizant. And it may be possible that what one of them is more cognizant of is not what another is more cognizant of.

Most people who pursue happiness pursue what is imagined, not what they form a concept of. Similarly, the principles such as to be accepted, imitated, extolled, and exalted are accepted by most people as they imagine them, not as they form a concept of them. Those who pursue happiness as they form a concept of it and accept the principles as they form a concept of them are the wise, whereas those in whose souls these things are found as they are imagined and who accept them and pursue them as though they are like that are the faithful.

91. The objects by which these things are represented vary so that some are wiser and more complete in imagination and others more defective, some are closer to the truth and others further from it. With some, the topics of contention are few or concealed; or it is difficult to contend against them. With others, the topics of contention are many or apparent; or it is easy to contend against and to refute them.

It is not impossible that the things by which these are presented imaginatively to the inhabitants be different objects and, in spite of their difference, be linked to one another—that is, that there be objects used to represent those things, other things to represent these objects, and yet a third set of objects to represent these things—or that the different objects used to represent those things—I mean, the principles of the existents, happiness, and its rankings—be equivalent in their representation.

If [87] all of them were equivalent with respect to the goodness of their representation or the topics of contention in them being few or concealed, all or any one of them chanced upon would be used. And if they were to vary, those chosen would be the ones most complete in representation or those in which the topics of contention were either nonexistent at all, trifling, or concealed; then would come those closest to the truth. Representations other than these would be discarded.

[C. The Different Kinds of Nonvirtuous Cities]

[1. THE CITIES CONTRARY TO THE VIRTUOUS CITY]

92. Contrary to the virtuous city are the [a] ignorant city, [b] immoral city, and [c] errant city. Then there are [d] the weeds in the virtuous city; for the status of weeds in cities is that of darnel in wheat, the thorns of plants within the crop, or the rest of the grasses that are useless or harmful to the crop or seedlings.

Then there are [e] the people who are bestial by nature.[44] Now those who are bestial by nature are not citizens, nor do they have any civic associations at all. Rather, some of them are like domesticated beasts and some like wild beasts. And some of the latter are like predatory animals. Similarly, among them is to be found those who abide separately in the wilderness, those who abide in associations while cavorting like predatory animals, and those who abide close to cities. Among them are those who eat only raw meat, those who graze on wild plants, and those who ravish [their prey] as do the predatory animals. These are found at the extremities of the inhabited dwelling-places, either at the northern or the southern tips. And they ought to be treated as beasts. Now any one of them who is domestic and useful in some way to the cities is to be spared, enslaved, and used as beasts are used. What is done to the rest of the harmful animals is to be done to any of them who is not useful or is harmful. The same ought to be done to any children of the inhabitants of the cities who happen to be bestial.

[2. THE DIFFERENT CATEGORIES OF THE IGNORANT CITY]

93. The inhabitants of the ignorant [cities] are citizens,[45] and their cities and civic associations are of many manners: [88] among them are [a] the necessary associations, [b] the association of depraved inhabitants in the depraved cities, [c] the vile association in the vile cities, [d] the association of [seekers of] honor in the timocratic cities, [e] the association of domination in the city of domination, and [f] the association of freedom in the democratic city[46] and the city of the free.

44. There is no further discussion of these people or their subgroups.
45. Or "city people" (*madaniyyūn*).
46. Literally, "the associational city" (*al-madīna al-jamāʿiyya*). See below, secs. 113–119.

[a. The Necessary City]

94. The necessary city or necessary association is the one in which there is mutual assistance for earning what is necessary to constitute and safeguard bodies. There are many ways of earning these things such as farming, herding, hunting, stealing, and others. Both hunting and stealing involve wiliness and openness. Among the necessary cities, there may be some that bring together all of the arts that procure what is necessary. With others, earning what is necessary comes about by a single art such as farming alone or another single one [of the arts].

According to them,[47] the most virtuous one is he who is most excellent at [a] using stratagems for, [b] governing, and [c] making available the ways by which the inhabitants of the city arrive at earning what is necessary. Their ruler is the one who has fine governance and excellent stratagems for using them so that they gain the necessary things and fine governance in preserving these things for them or who bestows these things on them from what he has.

[b. The Plutocratic City]

95. The depraved city or association of depraved inhabitants is the one in which they assist one another in gaining prosperity and wealth, being excessive in acquiring the necessities and what takes their place with respect to dirhams and dinars, and accumulating them beyond [89] the extent they are needed. [This is] for nothing other than love of, and greed for, wealth, while spending of it only what is necessary to constitute bodies. That comes about either by all of the means of earning or by the means available in that country.

According to them, the one most virtuous is the most wealthy and most excellent at using stratagems to obtain prosperity. Their ruler is the human being capable of excellently governing them so that they earn wealth and preserve it always. Wealth is gained through all the ways by which what is necessary is gained—namely, farming, herding, hunting, and stealing—and then voluntary interactions such as commerce, leasing, and others.

[c. The Hedonistic City]

96. The city of vileness or association of the vile is the one in which they assist one another in the enjoyment of sensual pleasure or imaginary

47. That is, the inhabitants of the necessary city or association.

pleasure—such as play or jesting—or both together, as well as in the enjoyment of the pleasure of eating, drinking, and sexual intercourse. The most pleasant of these is chosen in order to seek pleasure not, by means of it, to seek what constitutes the body or is useful to the body in some way, but only to be pleased by it. And so, too, with play and jesting.

According to the inhabitants of the ignorant [cities], this city is the happy and delightful one, because it is possible for them to obtain the purpose of this city only after having attained what is necessary and after having attained wealth.

[d. The Timocratic City]

97. The honor-seeking city or the association of [seekers of] honor is the one in which they aid one another to arrive at being honored in speech and in action. That is either by the inhabitants of other cities honoring them or by some of them honoring others. The honor some accord others is either equal or varied.

Equal honor is simply [90] that they exchange honor with one another by one bestowing one species of honor on another at a particular moment so that at another moment the other bestows on him that species of honor or another species whose power according to them is the same as that [first] species. The varied [exchange of honor] is for one to bestow on another one species of honor and the other to bestow on the first honor of greater power than the first species. All of this proceeds among them in that way according to merit in that the second merits honor of a certain extent and the first merits greater honor—that being in keeping with what is meritorious according to them.

98. Now according to the inhabitants of the ignorant cities, what is meritorious is not virtue, but [a] wealth, [b] making available for one another the causes of pleasure and play and obtaining the most of these two, [c] obtaining the most of what is necessary such that a human being is sufficiently served with all he needs of what is necessary, or [d] a human being acting in a useful manner—that is, doing good—to others with respect to these three things.

There is [e] another thing very beloved of many of the inhabitants of the ignorant cities, namely, domination. According to many of them, the one who achieves it is to be admired. Therefore, that ought also to be counted among what is meritorious for the ignorant cities. For, according to them, the most exalted thing a human being is to be honored for is being well-known for domination over one, two, or many things; not being dominated either due to himself, because his supporters are many or powerful, or both of these; and not being subjected to what is loathsome, while subjecting someone else to what is loathsome when he wills. This, according to them, is one of the conditions of delight for which, according to them, a human being merits honor. The more virtuous he is in this [91] object, the more he is honored.

Or [vi] for a human being to have distinguished ancestry, according to them. According to them, distinguished ancestry goes back to one of the things that preceded, that is, that his fathers and grandfathers were either wealthy, had much pleasure and the causes for making it available, had domination over many things, were useful to others with respect to these things—either to an association or to inhabitants of a city—or that available to them were the instruments for these such as nobility, endurance, or contempt for death. For these are the instruments of domination.

99. Equal honor sometimes has to do with merit coming from another, external thing. Sometimes honor itself is the merit, so that the human being who begins and honors another thereby merits being honored by the other, as takes place with market interactions. According to them, the one who merits more honor is the ruler over someone such as to be honored less. This variation does not cease ascending until it terminates at the one who merits more honor than anyone other than him in the city. That one comes to be the ruler of the city and its king. Since it is like that, that one ought to have more merit than anyone other than himself. What, according to them, are meritorious things are the ones we have enumerated.

100. If it is like that and if, according to them, rulership comes only through distinguished ancestry, then he [the ruler] ought to have more distinguished ancestors than anyone else. And, similarly, if honor according to them comes only through wealth. Then people vary and are ranked according to their extent of wealth and distinguished ancestry. Someone who has no wealth or any distinguished ancestors has no access to rulerships or honors. It is like that when the meritorious things are [92] objects whose good does not extend beyond him, and these are the vilest among the rulers of honor. And if he is honored only for the sake of his usefulness to the inhabitants of the city with respect to the endeavor and passion of the inhabitants of the city, that occurs insofar as he is useful to them

with respect to wealth, pleasures, arriving at having others honor them or at other things among the desires of the inhabitants of the city—either bestowing these things on them from what he has or gaining them for them through his fine governance and preserving them for them.

101. According to them, the most virtuous of these rulers is the one who gains these things for the inhabitants of the city and does not bother himself with anything other than honor alone—such as his gaining wealth for them and not seeking wealth, or his gaining pleasures for them and not seeking pleasures—but seeks honor alone and being praised, extolled, and magnified in speech and action so that his name becomes well-known for that among the rest of the nations during his time and afterward and memory of him remains for a long time. This is the one who merits honor according to them. Many times, this one needs money and wealth to bestow in getting the inhabitants of the city to arrive at their desires concerning wealth or pleasure and in preserving it for them. When these deeds of his are greater, he ought to be wealthier; and that wealth of his comes to be a reserve for the inhabitants of the city.

102. So some of them seek wealth for this reason and are of the opinion that these expenditures of theirs are due to generosity and liberality. They take that money from the city either in the manner of a tax or they dominate a faction other than the inhabitants of the city for their money, bring it to the treasure-house, and use it as a reserve for making great expenditures in the city so as to gain greater honor.

When someone loves honor by whatever means it chances to come about, it is not impossible for him to establish a [93] distinguished ancestry for himself and his offspring after him. And in order that memory of him remains after him through his offspring, he places ownership in his offspring or in his family.[48] Then it is not impossible for him to establish wealth for himself to be honored for it, even if it is of no use to anyone else. Then he also honors a faction so that they will also honor him. Thus he brings together all the things for which it is possible that people will honor him, then keeps particularly for himself things for which, according to them, he will have splendor, radiance, eminence, and magnificence—such as buildings, clothing, medals, [and] then being inaccessible to the people.

48. Literally, "in his genus" (*fī jinsih*). When the term "family" occurs later in this section, it is also literally "genus."

Then he legislates traditional laws[49] concerning honors. When rulership devolves upon him and the people are accustomed to him and his family being their king, he then ranks the people in such a way as to attain honor and magnificence. For each ranking, he legislates a kind of honor and what merits honor—such as wealth, buildings, clothing, medals, mounts, or other things that make his command magnificent. And he sets that down according to an order. After that, he tends to prefer the people who honor him more or assist him more in that magnificence of his. And he honors and gives honors on that basis. Now the inhabitants of his city who love honor interact in this way with him so that he will increase the honors he bestows on them. Due to that, the inhabitants of the rankings beneath them and above them honor them.

103. Due to these things, this city is similar to the virtuous city, especially if the honors and the rankings of the people with respect to honors are for the sake of what is more useful for others—such as wealth, [94] pleasures, or any other thing for which the one who seeks useful things has a passion. This city is the best among the ignorant cities.[50] It is the one whose inhabitants—unlike the inhabitants of the other cities—are [properly] called "ignorant" and similar names. However, if the love of honor in it becomes very excessive, it becomes a city of tyrants and is fit for being transformed into becoming a city of domination.

[e. The City of Domination]

104. The city of domination and the association of domination are the ones whose inhabitants assist one another so that they have domination. They are like that when they all have love of domination in common. Yet they diverge from one another insofar as they love it less or more, and they diverge from one another with respect to the kinds of domination and the kinds of things for which they dominate people. Some, for example, love to dominate to spill a human being's blood, some love to dominate for his money, and some love to dominate over his soul so as to enslave him. People are ranked with respect to it[51] according to the great

49. Here and in what follows, the term is *sunna*; see above, sec. 82, n. 39.
50. Bracketing, for sense, *ahl* ("inhabitants"), so that the phrase reads *khayr mudun al-jāhiliyya*. The phrase *khayr mudun ahl al-jāhiliyya* is bewildering.
51. Understanding the prepositional clause *fīhā* to refer to domination (*ghalaba*); but it can also be construed as referring to the city itself, in which case it should read "people are ranked in it."

if one loves domination, they will not be satisfied w/ anything else

extent of domination one person loves [to exercise] and the paucity of it that most love [to exercise]. Their love to dominate others is directed at their blood [so as to spill it] and their spirits [so as to extinguish them], their souls so as to enslave them, or their money so as to wrest it from them. Their love and their purpose in all of that are domination, conquest, humiliation, and that the conquered possesses neither himself nor any other thing for the sake of which he has been dominated but is subject to obeying the conqueror in whatever passion he has. Thus when one of those who love domination and conquest has an ambition or passion for a certain thing, then gains it without conquering any human being for it, he does not take it and pays no attention to it.

People differ in how they like to dominate and refrain from dominating those they other dominators in order to survive

105. Among them are those of the opinion that they should conquer by wiliness, those of the opinion that they should conquer only by severity, and some of the opinion [95] that they should conquer by both manners—by wiliness and by severity. Therefore, many of those who conquer so as to spill blood do not kill a human being when they find him sleeping nor take money from him until they awaken him; rather, they are of the opinion that they should take it by severity and have the other actively resist so that they conquer him and inflict on him what he loathes. Every one of these loves domination and thus loves to dominate all others, whether they are inhabitants of the city or others. However, they refrain from dominating one another with respect to spilling their blood or taking their money due to the need they have of one another so as to survive, to assist one another in dominating others, and to prevent others from dominating them.

106. Their ruler is the one among them who is most powerful in governing well by using them to dominate others, the one most excellent at using stratagems, and the one most perfect in opinion about what they ought to do so as always to be seen as dominators and to prevent others from dominating them. He is their ruler and their king. And they are enemies of all others. All of their traditional laws are traditional laws and prescriptions such that, when adhered to, they are fit for dominating others. Their rivalry and boasting is either about the frequency of their domination, its greatness, or their abundant acquisition of the equipment and instruments of domination.

Equipment and instruments of domination consist either in a human being's opinion, in his body, or in what is external to his body—in his body, endurance, for example; external to his body, having weapons;

and in his opinion, having excellent opinion about what allows him to dominate another. These human beings tend to be crude, cruel, irascible, haughty, and gluttonous in stuffing themselves with food and drink, overindulging in sexual intercourse, and dominating one another for all the goods. And that should come about through conquering and humiliating whoever has any of them. They are of the opinion that they should dominate everything and everybody. [96]

107. Sometimes the whole city is like this so that they are of the opinion that, due to their need for association and not for any other thing, they should be intent on dominating anyone not from the city.

Sometimes the ones dominated and the conquerors are neighbors in a single city. Then the conquerors either love to conquer and dominate in an equal degree and have equal rankings in the city or they have [different] rankings, with each one dominating over the conquered neighbors about something and doing so less or more than another. Similarly, with respect to the powers and opinions by which they dominate, they draw close to the king who rules them and governs the conquerors' affairs as concerns the instruments by which they arrive at conquest.

Sometimes the conqueror is only a single person with a faction as his instruments for conquering the rest of the people. Their endeavor is not to dominate something and take it for someone else, but to dominate a thing so that it will belong to that single person. In turn, what that single person uses to maintain his life and endurance is sufficient for him; he gives [the rest] to others and dominates for others, as do dogs and falcons. Likewise, the rest of the inhabitants of the city are slaves serving that single person in whatever he has a passion for; humiliated and submissive, they possess nothing of their own at all. Some of them cultivate the soil for him, others trade for him. His intention in that is nothing more than seeing a faction be conquered, dominated, and humiliated by him alone, even though he gains no other use from them nor any pleasure except that they be humiliated and conquered.

By its king alone is this a city of domination. The rest of the inhabitants of the city are not ones who dominate. The one previous to this is a city of domination by half of its inhabitants, and the first is one by all of them.[52]

52. By "the one previous to this" Alfarabi means the city in which "the ones dominated and the conquerors are neighbors in a single city"; and by "the first city" he means the one where "the whole city is . . . of the opinion that . . . they should be intent on dominating anyone not from the city." For these, see the accounts in the first two paragraphs of this section.

city of domination=
only when enjoy domination
for the
sake of it,
not for
the sake
of the
pleasures
its lovings

108. So the city of domination may be of this sort in that it endeavors by one of these means only to dominate and to take pleasure in doing so. If it loves domination only so as to attain the necessary things, wealth, [97] enjoyment of pleasures, honors, or all of these, then that is a city of domination of a different sort. These [inhabitants] belong to those other cities mentioned above. Though many people call these cities the city of domination, the one most deserving of this name is the one that wants [to obtain] all three of these by conquest.[53] And these cities are of three sorts, namely, [domination] by one of the inhabitants, by half of the inhabitants, or by all of the inhabitants.[54] Thus, these inhabitants pursue conquest and mistreatment, not for their own sake, but with an intention and a purpose for something else.

109. There are yet other cities intent on these [things] along with domination. In the first, which is intent on domination however it comes about and for anything whatsoever, someone may chance to harm another without any benefit coming to him from that—like killing for no reason[55] other than the simple pleasure of conquest. And in it there is domination for

1) love
domination

vile things, as is recounted about a faction among the Arabs.

2) love b/c
things

With the second, there is love of domination for the sake of things that, according to them, are highly praiseworthy and are not vile. When they gain these things without conquest, they do not resort to conquest.

3) don't love,
only for
things

In the third city, there is harming and killing only insofar as it is known that it is useful for one of the venerable things. When the things one [of the inhabitants] is intent on are made available to him without domination or conquest—by, for example, a treasure existing, someone else sufficing, or some human being bestowing that thing on him obediently—he does not destroy others, pay any attention to them, or take from them. These people are also called high-minded and prideful. [98]

---

53. Though Najjar thinks the word "three" (*al-thalāth*) may be an interpolation, he notes its presence in all the mss. and suggests an interpretation based on the punctuation of Feyzullah 1279, where the goods to be attained by domination—listed two sentences earlier—fall into three groups: "the necessary things, wealth, or enjoyment of pleasures; honors; or all of these"; see "Alfarabi: The Political Regime," in *Medieval Political Philosophy: A Sourcebook*, ed. Ralph Lerner and Muhsin Mahdi, 1st ed. (New York: Free Press of Glencoe, 1963), 48, n. 5.

54. See above, sec. 107, end, and n. 52.

55. The term is *sabab*; heretofore, it has been translated as "cause." Its cognate, *'illa* does not occur in this book.

110. The inhabitants of the first city restrict themselves to such conquest as is necessary so as to attain domination. Sometimes they contest and struggle mightily when prevented from getting money or a soul, and they quarrel until they are triumphant and can implement their judgment and passion on it, then abandon it and do not take it. These, too, may be praised, honored, and extolled for this. Those who love honor may use many of these things so as to be honored for them. The cities of domination are more often tyrannical than honor-seeking.

111. It may occur that the inhabitants of the city of wealth and the inhabitants of the city of play and jesting presume themselves to be delightful, happy, masterful, and more virtuous than the inhabitants of the rest of the cities. Because of what they presume of themselves, it may occur that they have contempt for the inhabitants of other cities, consider those other than them to have no value, and expect love and honor for what—according to them—makes them happy. So it occurs that they become conceited, haughty, boastful, praise-loving; that [they presume] others cannot reach what they have reached; and [presume] that they are therefore too stupid to get even one of these two kinds of happiness.[56] They create for themselves names that embellish their ways of life—for example, that they are the naturally gifted and elegant ones and that those other than them are the crude. Therefore it is presumed that they possess pride, magnanimity, and authority. Sometimes they are called high-minded.

112. When it chances that the lovers of wealth, pleasure, and play attain none of the arts by which wealth is earned except the power to dominate and they arrive at wealth and play by conquest and domination, they become more intensely prideful and enter into the troop of tyrants. The first are simpletons.[57]

Similarly, it is not impossible for there to be among those who love honor someone who loves it not for its own sake, but for wealth. Now many of them want others to honor them so as to gain wealth, either from those [who honor them] or from someone else. They want rulership over, and obedience from, the inhabitants of the city so as to arrive at wealth. And many [99] of them want wealth for play and pleasure. So it happens that many of them seek rulership and to be obeyed in order to attain

56. Namely, wealth or play and jesting; see the beginning of this section.
57. That is, those discussed above in sec. 111.

wealth to use in play. They are of the opinion that the greater and more complete their rulership and the obedience of others to them, the more increase they will have in these things. So they seek to be the only ones to rule over the inhabitants of the city so as to attain the magnificence by which they can arrive at such great wealth that none of the inhabitants can approximate it, then to use that wealth in play and to gain from play and the pleasures of food, drink, and sexual intercourse what no one else gains with respect to both quantity and quality.

[f. The Democratic City]

113. The democratic city is the city in which every one of its inhabitants is unrestrained and left to himself to do what he likes. Its inhabitants are equal to one another, and their traditional law is that no human being is superior to another in anything at all. Its inhabitants are free to do what they like. One [inhabitant] has authority over another or over someone else only insofar as he does what heightens that person's freedom.

Thus there arise among them many moral habits, many endeavors, many desires, and taking pleasure in countless things. Its inhabitants consist of countless similar and dissimilar groups. In this city are brought together those [associations] that were kept separate in all those [other] cities—the vile and the venerable ones. Rulerships come about through any chance one of the rest of those things we have mentioned. The public, which does not have what the rulers have, has authority over those who are said to be their rulers. The one who rules them does so only by the will of the ruled, and their rulers are subject to the passions of the ruled. If their situation is examined closely, it turns out that in truth there is no ruler among them and no ruled.

114. Yet those who are praised and honored among them are [a] those who bring the inhabitants of the city to freedom and to everything encompassing their passions and desires and [b] those who preserve their freedom and their diverging, differing desires [100] from [infringement] by one another and by their external enemies while restricting their own desires only to what is necessary. These are the ones among them who are honored, [deemed] most excellent, and obeyed.

Any of the other rulers is either equal to them or inferior to them. He is their equal when, in return for his producing the goods they will and desire, they bestow on him honors and money equivalent to what he does for them. Then they are not of the opinion that he has superiority over them. They are superior to him when they bestow honors on him and establish a share of their money for him without receiving any benefit from him.

So it is not impossible for there to be a ruler of this sort whose condition is that he chances to be magnified by the inhabitants of the city either because the inhabitants of the city have a passion for him or because the right of his forefathers, who had praiseworthy rulership over them, is preserved in him so that he rules. Then the public is in authority over the rulers.

All the endeavors and purposes of the ignorant [cities] are present in this city in the most perfect manner, and more.

115. Of [all] their cities, this is the marvelous and happy city. On the surface, it is like an embroidered garment replete with colored figures and dyes. Everyone loves it and loves to dwell in it, because every human being who has a passion or desire for anything is able to gain it in this city. The nations repair to it and dwell in it, so it becomes great beyond measure. People of every tribe are procreated in it by every sort of pairing off and sexual intercourse. The children generated in it are of very different innate characters and of very different education and upbringing.

Thus this city comes to be many cities, not distinguished from one another but interwoven with one another, the parts of one interspersed among the parts of another. Nor is the foreigner distinguished from the native resident. All of the passions and ways of life come together in it. [101] Therefore, it is not impossible as time draws on that virtuous people emerge in it. There may chance to exist in it wise men, rhetoricians, and poets concerned with every type of object. It is possible to glean from it parts of the virtuous city, and this is the best that emerges in this city. Thus, of the ignorant cities this city has both the most good and the most evil. The bigger, more prosperous, more populous, more fertile, and more perfect it becomes for people, the more prevalent and greater are these two.[58]

116. What the ignorant rulerships are intent on is as numerous as are the ignorant cities. For each ignorant rulership is intent on gaining control over what is necessary; wealth; enjoyment of pleasures; honor, fame, and praise; domination; or freedom. Therefore, these rulerships are bought for money—especially the rulerships that come about in the democratic city.

58. Namely, good and evil.

everyone equal so the best don't rule

For no one there is more deserving of rulership than another. So when rulership in it is surrendered to someone, it is either because the inhabitants granted it to him or that they took money or some other recompense from him.

117. According to them, the virtuous ruler is the one who is excellent at deliberation and fine at using stratagems to gain them their different and variegated desires and passions, preserving that from their enemies, and not depriving [them] of any of their money but restricting himself only to what is necessary for his power.

The one who is virtuous in truth—namely, the one who, when he rules them, determines their actions and directs them toward happiness—is not made a ruler by them. If he chances to rule them, he is soon deposed or killed, or his rulership is disturbed and challenged. The same holds for [102] the rest of the ignorant cities: each of them wants only to be ruled by someone who sets its choices and desires before it, makes the path to them easy, gains them for them, and preserves them for them. They reject the rulership of the virtuous and censure it. However, it is more possible and easier for the virtuous cities and the rulership of the virtuous to emerge from the necessary and democratic cities than from the other [ignorant] cities. *they want an easy life and dispose of rulers who aren't perfect*

[g. Summary]

118. What is necessary, wealth, enjoyment of pleasures and play, and honor may be gained by conquest and domination and may be gained by other means. So the four cities[59] are divided in this manner. Similarly, of the rulerships intent on these four [things] or [any] one of them, some are intent on obtaining it by domination and conquest and some by means other than these. Those [individuals] who procure these things by domination and conquest and safeguard what they attained by resistance and conquest need to have strong and powerful bodies; to be cruel, crude, coarse, and contemptuous of death in their moral habits; to be of the opinion that it is not worth living without gaining what is important; to have an art of using weapons; and to be good in deliberating about how to conquer others. This is common to all of them.

---

59. Namely, the necessary, depraved or plutocratic, vile or hedonistic, and timocratic cities.

119. In addition to these [things], those who pursue the enjoyment of pleasure happen to be voracious and to love eating, drinking, and sexual intercourse. Among them are those [a] who are so dominated by softness and luxury that their irascible faculty disintegrates, and nothing of it at all or [only] a trifling extent is to be found in them.

And among them are those [b] who are overwhelmed by anger, with its psychological and bodily instruments, and by desire, with its psychological and bodily instruments, to the point that these two are strengthened and increased, thus making it possible to carry out their actions. Their deliberation is devoted to the actions of these two, and their souls are equally subservient to them.

And among these are those who are ultimately intent on the actions of desire. They put their irascible faculties and actions as instruments for arriving [103] at the desires, thereby putting their higher and loftier faculties in the service of what is more vile. That is, they put their rational faculty in the service of the irascible and desiring [faculties] and then their irascible faculties in the service of their desiring faculties. They devote their deliberation to inferring what makes the actions of anger and desire complete; and they devote the actions of their irascible faculties and their instruments to what gains the pleasure to be savored from eating, drinking, and sexual intercourse, as well as to the rest of the things to be dominated and preserved for themselves—as is seen among the notables of the Turk and Arab inhabitants of the wilderness.

For common to the inhabitants of the wilderness is love of domination and great gluttony with respect to eating, drinking, and sexual intercourse. Therefore, women are of great importance according to them. Many of them approve of licentiousness and are not of the opinion that it is degenerate and vile, since their souls are subservient to their desires. You see many of them being pleasing to women in all they do, doing so in order to magnify their standing among women. They hold as shameful what women deem shameful, and what women find fair is fair for them. In all things, they adhere to the desires of their women. Women are in authority over many of them and are responsible for the affairs of the household. For this reason,[60] many of them accustom their women to luxury and do not give them over to toil; rather, they keep them in luxury and comfort, while themselves undertaking everything that requires labor, toil, and undergoing hardship.

60. The term is *sabab*; see above, sec. 109 and n. 55.

[3. THE IMMORAL CITIES]

120. The immoral cities are the ones whose inhabitants believed in, and formed a concept of, the principles [of the existents]. They had an image of happiness and believed in it. They were guided toward, were cognizant of, and believed in the actions by which they could gain happiness. Yet they did not hold fast to any of those actions, but through their passion and will inclined toward a particular feature among the purposes[61] of the inhabitants of the ignorant cities—either status,[62] honor, domination, or something else—and they established all of their actions and faculties to be directed toward those purposes.

The kinds of these cities are as numerous as the kinds of ignorant cities, because all the actions of their inhabitants are the actions [104] of the inhabitants of the ignorant cities and their moral habits the moral habits of those inhabitants. They are distinct from the inhabitants of the ignorant cities only by the opinions in which they believe. No one at all among the inhabitants of these cities gains happiness.

[4. THE ERRANT CITIES]

121. The errant cities[63] are the ones whose inhabitants receive representations of objects other than the ones we have mentioned—that is, the principles set before them and represented for them are other than those we have mentioned. The happiness set before them is other than the one that is happiness in truth, and a happiness other than that one is represented for them. And the actions and opinions prescribed for them gain nothing of happiness in truth.

[5. THE WEEDS IN THE VIRTUOUS CITIES]

122. The weeds in the virtuous cities are of many sorts. Among them is a sort [a] that holds fast to the actions by which happiness is gained, except that in what they do they are intent not on happiness but on some other thing a human being may gain through virtue—such as honor, rulership, wealth, or something else. These [people] are called hunters.

61. Literally, "a particular thing from the purposes" (*shay' mā min aghrāḍ*).
62. Status (*manzila*), which has not heretofore been cited as one of the purposes of the ignorant cities, takes the place here of necessity, wealth, enjoyment of pleasure, and freedom.
63. For a more precise indication of what characterizes these cities, see n. 68 below.

And among them [i] are those who have a passion for one of the ends of the inhabitants of the ignorant cities, but the Laws of the city and its religion prevent them from it. So they apply themselves to the utterances and statements of the lawgiver[64] for his precepts and interpret them so as to agree with their passion, thereby embellishing that thing by their interpretation. These [people] are called distorters. *of the law*

And among them are [ii] those who are not intent on distortion. But due to their poor understanding of the lawgiver's intention and their defective grasp[65] of his statements, they understand the Laws of the city differently from the way the lawgiver intended. So their actions fall outside the intention of the first ruler and they err without being conscious of it. These people are called schismatics. *don't understand the virtuous law*

123. Another sort [b] has already imagined the things we have mentioned, except that they are not persuaded by what they have imagined. So, for themselves and for others, they show those things to be false by arguments. In doing so, [105] they are not contending against the virtuous city. Rather, they are asking for guidance and seeking the truth.

Whoever is like this has his level of imagination elevated to things that the arguments he brings forth do not show to be false. If he is persuaded in thus being elevated, he is left there. But if he is not persuaded by that either and falls upon topics he can contend against, he is elevated to another level. It goes on like this until he is persuaded by one of these levels. But if he does not chance to be persuaded by one of the levels of imagination, he is elevated to the ranking of truth and made to understand those things as they are. At that point, his opinion becomes settled. *Question the city ↓ come upon the real truth*

124. Among them, another sort [c] presents as false what they imagine. Whenever they are elevated in rank, they present it as false—even when they obtain the ranking of truth. They do all this in seeking domination alone or in seeking to embellish one of the purposes of the inhabitants of the ignorant cities to which they are inclined. So they present as false [what they imagine] in every way they can. They do not like to hear anything that strengthens happiness and truth in the soul nor any argument that embellishes them and prescribes them for the soul, but meet them

64. Here and in what follows the term translated as "lawgiver" is *wāḍi' al-sunna* and should therefore be understood as the one who sets down traditional laws. See above, sec. 82, nn. 38 and 39.

65. Literally, "defective concept" (*nuqṣān taṣawwurih*).

with sham arguments that they presume will discredit happiness. In doing that, many of them are intent on appearing to be excused for inclining to one of the purposes of the inhabitants of the ignorant cities.

125. Among them is a sort [d] that imagines happiness and the principles [of the existents], but it is not within the power of their minds to form a concept of them at all. Or it is not within the power of their understanding to form a sufficient concept of them. So they present as false what they imagine and seize on the topics of contention in them. Whenever they are elevated to a level of imagination that is closer to the truth, they present it as false. It is not possible for them to be elevated to the level of truth, because it is not within the power of their minds to understand it. It may chance that many of these people present as false much of what they imagine, not because there are truly topics of contention in what they imagine, but because their imagination is defective. So, due to their poor understanding, they present that as false—not because there is a topic of contention in it. [106]

When unable to imagine something sufficiently or to grasp the true topics of contention in the places in which there are topics of contention and when unable to understand the truth, many of them presume that the one who apprehends the truth and says he has apprehended it is lying deliberately in a quest for honor or domination. Or they presume that he is a deluded zealot who also wants to present the truth as false and to vilify the one who has apprehended it. That leads many of them to presume that all people are deluded about everything they claim to have apprehended.

And that leads [i] some of them to perplexity about all objects.

And that leads [ii] some of them to be of the opinion that there is nothing accurate at all in what is apprehended and that whenever someone presumes he has apprehended something, he is lying about that[66] without being sure or certain of what he presumes. According to intelligent persons and in relation to the philosophers, these people are in the position of ignorant simpletons. Due to that, it is obligatory for the ruler of the virtuous city to watch over the weeds, keep them busy, and cure each sort by means of what is particularly suited to it—either expulsion from the city, punishment, imprisonment, or assigning them tasks even though they do not strive after them.

66. At this point all of the mss. except Feyzullah 1279 end.

And [iii] some of them presume that the truth is what appears to each person and what he presumes at each moment and that the truth about each thing is what someone presumes it to be.

And [iv] some of them exert themselves in making it seem that whatever has been presumed to have been apprehended up to this point is completely false and that even if there is something accurate and true, it has not yet been apprehended.

And [v] some of them imagine—as in a sleeping person's dream or as with a thing seen from afar—that there is a truth here, and it occurs to them that those who claim to have apprehended it have perhaps apprehended it or that there is among them someone who has perhaps apprehended it. In themselves, they sense that it has eluded them either because [107] apprehending it requires a long time as well as toil and hardship whereas they do not have adequate time for it nor the power to toil and persevere, because they are busy with pleasures and other things to which they have become accustomed and which it is hard for them to discard, or because they have sensed that they would not [be able to] apprehend it even if all its causes were made available to them.

Sorrow and grief occur to them due to their presuming that it is possible someone else may have seized on it. Due to envy about someone having perhaps apprehended the truth, they form the opinion to struggle by means of sham arguments to make it seem that the one who says he has apprehended it is either deluded or a liar who, in what he purports, is searching for honor, wealth, or some other thing such as to incite passion.

Many of these people sense their own ignorance and perplexity. They are pained and hurt by what they feel in themselves,[67] and that grieves and torments them. They find no way to remove this from themselves by means of a science that would seize on the truth, the apprehension of which would earn them pleasure. So they form the opinion to take a respite from that through recourse to the rest of the ends of the ignorant cities and to jesting and playful things. They set those down as consolation until death comes to relieve them of their lot.

Some of these people—I mean those who seek to take a respite from the torments they find in ignorance and perplexity—sometimes fancy that the [true] ends are the ones they choose and prefer, that happiness consists of these, and that the remaining human beings are deluded in what they believe. They struggle to embellish ignorant things and

67. That is, the inadequacy or lack they feel in themselves.

[ignorant] happiness. They fancy that they have come to prefer this after a long investigation of everything others purport to have apprehended, that they have rejected it only after grasping that it is not to be attained, and that they have come to this through an insight that these are the ends—not the ones those other people purport to be.

126. These, then, are the sorts [of weeds] growing among the inhabitants of the city. From their opinions, no city at all is attained, nor a large association from the multitude. But they are embedded among the inhabitants of the city as a whole.[68]

68. This marks the end of the discussion of the cities contrary to the virtuous city that began at sec. 92, above. Feyzullah 1279 contains an additional paragraph that is almost identical with a passage from Alfarabi's *Virtuous City*. In Richard Walzer's edition and translation, the passage occurs at the beginning of section 6, chapter 18, 286:2–288:3; and in Friedrich Dieterici's edition, *Risāla fī Ārā' Ahl al-Madīna al-Fāḍila* (Leiden: E. J. Brill, 1895; repr. 1964), it occurs at 71:23–72:10.

As Najjar points out, the paragraph may simply be misplaced; and the text can therefore be considered complete at this point. If it does belong to the text, then the work as a whole must be considered incomplete since the paragraph terminates with an unfinished sentence and omits the part corresponding to the rest of the passage in the *Virtuous City*, namely, the rest of section 6, chapter 18 plus all of section 6, chapter 19 (288:3–328:12) in Walzer's edition and 72:10–85:7 in Dieterici's edition. Here is the passage in question: "The errant cities are generated when religion is built on some of the corrupt ancient opinions. Among them is that a faction says: 'We see that the existents we observe are contrary to one another, and each seeks to destroy the other; and we see that when each of them attains existence, along with its existence it is given something with which to preserve its existence from destruction and defend and safeguard itself from its contrary and something by which it is able to put the rest of things into its service concerning what is useful for its most excellent and continuous existence. And for many of them, there is set down that by which they conquer whatever resists them. That is set down for every contrary with respect to its contrary and whatever else is in this condition, so that every one of them is intent on safeguarding for itself the most excellent existence apart from the others. Therefore, there is set down for it what destroys.'" Whether the passage from Feyzullah 1279 is accepted as part of the text or not, it must be noted that the conclusion at sec. 126 is premature insofar as nothing has been said yet of "people who are bestial by nature" who were part of the original taxonomy set forth above in sec. 92.

Summary of Plato's Laws

Introduction

The Translation

The Arabic text of Alfarabi's *Plato's Laws* was first published by Francesco Gabrieli, who also translated it into Latin.[1] Almost a decade after its appearance, Muhsin Mahdi subjected Gabrieli's text to a detailed examination and presented additional evidence with a view to a new edition.[2] Thérèse-Anne Druart took on the task and brought a painstakingly careful edition of the text to light about a decade and a half ago—its publication having been delayed for several years, a circumstance to which she alludes at the very beginning of the published text. As Druart graciously notes in the introduction to the edition, she was aided in no small measure by Mahdi pointing her to one manuscript and providing a microfilm copy of another.[3] The present translation is based on this edition with minor modifications noted when they occur.

A translation of the introduction plus the first and second treatises of the *Summary* was published by Muhsin Mahdi over half a century ago.[4]

1. *Alfarabius, Compendium Legum Platonis*, trans. and ed. Franciscus Gabrieli, Plato Arabus, vol. 3 (London: Warburg Institute, 1952).

2. Muhsin Mahdi, "The *Editio Princeps* of Farabi's *Compendium Legum*," *Journal of Near Eastern Studies* 20, no. 1 (1961): 1–24.

3. "Le sommaire du livre des 'Lois' de Platon (*Ǧawāmi' Kitāb al-Nawāmīs li-Aflāṭūn*) par Abū Naṣr al-Fārābī," trans. and ed. Thérèse-Anne Druart, in *Bulletin d'Études Orientales* 50 (1998): 109–155.

4. See *Medieval Political Philosophy: A Sourcebook*, ed. Ralph Lerner and Muhsin Mahdi, 1st ed. (New York: Free Press of Glencoe, 1963), 83–94. The introduction has been republished in the new edition of that work, *Medieval Political Philosophy: A Sourcebook*, 2nd ed., ed. Joshua Parens and Joseph C. Macfarland (Ithaca, NY: Cornell University Press, 2011), 72–73.

Moreover, about ten years after that, Mahdi prepared an early version of this translation for use with students. Revisited from time to time over the years, it has now been thoroughly revised in the light both of Druart's new edition and more recent translations of Alfarabi's other writings by both Mahdi and myself.

Mahdi's division of the text into numbered sections, as well as into paragraphs within those sections, has been preserved. The same holds largely for the internal divisions of the paragraphs into sentences. Numbers in brackets in the body of the text refer to the pages of Druart's text, Gabrieli's original edition now having been surpassed by Mahdi's emendations and Druart's edition. The numbers in brackets at the beginning of some of the numbered sections and paragraphs refer to the pages and their divisions in Henricus Stephanus's 1578 edition of the Greek text of Plato's *Laws*. Similarly, brackets have been used to indicate what seem to be an introduction and conclusion, even though they are not set apart as such in the available manuscripts.

The only other translation of the *Summary* known to me is that into French by Stéphane Diebler.[5] Appealing in linguistic elegance, inconsistent rendering of key terms diminishes its value as a faithful representation of Alfarabi's text.

In this version, every effort has been made, consistent with good English, to translate the same Arabic word by the same English word and to render Alfarabi's style in a faithful manner. Differently stated, although the goal is to provide a literal version of Alfarabi's text, the need for the translation to make good sense in English has never been forgotten. Thus, it has sometimes been necessary to make explicit the antecedent referred to merely by a pronoun or to repeat a term that Alfarabi passes over in silence because Arabic syntax allows such indirectness. Students of Alfarabi are all too aware that this accords very well with his own penchant for elliptical expression. Brief notes are used to explain how key terms have been rendered and to draw attention to instances when liberties have been taken with the rendering of words or clauses. Interested readers may also find the Arabic-English and English-Arabic glossaries at the end of the volume helpful.

5. See *Le compendium des Lois de Platon*, trans. Stéphane Diebler, intro. Pauline Koetschet, in *Al-Fārābī, Philosopher à Baghdad au Xe siécle*, ed. Ali Benmakhlouf and Pauline Koetschet (Paris: Éditions du Seuil, 2007), 130–191.

The Teaching of the Text

Alfarabi's *Summary of Plato's Laws* consists of an introduction, accounts of the first nine books of Plato's *Laws*, and a conclusion. In the introduction, Alfarabi explains Plato's art of writing in general and the method he follows in writing the *Laws* in particular. Alfarabi also sets forth his own method of summarizing Plato's *Laws*, points to the two groups of readers for whom the work was written, and indicates the benefit each might derive from reading it. Elsewhere—namely, in the *Political Regime*, the *Enumeration of the Sciences*, chapter 5, and the *Book of Religion*—he examines the place of legislation and laws in the broader context of political philosophy. Here, however, the question of laws, as well as how and why they are formulated, becomes the object of a specialized study. Of particular importance for Alfarabi is the relevance of Plato's investigation concerning Greek divine laws for the study and understanding of all divine laws. Indeed, Zeus's role in setting down Greek laws is emphasized at the very beginning of the commentary and reiterated in subsequent passages.[6]

Although Alfarabi never speaks directly of Islam or its divine law in the *Summary*, no less a successor than Avicenna draws attention to this link in his popular epistle entitled *On the Division of the Rational Sciences*. He depicts Plato's *Laws* as treating prophecy and the divine law generally, then explains how Arab and Muslim philosophers understand the treatise and the subjects raised in it. Avicenna strives, above all, to explain what the philosophers mean when they speak of law—the term in question being *nāmūs*, the Arabic transliteration of the Greek *nomos*. Adamant that they do not use it with a view to deceiving or misleading the people, he contends that when they speak of law or *nāmūs*, it is traditional law (*sunna*) that they have in mind.[7] This perspective allows him to infer that

6. *Summary*, 1.1 with 1.7 and 1.9.

7. Avicenna adds that by traditional law, the philosophers mean "established and fixed example" as well as "the coming-down of revelation," then notes that "the Arabs also call the angel that brings down the revelation a *nāmūs*"; see *Fī Aqsām al-ʿUlūm al-ʿAqliyya*, in *Tisʿ Rasāʾil* (Cairo, 1908), 108:2–6; English, "On the Division of the Rational Sciences," trans. Muhsin Mahdi, in *Medieval Political Philosophy: A Sourcebook*, 97:21–25 (1st ed.) or 75b:35–76a:5 (2nd ed.).

Those who agree with Avicenna that *nāmūs* signifies the messenger who brings revelation often cite a discussion between Muhammad and Waraqa bin Nawfal, the uncle of his wife Khadija. According to Ibn Hisham, Khadija took Muhammad to meet Waraqa, who was then Christian, to inquire about the being who spoke to Muhammad in the Cave of Hira. On hearing his description, Waraqa is reported to have said, "There hath

> through this part of practical wisdom, one becomes cognizant of the necessity for prophecy and the need the human species has of Law [*sharīʿā*] for its existence, preservation, and life to come. Through it, one becomes cognizant of the wisdom in the universal penalties [*al-ḥudūd al-kulliyya*] common to [all] Laws and in those [penalties] particular to one Law or another having to do with one people or another and one time or another. And it makes known the difference between divine prophecy and all of the false claims to it.[8]

This, from the philosophical perspective, is the context for seeking to understand the way Alfarabi speaks of law in his *Summary* of what he contends Plato had to say about the divine—and also the human—origin of Greek laws, that is, the way he speaks not only of laws, but also of traditional law and of Law. In asserting that by *nāmūs* philosophers mean *sunna*, and then linking the latter with *sharīʿa*, Avicenna suggests that, at least for them, law is simply conventional. It therefore becomes imperative to investigate what it means to speak of law as coming about through prophecy and revelation. Alfarabi's skillfulness at presenting all sides of complex issues makes him a most helpful guide in this quest.

Alfarabi's Access to Plato's *Laws*

In recent times, scholarly debate over whether Alfarabi expounds Plato's text or merely an abridged version of it has engendered doubt about

come unto Muhammad the greatest Nāmūs, even he that would come unto Moses." See Martin Lings, *Muhammad: His Life Based on the Earliest Sources* (New York: Inner Traditions International, 1983), 44. In an explanatory footnote to the word *nāmūs*, Lings says: "The Greek Nomos, in the sense of Divine Law or Scripture, here identified with the Angel of Revelation."

Indeed, Christian Arabs use *nāmūs* to refer to the archangel Gabriel and understand the term to mean "the carrier of the secret." Thus, Cyril Glasse identifies it as "an archaic term, borrowed from the Christians, for Being, or the personal God." He continues: "It was personified as an Angel who imparted knowledge or brought revelations. This was the Angel, one could say, of *intellection*, or knowledge obtained through the universal contents of the mind being brought into consciousness in the lightning flash of recognition, a 'natural' revelation. . . . Waraqah . . . identified the Angel bringing revelations to the Prophet as the Namus" (Glasse's italics). See Cyril Glasse, article *nāmūs*, in *Concise Encyclopaedia of Islam* (San Francisco, CA: Harper & Row, 1989).

Others think the term refers only to the message itself or to the Law revealed to Muhammad. Key for them is that the Quran invariably identifies the one who delivers the message as *al-rūḥ al-amīn*, *rūḥ al-qudus*, *al-rūḥ*, or simply Jibrīl. Alfarabi's discussion of the active intellect in the *Political Regime*, above (sec. 3, n. 3), likening it to *al-rūḥ al-amīn* and *rūḥ al-qudus*, may be an allusion to that opinion.

8. *Aqsām*, 108:6–10; "Division," 97:26–32 or 76a:5–b:7.

the value of this treatise. Alfarabi's unique account of Plato's approach presented in the introduction to the *Summary*, subsequent innovative explanations of the text, and willingness to make direct as well as indirect departures from it have prompted the suspicion that he may have been responding to something other than Plato's *Laws*. Even though there is ample evidence that two Arabic translations of the *Laws* were easily available to Alfarabi, one by his student Yaḥyā ibn ʿAdī,[9] neither is now extant. It is not possible, therefore, to determine through textual comparisons which of the two he may have used or whether he actually used either one. Nor is it possible to identify the abridged version of the text he may have used or any other source that may have influenced him. It is known that an Arabic translation of Galen's *Synopsis of Plato's Laws* existed at the time Alfarabi was writing, but that is now lost as well. Precisely because these uncertainties have prompted controversy as to how the *Summary* is to be read and interpreted—that is, whether one can seek to learn something about Plato's *Laws* from Alfarabi's *Summary* with confidence or must instead be limited to conjectures about its role in the transmission of Greek texts into Arabic—the history of the question deserves attention here.

For our purposes, it begins with Francesco Gabrieli, the first editor of Alfarabi's *Summary of Plato's Laws*. Taken aback at Alfarabi's novel explanations and unusual terminology, he accounted for them by postulating that Alfarabi was more beholden to Neoplatonic and Syriac intermediary accounts than to his own investigations of Plato's text. Although Gabrieli was aware of Leo Strauss's probing interpretation of Alfarabi's *Philosophy of Plato*, he dismissed the suggestion that this work contained an esoteric teaching as stemming more from Strauss's ingenuity than scholarly exegesis. Strauss's success in illuminating Alfarabi's insights into Plato's fuller teaching and admirably detailed examination of the arguments within the text notwithstanding, Gabrieli thought he paid insufficient attention to the influence putative Neoplatonic and Syriac sources could have had on Alfarabi. For him, nothing was to be learned from Alfarabi about Plato or Plato's teaching. The suggestion that Alfarabi might be indirectly addressing the relationship between philosophy and religion and also between philosophy and politics occasioned no more pause than Strauss's critique of the textual historian who, blind to the possibly nonhistorical philosophical character of Alfarabi's text, fails to read him with the same

9. See Ibn al-Nadīm, *Kitāb al-Fihrist*, ed. Gustav Flügel (Beirut: Maktabat Khayyāṭ, 1964), 246.

care as Avicenna and Maimonides do. Even Strauss's illustration of how contradictions and repetitions in Alfarabi's text could be unraveled or more thoroughly explained by recourse to Maimonides fell on deaf ears.[10]

Shortly thereafter, Strauss indicated how one might read Gabrieli's own edition of the *Summary* in order to elucidate the work's fuller teaching. He indicated the flaws in Gabrieli's assumptions about influences and—through detailed attention to particular themes relevant to lawgiving addressed by Alfarabi—identified the major subjects addressed in the text, then showed their affinity to questions raised in the *Philosophy of Plato*. Here, too, detailed analysis of the text itself and precise references to Alfarabi's arguments allowed Strauss to reveal how much one could learn from careful and thoughtful reading. Muhsin Mahdi's lengthy review of Gabrieli's edition, emphasizing Alfarabi's grasp of Plato's teaching and the broad extent of his influence on the tradition of medieval Arabic-Islamic philosophy, appeared not long after. Taking a cue from textual historians, Mahdi used their own tools to show precisely what could be learned from Alfarabi's medieval contemporaries. Moreover, examining more closely the single manuscript—Leiden Or. 133—used by Gabrieli, plus unpublished material from the renowned Arabist Paul Kraus, Mahdi corrected several errors and misreadings in Gabrieli's edition.[11]

The decorum and civil address that stand as hallmarks of these exchanges notwithstanding, the fundamental question at issue about how past authors are to be studied and understood is readily evident. Clearly intent on discerning what in Alfarabi's exposition so intrigues subsequent thinkers within this medieval Arabic-Islamic and Arabic-Jewish tradition and open to learning something new about Plato from Alfarabi, Strauss and Mahdi strove to grasp Alfarabi's philosophic teaching. Conversely, Gabrieli and those who follow his lead intimated that their grasp of Plato's teaching is so accurate as to necessitate explaining deviation from it by a commentator—even one of Alfarabi's stature—in terms of influence from outside sources. To them, Alfarabi is a merely derivative thinker. The interpretive skills as well as enviable grasp of Plato's teaching plus

10. See *Alfarabius, Compendium Legum Platonis*, ix–xii and xiii, n. 6, with Leo Strauss, "Farabi's *Plato*," in *Louis Ginzberg Jubilee Volume* (New York: American Academy for Jewish Research, 1945), 357–393, esp. 363–385 (note Strauss's explicit digression at 375–377) and 389–393.

11. See Leo Strauss, "How Fārābī Read Plato's *Laws*," in *What Is Political Philosophy* (Glencoe, IL: Free Press, 1959), 139–144, 147–150, 150–152; also Mahdi, "*Editio Princeps*," 2–10, 10–15, 15–24.

medieval Arabic-Islamic philosophy displayed by Strauss and Mahdi laid bare the tenuous character of the arguments about extraneous influences on Alfarabi and showed that it was possible to learn about Plato from him, but did not suffice to make the question prompting Gabrieli's original doubt disappear. Not even the conjectures of Richard Walzer—usually ranked among the partisans of explaining texts by seeking their supposed sources—that Alfarabi must have had access to Plato's *Laws* gave pause to those who doubted.[12]

Quiescent for a number of years, the controversy erupted anew following the appearance of Thérèse-Anne Druart's research note concerning one of the two additional manuscripts—Escurial ms. 888 (Casiri 883) and Kabul ms. 217—she had consulted for her new edition of the *Summary*. Comparison of the manuscripts suggested to her that Escurial 888 is an abridgement of the full version of the text such as that found in Leiden 133. For what follows, it is important to note that she nowhere claimed Escurial was an abridgement of Leiden—a point she emphasized in her subsequent edition. Moreover, Druart pointed out that Escurial is about a century earlier than Leiden.[13] As noted, factors beyond her control delayed publication of her new edition for two decades, but she shared the unpublished version with fellow scholars—in particular, Dimitri Gutas and Joshua Parens, both of whom were working on the *Summary*.[14]

From his own study of the manuscripts, Gutas determined that Escurial could not be a shorter version of Leiden and incorrectly represented Druart as having made a claim to that effect. Then, averring that the treatises found in both manuscripts had to be independent works drawing on a common source, he denied it could be a version of Alfarabi's *Summary* and insisted, rather, that it must be Galen's *Synopsis* of Plato's *Laws*. To support his contentions, he pointed to readings from Plato's *Laws* found in Escurial, but not in Leiden, as well as to other readings in Escurial found neither in Plato's *Laws* nor in Leiden. The features common to both manuscripts suggested to Gutas that even though Escurial and Leiden

12. Richard Walzer, "Platonism in Islamic Philosophy," in *Greek into Arabic: Essays on Islamic Philosophy* (Cambridge, MA: Harvard University Press, 1962), 238, 243–247.

13. Thérèse-Anne Druart, "Un sommaire du sommaire Farabien des *Lois* de Platon," in *Bulletin de Philosophie Médiévale* 19 (1977): 43–45. The Escurial ms. is from the end of the twelfth century or beginning of the thirteenth CE, while the date found in the Leiden ms. (692 AH) shows it to be from the end of the thirteenth. The Kabul ms. is much later, 999–1000 AH (1590–1592 CE). See also Alfarabi, "Le sommaire," 116.

14. See Alfarabi, "Le sommaire," 109, note to title.

(which he presented as Alfarabi's text) must have used the same source, Alfarabi had surely altered it. For Gutas, then, Alfarabi expands on the common source in ways not reflected in Escurial and takes far greater liberties with it than the author of the earlier manuscript does. Finally, focusing on the way Alfarabi emphasizes acquiring moral virtues toward the middle of the commentary, but somehow overlooking the way the same topic is developed at the very beginning, where Alfarabi explains the goal of Plato's *Laws*, Gutas asserted this to be evidence of his debt to Galen and concluded that "the common source . . . was either Galen's *Synopsis of the Laws*, as it left the pen of its translator . . . or very closely related to it; the precise relationship has yet to be determined." Oblivious to how he was thereby donning the mantle of the philosophically myopic textual historian caricatured half a century earlier by Strauss, Gutas went on to proclaim his desire to "study in greater detail the Greek exegetical tradition and reception of Plato's *Laws* from Posidonius to Galen" and "highlight the precise ways in which Fārābī molded transmitted material to fashion his own philosophy."[15]

In 1991, that is, some years before the article appeared, Gutas shared with Parens a draft in which these insights or conjectures were formulated. On the basis of the draft, Parens contended that Gutas had misunderstood Druart's description of the relationship between Escurial and Leiden, as well as of what each represents; provided insufficient evidence for identifying Galen's *Synopsis* as the common source of which both purportedly provide an account; and—in characterizing Alfarabi as merely abridging Galen's text—failed to appreciate his role as a commentator. Recurring to the very sources cited by Gutas, especially Posidonius and Galen, Parens suggested why Alfarabi may well have known more about Plato's *Laws* than he admits.[16] Parens acknowledged that pointing to the flaws and logical inadequacies in Gutas's interpretation was not sufficient to prove Alfarabi did have access to Plato's *Laws*, but then went on to present a detailed interpretation of the *Summary* based on a comparison with the *Laws* as the needed evidence.

15. Dimitri Gutas, "Galen's *Synopsis* of Plato's *Laws* and Fārābī's *Talkhīṣ*," in *The Ancient Tradition in Christian and Islamic Hellenism: Studies on the Transmission of Greek Philosophy and Sciences*, ed. Gerhard Endress and Remke Kruk (Leiden: Research School CNWS, 1997), 103, 109–110, 117–119. For Alfarabi's discussion of the importance of moral virtue, see the translated text below, 5.7 (treatise 5, section 7); his earlier remark about the salience of this issue occurs at 1.16 (with n. 8) and apparently refers to Plato, *Laws* 1.641b–d.

16. Joshua Parens, *Metaphysics as Rhetoric: Alfarabi's Summary of Plato's "Laws"* (Albany: SUNY Press, 1995), xxxi–xxxiv.

In the subsequently published article, Gutas nowhere alluded to his earlier exchange with Parens. However, the last footnote did repeat the penultimate sentence of a harsh, ad hominem attack on Parens that appeared in the guise of a book review a year after the article.[17] In the review, Gutas not only referred to the exchange; he also scolded Parens like a schoolboy for rejecting his arguments. But he never addressed the reasons set forth by Parens for doing so. Moreover, eschewing consideration of the detailed textual analysis set forth by Parens, he focused solely on the impossibility that Alfarabi might have had access to Plato's *Laws*. On the few occasions he did note in passing particular aspects of the interpretation presented by Parens, he revealed patent misunderstanding of Parens's particular goal and how it related to Plato's and Alfarabi's philosophical inquiries. Indeed, at the beginning of the review, he simply asserted that the mainstream opinion about Plato as set forth by Charles Kahn and Glenn Morrow—namely, that for Plato all politics and morals rest on metaphysics—is the only valid opinion.[18]

Thus, although the discussion centered on Alfarabi's merit as an interpreter of Plato and Aristotle continues unabated, a sharper and more discordant tone has now been introduced. Absent Steven Harvey and his salutary efforts to reconcile the warring parties, that might mark the end of the story and, therewith, intelligent, courteous, scholarly exchange. With clear reasoning and gentle speech, he has reexamined the arguments of Gutas and Parens by focusing on the third manuscript Druart used for her edition—Kabul, Library of the Ministry of Information, no. 217. Variant readings found in it corroborate the claims by Druart and Parens that Leiden and Escurial are derived from an early version of the same text, Alfarabi's *Summary*, and invalidate the efforts by Gutas to view the latter as an abridgment of Galen's *Synopsis*. Yet, as Harvey readily acknowledges, such variants raise an important question whose solution might strengthen Gutas's position, namely, the need to explain what accounts for the variants in the Leiden and Kabul versions as contrasted with those in the Escurial version. In effect, both approaches are conjectural. While the discovery of yet another manuscript might well give new life to the

17. Dimitri Gutas, "Fārābī's Knowledge of Plato's *Laws*," *International Journal of the Classical Tradition* 4, no. 3 (1998): 405–411.

18. Thoughtful readers interested in the problems besetting textual interpretation, especially concerning philosophical texts of such complexity, will profit greatly from the guidelines Parens sets forth in his introduction about how to read this particular text of Alfarabi; see *Metaphysics as Rhetoric*, xxvi–xxviii. A more balanced review of the book appeared in *Speculum* 73, no. 3 (July 1998): 881–883.

objections and presumptions raised by Gutas, it could also have the opposite result. By chance, Harvey was able to point to a Hebrew text that bears witness to just such a manuscript.[19]

As the title of his article suggests, this was not Harvey's main point. Rather, based on anomalies he found in the *Summary*—Alfarabi's failure to indicate that Plato's text is a dialogue between three individuals, the constant use of "he" as though the text were a treatise by Plato, and the overwhelming occurrence of the particle "then" (*thumma*) followed by a third-person singular verb—he concluded that Alfarabi was most likely not commenting on Plato's *Laws*. It is a judgment Harvey arrived at hesitantly and with apparent trepidation, for he quickly noted that it "does not mean that Alfarabi's *Summary* cannot help us to understand Plato's *Laws*." Rather, its import for Harvey is "that we must exercise great caution before making or accepting any arguments from silence or other such arguments (just as we ought not to dismiss them too readily)." In this sense, "the importance of the *Summary* as a guide to the *Laws* does not wholly depend on whether Alfarabi read the *Laws* or a good summary or paraphrase of it."[20] Harvey then proceeded in a subsequent article to show how one can read Alfarabi's *Summary* with profit—learning from it about Plato's *Laws*, as well as about different emphases Alfarabi brings to Plato's text, but refusing to conjecture about what Plato says that Alfarabi passes over in silence.[21]

Commendable as these two articles are and instructive as Harvey's example about how to read Alfarabi's *Summary* may be, his reasons for deciding against Alfarabi having read Plato's *Laws* are not unproblematic. In none of Alfarabi's discussions of Plato now extant does he speak about the dialectical character of Platonic dialogues. Likewise, in his commentary on the *Republic*, Averroes explicitly ignores its dialectical arguments in order to focus on what he calls its scientific statements.[22] Moreover, he also uses the pronoun "he" or speaks as though the text being discussed

19. Steven Harvey, "Did Alfarabi Read Plato's *Laws*?" in *Medioevo: Rivista di storia della filosofia medievale* 28 (2003): 54–61, 65–68.

20. Ibid., 64–65.

21. Steven Harvey, "Can a Tenth-Century Islamic Aristotelian Help Us Understand Plato's *Laws*?" in *Plato's Laws: From Theory to Practice*, ed. S. Scolnicov and L. Brisson (Sankt Augustin: Academia Verlag, 2003), 325–330.

22. Averroes, *Averroes on Plato's "Republic,"* trans. Ralph Lerner (Ithaca, NY: Cornell University Press, 1974), 21:3–4.

is a treatise by Plato. Finally, in both the *Philosophy of Plato* and the *Philosophy of Aristotle,* Alfarabi uses the particle "then" (*thumma*) followed by a third-person singular verb (referring to Plato in the first instance and Aristotle in the second) to signal the different steps in his own exposition. Our ignorance about Alfarabi's awareness of Platonic dialogues notwithstanding, we do know he had direct access to Aristotle's treatises. So this stylistic idiosyncrasy cannot be viewed as indicative of Alfarabi's uncertainty about a particular text. In short, the anomalies adduced by Harvey are not all that conclusive.

Still, the twists and turns of the debate show clearly that we simply do not know whether Alfarabi's *Summary* is based on the text of Plato's *Laws,* as he claims, or an abridged version of it. What we cannot fail to note, however, are the remarkable insights Alfarabi provides to this difficult text. Nor can we ignore the most unusual manner in which he approaches Plato's *Laws,* just as he explains he will do in the introduction. Such awareness must guide us as we strive to make sense of what he says about law and the way it comes to be as well as what that reveals about his understanding and interpretation of what Plato has to say about the same topics. Given that there are grounds to wonder how good a version of Plato's *Laws* Alfarabi might have had before him, it will be prudent to follow Harvey's advice here and focus on what Alfarabi actually says about Plato's statements while remaining circumspect about his silence concerning this or that passage in the text. To adopt such an approach for the purposes of this introduction is in no way to impugn the quality—indeed, the brilliance—of Joshua Parens's interpretation. It provides a consummate illustration of how to pursue the deep philosophical questions raised in a text as complex as Plato's *Laws* through recourse to another text such as Alfarabi's *Summary* that examines many of those questions even while raising others.

Alfarabi's Approach to Plato's *Laws*

Alfarabi opens his *Summary of Plato's Laws* by distinguishing human beings as the species able to determine what is useful and pursue it. They do so, he asserts, by considering how particular incidents point to something more general. It is an observation that privileges inductive reasoning. Reflecting about discrete occurrences so as to infer rules of conduct, rather than striving first to discern the workings of the universe and then deducing what is good and useful, thus becomes primarily important.

This does not mean that Alfarabi jettisons the paradigms set forth in the *Political Regime, Virtuous City, Attainment of Happiness, Book of Religion*, and similar writings, which all point to good rulership as centering on philosophers or kings imbued with philosophic wisdom, but that the focus here on actual political life takes precedence. Consonant with this different emphasis, he draws attention throughout the treatise to the solidly human character of lawgivers and the shortcomings of those receiving their laws. He thus appears especially intent on identifying the components of a good, rather than a best, regime. Given Plato's—or at least the Athenian Stranger's, but Alfarabi pays scant heed to the dramatic features of the dialogue—declaration that the regime aimed at in the *Laws* is a lesser one, perhaps one that can be achieved, such an objective is not surprising.[23]

Nor does it imply a criticism of lawgiving generally or the divinely inspired lawgiver in particular. After all, as attested by several Quranic verses, imperfect political order stems from divine intention.[24] In the *Summary*, Alfarabi refers not once to the Quran, Islam, prophetic missions, or Muhammad. Much as that silence prompts the perspicacious reader to wonder how revelation does affect lawgiving or what distinguishes divinely inspired lawgiving from that which is not, those topics are not addressed.

Rather, Alfarabi's discussion of the way human beings reason culminates in elucidation of Plato's unusual writing style. The reader is not to presume that what Plato does occasionally is what he does always, or even what he does in the *Laws*. Such at least is the lesson to be derived from the tale of the pious ascetic who spoke truth while pretending to do the opposite and thereby escaped imprisonment, maybe even death, at the hands of an unjust ruler. Yet, if insight into reading Plato is derived from discerning what human error allowed the ascetic to escape, that awareness is equally important for learning to distinguish what is useful from what is useless and what is most imminent from what is less so. Reflection on the three topics raised in the opening sentences of the *Summary*—seizing on the useful as distinctly human, the need for experience, and greater experience increasing one's excellence—is made more salient by the intriguing tale of the ascetic, provided one apprehends that its point is the need to distinguish clearly and not the benefit of tricking people. A thoughtful human intent on wisdom must be ever alert to what leads to error. In addition to experience, he must discover how to reason correctly about the link between disparate events.

23. Plato, *Laws* 5.739a–b and c–e; cf. *Summary*, 4.1–3, 5.14–15, 6.1, 6.3, and the references to Greek regimes mentioned by Alfarabi's Plato at 3.11 and 4.6.

24. Quran 5:48, 10:19, 16:93, 42:8.

In using the story to explain how to read Plato, Alfarabi underlines Plato's reputation for recourse to symbols and riddles as well as his reticence about expressing his opinions in his own voice in the *Laws* and other dialogues, then focuses on the art or science of legislation discussed in the *Laws* and vows to extract such hints from it as will help both the one who wants to learn more and the one not able to study and reflect. This affords him an astute way of alluding to the indirect character of his own writing. As he notes early on in the *Summary*, an adept teacher can use even such apparently useless pastimes as play to instill habits ultimately of use to the one who wants to learn.[25]

Reflection on the laws that can benefit promising citizens or oneself leads to tangible results only insofar as one excels in applying "the faculty by which" a human being "distinguishes among the causes and objects he deals with and observes." In other words, one must pay attention both to the way things come to be and to the reason for their being. Just as Plato's *Laws* opens with the query of whom to credit with laying down the laws by which old cities are governed, so does Alfarabi's *Summary* note the importance of determining causality in such matters. For the Athenian Stranger, who plays such a central role in the *Laws*, that query quickly gives way to the more important one of what purpose different lawgivers sought to achieve by means of their legislation. Alfarabi also moves from the question of who made laws to the purpose they serve, passing over in silence that both are aspects of causality.[26]

25. *Summary*, 1.18, and consider the introduction to the *Enumeration of the Sciences* presented below in appendix A.

26. See Alfarabi, *Attainment of Happiness*, sec. 59, in *Alfarabi, Philosophy of Plato and Aristotle*, trans. Muhsin Mahdi (Ithaca, NY: Cornell University Press, 2001); the term translated there as "legislator," *wāḍi' al-nawāmīs*, seems to be used more precisely in the *Summary* to signify "lawgiver," and that is the way it is rendered. In "Quelques remarques sur la science politique de Maïmonide et de Fârâbî," *Revue des Études Juives* 197 (1935): 22, Leo Strauss loosely paraphrases Deuteronomy 30:11–14 to illustrate Maimonides' emphasis on seeking the purpose of the Law, rather than its origin, in *Guide of the Perplexed*, 2.39–40: "Que la révélation de la Tora soit un miracle ou un fait naturel, que la Tora soit venue du ciel ou non—dès qu'elle est donnée, elle est 'non pas au ciel' mais 'très près de toi, dans ta bouche et dans ton coeur afin que tu la pratiques.' Non pas le mystère de son origine, dont la recherche conduit ou bien à la théosophie ou bien à l''épicuréisme,' mais sa fin, dont la compréhension garantit l'obéissance à la Tora, est accessible à la raison humaine. Guidé par cette conception, Maïmonide, après avoir exposé que la prophétie de Moïse se distingue en tant que prophétie législatrice de celle des autres prophètes, aborde au chapitre suivant (40) la question fondamentale concernant la fin, la raison de la loi." Consider also Strauss's January 20, 1938 letter to Jacob Klein, *Leo Strauss Gesamelte Schriften, Band 3: Hobbes' politische Wissenschaft und zugehörige Schriften-Briefe*, ed. Heinrich Meier and Wiebke Meier (Stuttgart: J. B. Metzler, 2001), 545: "Maimonides wird immer aufregender. Er war ein wirklich freier Geist. Er hat natürlich die Legende von der

The remarks of Avicenna cited above confirm that he believed the study of laws and lawgiving to be best approached in such a manner. Alfarabi's *Summary* reveals how assiduously he pursues the question posed by Plato's spokesman in this treatise, namely, discovering the best laws for ruling human beings. One sign of this is his identifying the laws set down by Zeus and Apollo as both *nawāmīs* and *sharāʾiʿ*. The names accorded them matter less to him than the link uniting them in what they aim to establish. Consequently, he goes on to use the terms interchangeably in his *Summary* and hesitates not the least to term nomos and traditional law "divine."[27] Achieving clarity about a city such as actually to arise requires awareness of the laws good for particular humans living in determinate times and places. Such an inquiry, set forth in the *Summary*, is distinct from one that searches for the general ends pursued in different kinds of polities or in a city that may exist only in speech—namely, one resembling the inquiry recorded in Plato's *Republic* or in the *Political Regime* and other writings of Alfarabi. Part of what distinguishes the *Summary* from the *Political Regime* is Alfarabi's insistence in the latter on identifying law only as *sharīʿa* or *sunna*. His more inclusive approach in the *Summary* better serves his stated goal of presenting what Plato "intended to explain" in the *Laws* about laws, lawgiving, and the purposes of both.[28]

At the beginning of all but the first and third treatises of the *Summary*, Alfarabi provides a synopsis of the discussion to follow. The seventh treatise stands out as the only one lacking discernible links between its sections and the corresponding book in Plato's *Laws*. Treatise 9 opens with the observation that the exposition of the prior eight treatises has centered on the roots of the laws, a term Alfarabi then equates with regulations. Its

jüdischen Herkunft der Philosophie *nicht* geglaubt. Was war dann aber Moses für ihn? Es ist tatsächlich schwer zu sagen. Die cruciale Frage war für ihn *nicht* Weltschöpfung oder Weltewigkeit (denn er war von der Weltewigkeit überzeugt), sondern, ob der ideale Gesetzgeber Prophet sein muss. Und diese Frage hat er—verneint, wie Farabi vor ihm und Averroës gleichzeitig getan haben. Es ist sehr schwierig, das zu beweisen, da er die Fragen in exegetischer Form diskutiert." (Emphasis in the original.)

27. See *Summary*, 1.1, 1.9 (Zeus and Apollo); 1.9, 2.8, 4.13, 7.2 (*sharīʿa/sharāʾiʿ*, *nāmūs/nawāmīs*); 1.7, 1.12, 2.1 (in two places), 3.4 (*nāmūs* as "divine"); 4.4, 5.1, 5.12, 5.18 (*sunna* as "divine"). Similarly, in the *Book of Letters*, he evinces no compunctions about speaking of the laws legislated (*sharraʿa*) by God as *nawāmīs* or nomoi; see Alfarabi, *Book of Letters*, part 1, chap. 17, sec. 106, trans. Charles E. Butterworth (forthcoming); for the Arabic text, see *Abū Naṣr al-Fārābī, Kitāb al-Ḥurūf*, ed. Muhsin Mahdi (Beirut: Dār al-Mashriq, 1969). A revised edition of the Arabic, based on new manuscript evidence, will accompany the forthcoming English translation.

28. See *Summary*, "Conclusion"; also Strauss, "How Fārābī Read Plato's *Laws*," 141; *Thoughts on Machiavelli* (Glencoe, IL: Free Press, 1958), 15.

subject is not, however, the roots of the laws or regulations in any sense, but the things that adorn the laws—a task to be carried out by the virtuous legists. Anomalies notwithstanding, nothing in the accounts of these treatises links them more tightly or evokes a separate teaching.

Alfarabi opens treatise 1 by commenting on how laws are caused, namely, by a lawgiver. He does so, not in his own name, but as an account of what is said in the *Laws*. This practice he follows throughout the *Summary*. When he does voice a comment, appreciation, or explanation of his own, it is almost in passing—such that his observations and remarks appear to be mere reports of matters discussed in the *Laws*. Here, then, he explains that the Greeks hold Zeus, whom they deem the father of mankind, to be the cause of their laws. It appears that all peoples consider their laws to have a divine origin. Yet, as Alfarabi notes immediately afterward, they do so less to identify who set down which set of laws or how that person determined what laws to set down than to denote their uniqueness. Thoughtful citizens will go beyond civic pride so evinced to investigate the purpose of the laws in question.

The Arabic terms translated as "lawgiver" in what follows are *wāḍiʿ al-nāmūs* and *wāḍiʿ al-nawāmīs*, while *wāḍiʿū al-nawāmīs* is translated as "lawgivers"; the term *wāḍiʿū al-nāmūs* does not occur in the *Summary*, nor do the terms *wāḍiʿ al-sharīʿa* or *wāḍiʿ al-sharāʾiʿ* occur. (Whether it would be reasonable to speak of either in the plural—that is, of *wāḍiʿū al-sharīʿa* or *wāḍiʿū al-sharāʾiʿ*—the terms do not occur.) The Arabic terms rendered as "legislator" are *ṣāḥib al-nāmūs* and *ṣāḥib al-nawāmīs*, while the plural is either *aṣḥāb al-nāmūs* or *aṣḥāb al-nawāmīs*. For "legists," the Arabic term is *ahl al-nāmūs*; but the term *ahl al-nawāmīs* is never used. Only once does the Arabic term *ḥurrās al-nawāmīs wa al-siyāsāt* occur; translated as "custodians of the laws and regimes," it comprises judges, preachers, governors, and advisers.[29] The term *sharīʿa*, either as a singular or plural, is not to be found in conjunction with *ṣāḥib* or *aṣḥāb*. Simply put, Alfarabi refers no more to someone setting down a *sharīʿa* than legislating one. As already

29. The term "lawgiver" occurs seven times and "lawgivers" twice, with the latter being referred to indirectly once. For "lawgiver," see *Summary*, 1.7, 1.14, 1.15 (twice), 2.1, 3.2, 3.13. For "lawgivers," see 1.2, 1.20; the indirect reference is at 1.12. Dominating the discussion is the term "legislator," for it occurs in the singular and plural sixty times and is referred to indirectly 3 times: 1.7 (twice), 1.8, 1.19, 1.21, 1,25, 2.1 (five times), 2.2, 2.8, 3.7 (twice), 3.13 (twice), 3.14 (twice), 4.3, 4.13, 4.14, 4.16, 5.3, 5.14, 5.18, 6.1, 6.2, 6.3 (three times), 6.6, 6.8, 6.12, 6.14, 6.15, 6.18, 6.20, 7.1, 7.5, 7.7, 7.10, 7.11 (four times), 7.12 (twice), 7.13 (three times), 7.14, 8.5, 8.6, 8.7 (twice), 8.12, 8.13, 9.1, 9.7. The indirect references occur at 2.2, 6.5, 7. 2. The term "legists" occurs only at 6.17 and 9.2; and the term "custodians of the laws and regimes" occurs only at 6.10.

mentioned, he does not shy away from identifying the body of law set down by Zeus and Apollo as both a nomos (*nāmūs*) and a *sharī'a*.[30] That—given his silence about Islam, prophetic missions, and Muhammad—raises the questions of why some nomoi are denoted as *sharā'i'* (that is, some laws as Laws), while others are spoken of as only one or the other, and what the distinction signifies.

The opinion among Greeks that Zeus and Apollo are gods who set down laws must be what prompts Alfarabi to call their nomoi *sharā'i'*. But that is not sufficient to justify calling the law imposed by a conquering king or traditional laws set down by legislators—as distinct from lawgivers—divine and terming what legislators bring forth as *sharā'i'*.[31] It requires attention to the purpose of the law. Taking the reference to Cypress trees as a Platonic ploy to probe more deeply into the laws "generally known in his time," Alfarabi transforms the inquiry that first arises, wars and the need to prepare for them, into one about the way such preparation promotes moral virtue among the citizens and even for the lawgiver. He says nothing about the shade offered by these trees, even though this was explicitly mentioned in Plato's dialogue; nor does he make any reference to the obscurity that accompanies shade and thus, by implication, the discussion that work presents.

Acknowledgment that not all the topics addressed here were actually raised by Plato signals Alfarabi's innovative procedure. The legal command to wage war is thus said to serve the goal of seeking peace and to promote camaraderie as well as self-control, while the focus of the lawgivers and legislators on educating the citizens in moral virtue and good conduct appears to exclude intellectual virtue, justice, and courage. Although the actions cited here as exemplary of moral virtue limit it at first to moderation, the purview is subsequently broadened. Still, more emphasis is accorded the earlier, limited portrayal of moral virtue than the broader one. Throughout, Alfarabi presents Plato as emphasizing that the law exhorts, rather than prescribes or compels, citizens to aim at what makes them better. Specific statutes encourage them to aim at what makes them better, that is, at moral well-being. Because human virtue—not divine virtue or piety—is the goal, acquaintance with the vices is one path to

30. Ibid., 1.9.
31. See ibid., 1.1, 1.9, with 3.4, 7.2, 5.18.

it. Another is guidance proffered by an agreeable judge who, by means of gentle rather than harsh means, provides for the immediate economic needs of all citizens. To be sure, the possibility of arriving at divine virtue through practice of human virtue is acknowledged. But no explanation of how that might occur is presented. Moreover, even though most of the human virtues are identified and discussed, nothing is said about the divine ones.[32]

That silence suggests they are not the concern of the law. Though the divine virtues are honored in speech, the sufficiency of properly ordered human virtues makes it unnecessary for them to be pursued. For this reason, it behooves the true legislator—as distinct, it seems, from just any legislator—to ensure the laws are so directed. The good of the political community as a whole, not the achievement of individual excellence, is the goal. A possible indication of just how important it is to pursue such a task is the occurrence of the term "causes" in the two sections immediately following this declaration.[33]

Two points appear clearly here. First, while the law is for the sake of humans obtaining the virtues, the ones aimed at are the moral virtue conducing to political harmony. Second, this is to be accomplished indirectly. Citizens are to be inculcated in actions that promote virtue rather than subjected to moral rules. Accordingly, lawgivers establish the principles whose application is ensured by the legislators. The causes identified help attain moderation above all, but also foster liberality, courage, gentleness, and asceticism—the latter serving to rein in the passions, nothing more.[34]

Moral virtue is pursued not for its own sake, but for health of the soul. Its relation to the soul is like that of gymnastics to the body. That said, no fuller image is presented here of a healthy soul than of a healthy body. There is no account of gymnastics for the one or a system of education for the other; and apart from a brief assertion of the need for intellectual

32. See ibid., 1.3–4, 1.6–9, 1.22, 2.1, 2.9, 4.2, 5.7–9, 5.18, 6.15, 8.5; and consider especially 2.7, 3.14, 5.14.

33. Ibid., 1.8, 1.9.

34. See ibid., 1.7–8, 1.19, with 6.14. By overestimating the role of formal institutions, Patricia Crone and Dimitri Gutas miss the significance of education in Alfarabi's political teaching. See "Al-Fārābī's Imperfect Constitutions" and "The Meaning of *madanī* in al-Fārābī's 'Political' Philosophy," in *Mélanges de l'Université Saint-Joseph*, 57 (2004), *The Greek Strand in Islamic Political Thought: Proceedings of the Conference held at the Institute for Advanced Study, Princeton, 16–27 June 2003*, ed. Emma Gannagé, Patricia Crone, Maroun Aouad, Dimitri Gutas, and Eckart Schütrumpf, 191–228 and 259–282, respectively.

acumen, nothing is said about the intellectual virtues or the development of the intellect.[35] The focus, instead, is on the moral virtues.

That the habits leading to the moral virtues often resemble their excesses and deficiencies complicates the quest for them. It thus becomes necessary to understand what is appropriate and permissible for each circumstance. Differently stated, the ends pursued do not permit employing just any means. Still, as noted above, to acquire moral virtue intelligently, one must have some awareness of moral vice. The excesses engaged in by others may be observed so as to learn why such actions are blameworthy, as long as the looking-on goes no further. After allowing for such vicarious titillation, Alfarabi immediately returns to the key point: virtue can be acquired only by a person first "driving away the vice that is opposed to it." The breech of strict moral conduct does, nonetheless, include a passing reference to the benefits disciplined wine drinking can provide.[36]

Justice must be the premier or most important moral virtue, for Alfarabi insists that none of the others is complete without it. All the same, it is not to justice but to affection or amicability and freedom that the legislator is urged to devote utmost attention. When they are achieved, it is easier for the other laws to be brought about. Although compulsion must sometimes be used in place of education and upbringing or domination have temporary sway, those are exceptions. For "goodness and happiness" to be achieved, rule must be "based on fundamental affection, thorough upbringing, and perfect intellect." These three are so central to rulership as to provide the sole exception to the precedence usually accorded the city. Indeed, they are as applicable to the household and individual as to the city, an intimation that legislation must consider the particular as much as the general and politics not neglect the individual. Moreover, whereas justice inevitably entails punishments and other consequences that are not noble, nothing of the sort attaches to these three. All the same, a caveat is in order: these three pertain to the rulers, not to

35. See *Summary*, 1.21 with 2.8, end; also 2.7. The importance of excellent discernment is explained in *Al-Fārābī, Kitāb al-Tanbīh ʿalā Sabīl al-Saʿāda*, ed. Jaʿfar Āl Yāsīn, 2nd ed. (Beirut: Dār al-Manāhil li-al-Ṭibāʿa wa al-Nashr wa al-Tawzīʿ, 1987), 77:4–78:14; for an English translation, see *Directing Attention to the Way to Happiness*, trans. Jon McGinnis and David C. Reisman, in *Classical Arabic Philosophy: An Anthology of Sources* (Indianapolis: Hackett, 2007), 117, secs. 31–32.

36. *Summary*, 1.24; also 1.22–23.

the citizen body as a whole. For the citizens, as noted, something less is quite acceptable.[37]

Properly construed, the law serves not only to improve the citizens but also to keep them in such a reformed condition. It sets the standards for praiseworthy conduct and enforces actions that maintain it. For standards to have any effect, the citizens must be so habituated to them that acting in accordance with them comes to be almost natural. Songs, praise, and blame serve to instill and reinforce the attitudes that promote these standards. The legislator orders all activity in the city with a view to how it affects the moral upbringing of the citizens, the goal being to teach respect for good conduct and scorn for any action that falls short of it.[38]

In addition to working out the details of the law set down by the lawgiver, the legislator sees to its application and forms the citizens so that they abide by it. Attention to these tasks requires legislators to act somewhat as lawgivers. The habits or traditions the former establish among the citizens so closely resemble those the latter set down that the distinction between the one and the other becomes blurred. Acknowledging, albeit cursorily, that legislators may alter the laws to make them more effective, Alfarabi pointedly emphasizes that awareness of what lawgiving or legislating entails and the skill requisite for becoming adept in either make them akin to practical arts. The point is evident. Less so is his contention that merit or skill alone counts, not actually exercising the art. His passing assertion of divine sanction needed for someone to be a true lawgiver is equally obscure.[39]

Such questions, tantalizing as they are—especially that of how one can be skilled in an art yet unable to exercise it—must give way to permit the larger one implied by them to be grasped—namely, that lawgivers or legislators do not arise spontaneously. Not only must they have practiced the laws they would prescribe, they must also possess insight into how

37. See ibid., 3.13–15, 4.4–6, 9.9, with 9.2–3, 6, 8. In *Selected Aphorisms*, aphs. 61–62, 63–65, Alfarabi links affection (or love, the Arabic term is *maḥabba*) with justice; see Alfarabi, *The Political Writings: "Selected Aphorisms" and Other Texts*, trans. Charles E. Butterworth (Ithaca, NY: Cornell University Press, 2001); Arabic text, *Abū Naṣr al-Fārābī, Fuṣūl Muntaza'a*, ed. Fauzi M. Najjar (Beirut: Dār al-Mashriq, 1971).

38. See *Summary*, 4.2, 4.16, 5.18, 8.7, 9.7.

39. Ibid., 1.14, 6.14, with 2.7. Aristotle's observation that knowing and understanding are more important to the practice of an art than experience, because they provide awareness of why a thing is and experience only that it is (*Metaphysics* 1.1, 981a23–30, 981a30–b9, 981b30–982a2; 5.1, 1013a25–b3; 6.1, 1026a18), should be considered here. See also Alfarabi, *Book of Letters*, part 2, chap. 19, secs. 112–113.

the citizens will be affected by them. To discern what constitutes lawgiving or legislating, the aura surrounding the lawgiver and legislator must be pierced and the considerations evoking this or that law, tradition, and habit identified. That must be done discretely, perhaps by a preposterous allusion such as to distract the casual reader from the problem of how the lawgiver or legislator comes to know what laws are needed. The education, training, and upbringing prescribed for those who will be formed by the laws must also be considered with a view to how the lawgiver and legislator apprehend what is needed so as to rule their fellows.[40] In sum, the blurring of the distinction between lawgiver and legislator makes Alfarabi appear to be intimating that the latter has the same kind of knowledge as the former, that he fathoms the lawgiver's goals.

That is, indeed, what he contends. It allows him to point to the mystery surrounding how the lawgiver comes to have those goals as well as the knowledge of how to train people in pursuing them. Answers to those questions are to be found no more in the *Summary* than in any of his other writings, for that is not what Alfarabi is intent on. His quest, rather, is the goals laws aim at and the particular statutes leading to their realization. The stipulation that it must be guided by reason, presented here as merely an assertion made by Plato, is key to Alfarabi's procedure in this treatise and reinforced by reference to the training or education legislators must receive in political matters from childhood on. Important as it is to identify these ends, Alfarabi says nothing precise about them. Instead, he introduces moral virtue as something like moderation or even self-control. Because political life is so fluid, a lawgiver or legislator must be able to face all eventualities with rational equanimity.

Constant in human life is the pull of the passions. To lead a life in accordance with reason, the one best for humans, that pull must be resisted. Training is needed to help the citizens approximate such conduct. Hence, whatever toils are exacted of them must be mixed with pleasures that encourage such effort. A division of labor between the lawgiver and legislator occurs here as well: the lawgiver investigates the natural origins of moral habits, whereas the legislator seeks the laws that induce citizens to acquire them. Alfarabi buttresses these recommendations and observations with assurances that they are merely lessons set forth by Plato in his presentation, then notes their usefulness and attractiveness to indicate his own approval.[41] The education, training, and encouragement in the kind

40. See *Summary*, 1.15–16, 18–19, 25.
41. See ibid., 1.20–24, 2.1, 3.7–12.

of moral conduct such as to strengthen the soul's discerning power comes from sound laws. They, explains Alfarabi, speaking now in his own name, come about through the power of discernment a few citizens acquire on their own or "the truth" that most others receive "from their lawgivers, those who follow in their path, those who speak the truth about their laws, those who are good, and those who are righteous."

Though indirect, the hierarchy must not be ignored. Indeed, it explains the absence of physical and intellectual education in Alfarabi's *Summary*. That most citizens do not receive training beyond what allows them to resist the pull of the passions fits with the lesser character of the regime provided for here. It is consonant as well with the way Alfarabi limits the upbringing that fosters intellectual development to legislators and rulers. Citizens of this new regime are to follow the laws set down for them, not engage in making such laws themselves. Nor will they attain a level of human perfection such as to free themselves from body or matter and move on to a noncorporeal existence along the lines alluded to in the *Political Regime*.[42]

Adaptation to differences in human character is behind the more audacious suggestion—presented, all the same, as Plato's—that "the good is only relative, not absolute." This is why laws vary according to the time, place, and temperament of those for whom they are promulgated. In his own name, Alfarabi modifies or corrects Plato's formulation. It is the path to the good, the things allowing citizens to achieve it, rather than the good itself, that changes with respect to the setting and people. A fixed standard for judging what is good remains intact, namely, what the intelligent person discerns. Moreover, the possibility of arriving at the ultimate good is never abandoned and is linked to the notion of leading citizens to be obedient to the gods. No explanation for this linking is offered, but it follows closely upon a lengthy digression about the necessity to know the whatness, essence, and indeedness of things like laws, arts, and sciences.[43]

Alfarabi's lack of precision about these matters meshes well with the way he discusses the actual founding of the city. He depicts Plato as trying to found a perfect city, terming it a "city in truth," but is silent about the practical considerations of where and how it is to be established. It must, however, meet three conditions or stipulations: observe the traditions of

42. See above, *Political Regime*, sec. 81, and introduction, 17–18. Appropriately, nothing is said about the goal aspired to by the pious ascetic mentioned in the opening lines of the *Summary*.

43. See *Summary*, 2.2–4, 7, 9. For the term "indeedness," see ibid., 2.7, n. 18.

"the regimes," have a divine governor, and be populated by citizens possessing praiseworthy moral habits. To comply with the first, the city in question must adopt the traditions of sound existing regimes. Yet none is cited as an example; nor is more said about this condition. The second, one unlikely to be realized, is not explained either—an indication that whatever might be meant by the term "city in truth," Alfarabi sees no need to speak more about it in this treatise. The only other reference to the kind of city Plato may have had in mind occurs in the subsequent treatise where Alfarabi purportedly cites Plato's affirmation "This, then, is the city whose existence we wanted from the outset." It is, from the context, one that provides material well-being for all citizens, ensures equitable distribution of goods, and guards against great disparities in personal wealth. Because justice prevails in this city, it is virtuous; and insofar as it is virtuous and just, it is divine. If acquiring virtue is thus tantamount to being divine, the second condition or stipulation is perhaps not as unattainable as first appears.[44]

Such an account of the good, the conditions requisite for a sound city, and the political sense of divinity are consonant with the way Alfarabi characterizes laws more generally. He evinces no hesitation in citing Plato's observation that the floods and calamities of the past, though obliterating peoples and memory of their cultures, allow new ones to come into being through time. Precisely because there is no assurance that the same will not occur again, it is necessary to reflect on such incidents. To corroborate the lesson, Alfarabi could draw on parallels from his own history and culture. His silence suggests that he discerns nothing distinguishing human beings in Plato's time from those in his own such as to affect laws and lawgiving or legislating.[45] It is warranted only if, as implied in two passages of the *Summary*, all laws—even traditional laws (*sunan*, the

44. See ibid., 4.1, 5.15, with 5.13–14; see also 4.7, 5.18. The term "divine" occurs twenty-five times in Alfarabi's *Summary*: 1.7 (six times), 1.12, 2.1 (three times), 3.4, 3.11, 4.1, 4.4, 4.7 (twice), 5.1 (three times), 5.9, 5.12 (twice), 5.18 (twice), and conclusion.

45. See ibid., 3.1–2. In the Quran, Sura Noah (Sura 71) relates Noah's failed attempt to save his people from the flood; and there are numerous other references to the story. See Quran 7:59–64, 10:71–73, 11:25–49, 19:58–63, 21:76–77, 23:23–32 and 33–41, 25:35–40, 26:105–122 and 123–140, 29:14–22, 37:75–82, 46:21–26, 51:46, 54:9–15, 57:26–27. The disasters befalling the people of Pharaoh and Lot are also enumerated, as are those that occurred to the people of Ād and Thamūd. Alfarabi's mention of "the original work on which this book [the *Laws*] is based," at *Summary* 3.2, may refer to Plato's *Timaeus* (22b–23c) or *Critias* (109d–e, 111e–112a). When he discusses these dialogues in the *Philosophy of Plato* (secs. 33–35), he is silent about the issue; see *Alfarabi, Philosophy of Plato and Aristotle.*

plural of *sunna*) and Laws (*sharāʾiʿ*, the plural of *sharīʿa*)—are to be understood as deriving from humans. Although Alfarabi presents the second text as a Platonic speech, neither one is echoed in Plato's *Laws*. He averts the radical inference to which these statements point by another invention, the claim that Plato deemed traditional law to consist of two sorts. One, adopted by legislators for particular instances, changes according to the circumstances; the other, not varying at all, is termed natural. While the first sort alters according to the people, the time, and the setting, the second is universal and inalterable. Alfarabi's recourse here to nature as a source of traditional law is astute, the limited scope accorded this particular sort of traditional law—interaction with family and those one has benefitted—notwithstanding.[46]

Still, traditional laws, however they come about—that is, as customs habitually pursued by human beings at all times and places or as practices they are induced to acquire by a gifted leader—are only that, traditional laws. Of more immediate significance are the laws set down to regulate human action. They are not universal, but particular. No body of laws is valid for all peoples, places, and times because—common features and universal traditional laws notwithstanding—there is such great variety among human beings, their settings, and the practices and rules they follow. Even the Law set forth in the Quran testifies to the necessity that particular incidents be addressed, and this is done in a manner that in no way distracts from—and perhaps contributes to—the more universal teaching. Some verses and, on occasion, whole Suras respond to circumstances faced by the Prophet himself or the fledgling community of Muslims as well as to specific questions. Nonetheless, to forge an interpretation of the Law that preserves the principle of it applying to all peoples, one must acknowledge that it—like any law having such a purview—can be fully implemented only after people have first been prepared to live by it. Differently stated, people must first be trained, educated, or brought up so as to be capable of following its precepts. That concern explains the emphasis on upbringing and education present—albeit in general rather than specific terms—throughout Alfarabi's treatise. Taking a cue from Plato, he notes that when "the people are good and virtuous," either by nature or due to this upbringing, "they do not need traditional laws or laws at all

46. See *Summary*, 5.18, 7.2, 7.14. See also Montesquieu, *On the Spirit of the Laws*, bk. 26, chap. 2; Jean-Jacques Rousseau, *Of the Social Contract*, bk. 2, chap. 12, end.

and are very happy." In other words, "only those whose moral habits are not valid and upright need laws and traditional laws."[47]

The reason for recourse to laws—understood as arising from convention, custom, nature, or divine intervention—is not only that most human beings lack "valid and upright" moral habits. It is also, perhaps primarily, because they fail to fathom that to live together in harmony they must subordinate their own private good to the common good. Cognizant as they are of the need for political community, they neither know how to achieve it nor are inclined to do what that task requires. Even those who do know enough to prefer the common to the personal have difficulty doing so. The penchant for pursuing their own good too often prevents them from recognizing that it is best obtained through communal effort, and this is especially true when such efforts entail some personal sacrifice.[48] Were an individual capable of helping humans overcome these proclivities ever to arise, prudence would urge that such a person's guidance be followed. Absent that, the best course is adherence to the law and the upbringing or education it provides.

Just before the end of the *Summary,* in commenting on a topic raised by Plato about punishment, Alfarabi avails himself of an unusual exclamation. Indeed, to declare "upon my life," as he does here is startling language and almost an epithet. Alfarabi has recourse to it on only one other occasion in this treatise, during an earlier discussion where he aligns himself with Plato's judgment that only those able to anticipate its consequences find the good pleasant. The observation is then dropped and accorded no further attention.[49] Here, Alfarabi proceeds to temper the enthusiasm he has

47. *Summary,* 9.7; see also ibid., 8.6–8. In *Kitāb al-Tanbīh ʿalā Sabīl al-Saʿāda,* Alfarabi notes that the science of politics (*ʿilm al-siyāsa*) thoroughly investigates how citizens can be led to develop virtuous moral habits either through an education that helps them perform noble actions and avoid base ones or by means of punishment; see 70:2–72:14, 72:14–73:2; English trans., 114–115, secs. 22–26. See also Muhsin S. Mahdi, *Alfarabi and the Foundations of Islamic Political Philosophy* (Chicago: University of Chicago Press, 2001), 136–137 and 138–139. Cf. Quran, Suras 8–9, 24, 30, 33, 48, 49, 58, 59, 63, 80, 105; also 1 Timothy 1:8–11; Niccolò Machiavelli, *Discourses on Livy,* bk. 1, chap. 3; Abraham Lincoln, first inaugural address, March 4, 1861: "No organic law can ever be framed with a provision specifically applicable to every question which may occur in practical administration. No foresight can anticipate, nor any document of reasonable length contain express provisions for all possible questions."

48. For Alfarabi, speaking in his own name, providing for common needs and levying taxes are "among the most important considerations of the city," whereas understanding how the virtues and vices "creep stealthily into the soul" is "one of the most important issues that the legislator ought to take care of completely"; see *Summary,* 6.17, 8.6.

49. See ibid., 9.9, 2.3.

just expressed by observing that Plato's discussion—one he characterizes as "expansive"—will be useful if it can be "truly expounded" or if "a true commentary on it is made." At issue is whether a person whose natural disposition apparently compels him to commit a crime must be punished either immediately or in the future. The question, fraught with religious implications, is best avoided. Alfarabi does just that. An equally sensitive subject figures prominently in the next book of Plato's dialogue. Insofar as Alfarabi's account does not extend that far, he is exempted from having to address it.

By affirming in the conclusion that his account is limited to the material having come to his attention and referring to the "disagreement among people as to the number of treatises in this book," Alfarabi intimates uncertainty about their exact number. Still, ought awareness of how deftly he sidesteps the topic of future punishment even while drawing attention to it as a problem, plus recollection of the way he utilizes the tale of the pious ascetic to draw lessons about Plato's art of writing, lessons he reiterates at the beginning of the first treatise, not raise some questions as to why he places emphasis on such indirectness or even a suspicion that he engages in something like it? Modest skill in arithmetic, for example, suffices to notice that the correct number of treatises in Plato's dialogue falls between the conflicting claims. Through recourse to additional stratagems, Alfarabi obliquely manages to express appreciation for some Platonic arguments and tacitly substitute his own opinions for others.

The care he takes to distinguish what Plato says or thinks about a particular issue from what he has to say or what he thinks has already been noted. Making editorial comments, expressing judgment about the merits of particular arguments, and ascribing his own speech to Plato are yet other ways Alfarabi personalizes what at first appears to be a conventional report on subjects raised in Plato's dialogue. Solitary and occasional, they by no means constitute a variant interpretation of the *Laws* as a whole. Rather, they draw the reader's attention to select issues raised in the dialogue and intimate how they might appear from another perspective. Having prompted the reader to pause and reflect for a moment, Alfarabi returns to his comments on the text.

There are about seven different sorts of editorial comments or remarks. On half a dozen occasions, Alfarabi makes explicit Plato's purpose or intention while reporting on what Plato had to say about a particular subject—once even deeming it pertinent to speak both of Plato's purpose and his intention in the same clause.[50] A similar number of times, he emphasizes that Plato "explained" a notion or subject and notes how he went about the task, namely, that he "explained another notion suited" to the subject under discussion, "explained a fair notion," "rushed on to explain," employed "useful, clear examples," "resolved to explain," or "elucidated this notion adequately."[51] Several other comments, almost two dozen, describe the way Plato speaks about one issue or another, albeit in a tone that evinces no judgment about his procedure. Thus, Alfarabi observes that Plato spoke "extensively," "at length," "effusively," "profusely," or "a great deal."[52] He does not hesitate to offer critical evaluations as well, charging Plato a few times with having "digressed" from the subject at hand and once of having "carried on an unconnected discussion."[53] Likewise, Alfarabi refers at one point to something Plato "mentioned obliquely" and at another to his having expounded a subject "eloquently."[54] Frequently, he praises Plato for having "mentioned a useful subject," pointed to a "useful notion" or subject of "great usefulness," or "commanded something useful."[55] In addition to referencing the usefulness of a subject or notion discussed by Plato, Alfarabi draws attention to their subtlety on two different occasions.[56]

Alfarabi is highly versatile in the way he expresses his own opinions or judgments. Thus, he employs the adjective "skilled" on several occasions. Once it is to explain what Plato expects of those who examine the "science being discussed" in his various dialogues, and at other times it is to recommend how a physician or legislator described in this manner is to act.[57] Early on in the *Summary*, when discussing the way in which the good

50. For "purpose," see ibid., 1.3, 2.8, 9.9; for "intention," 1.3, 5.14, 8.13.

51. See ibid., 2.9, 3.7, 3.15, 5.4, 6.1, 6.9.

52. For "extensively," see ibid., 2.6, 3.13, 5.4, 5.9, 5.18 (in two places), 6.3, 6.13, 6.19, 7.1, 7.10, 8.8, 9.8; for "effusively," 2.8, 4.10, 6.3c, 7.11, 7.14, 8.5, 9.9; for "at length," "profusely," and "a great deal," each mentioned only once, see 2.8, 6.19, 8.5.

53. Plato is said to have "digressed" at ibid., 6.12, 6.17, 7.7, 8.10, while the singular reference to his carrying on "an unconnected discussion" is at 9.9.

54. For the first, see ibid., 1.9; and 5.12 for the second.

55. References to Plato having "mentioned a useful subject" occur at ibid., 1.23, 2.8, 4.10, 5.4, 5.12, 6.8, 6.10, 6.12, 9.9 (twice), and conclusion; to him speaking of "a useful notion" at 3.14, 5.12, 6.8, 9.9 (twice); references to a subject of "great usefulness" and to Plato having "commanded something useful" are at 4.10 and 6.12, respectively.

56. See ibid., 6.7, 8.1. The discussion immediately following the latter comment is, itself, also subtle.

57. See ibid., introduction 2, 2.1 (twice), 4.3, 6.5, 8.8.

is said to be relative, Alfarabi declares: "This is a notion the legislator and likewise the poets and all those who write down their sayings ought to pay great attention to so that they will not be misunderstood." Much later, toward the end of the work, he qualifies the explanation of how virtues and vices unobtrusively take root in the soul as "one of the most important issues that the legislator ought to take care of completely."[58] His use of the exclamation "upon my life" on two occasions has already been mentioned along with his judgment that the discussion prompting his second recourse to the unusual phrase would be "exceedingly useful" were it to be "truly expounded." Alfarabi also describes Plato as a "sage" at two points in the *Summary*. Moreover, when discussing the numerous tasks to be assigned citizens so that a city functions properly, he declares the undertaking to be "equitable" or "an equitable law" and explains that this is "because assigning functions is enormously and completely useful."[59]

Indicative as are these editorial comments and judgments of Alfarabi's own thoughts as distinct from those of Plato, he goes further on two different occasions and attributes to him things he did not say. The first occurs in the opening treatise of the *Summary*. Explaining Plato's discussion of the qualifications a legislator or lawgiver is to have, Alfarabi introduces one that finds no parallel in Plato's text, namely, that "a true lawgiver" is "only the one whom God creates and equips for setting down laws." Immediately thereafter, his account comes back to what is found in the *Laws*. Further on, toward the middle of the *Summary*, in the course of discussing the distribution of land and goods needed by the citizens, Alfarabi declares: "Then, finally, he said, 'This, then, is the city whose existence we wanted from the outset.'" Nothing resembling such a declaration is to be found in Plato's *Laws*.[60]

Whatever text Alfarabi had at his disposal—a translation of the *Laws*, a translation of part of it, or a summary composed by someone else—he clearly studied it most carefully. Indeed, as he affirms in the conclusion to the *Summary*, he "reflected on it, leafed through it, and extracted those of its notions that dawned on us and that we knew the sage had intended to explain." Although he admits immediately thereafter that Plato "perhaps entrusted to his sayings from which we extracted these notions subtleties,

58. See ibid., 2.2, 8.6.

59. For the references to Plato as a "sage," see ibid., 5.18 and conclusion. The judgment concerning the assigning of functions occurs at 6.10.

60. See ibid., 1.14, 5.15.

details, and useful notions that are several times more than what we mentioned," he is nonetheless confident that "he did intend to explain what we brought forth." As is evident from a consideration of the several stratagems Alfarabi employed to emphasize one aspect of the text or another and to enhance it on occasion, he accomplished precisely what he sets forth here as his intention.

Alfarabi's investigations of laws and lawgiving demonstrate why such an inquiry is best begun from Plato's own discussion of these topics. Although Alfarabi alludes to their importance for revealed religion, especially that of his own day, he goes no farther here or anywhere else. If, to borrow a phrase from Leo Strauss, Alfarabi draws on "Platonic standards for judging, or criticizing, specific Islamic institutions," he does so only indirectly.[61] To be sure, a critique of Islam may be inferred from Alfarabi's silence about Islam insofar as the city outlined here is distinct from one guided by divine law or by a lawgiver who has received revelation. It is, moreover, less than a virtuous city or even one such that its citizens can aspire to the highest human excellence. Moderation is the highest virtue they can hope to achieve. To envisage the alternative to a city like this, it is necessary to reflect on the best or true city whose contours are presented in the *Political Regime*. Precisely because such an undertaking entails reflection on Alfarabi's other political writings, the teaching of this treatise points as much to an indirect defense and explication of the reasoning behind revealed religion as to a criticism of it. That he forces a thoughtful reader to raise such questions and to weigh judiciously the alternatives, even as he allows the inattentive one to ignore the enigmas that give pause, is at the heart of his appeal—something Leo Strauss learned from Averroes and Maimonides, then sought to pass on through his interpretation of Alfarabi. Central to Strauss's exposition in "Farabi's *Plato*," for example, is an account of how Alfarabi presents philosophy

61. See Strauss, "How Fārābī Read Plato's *Laws*," 144: "The *Laws* is not a book of whose content one can merely take cognizance without undergoing a change, or which one can merely use for inspiring himself with noble feelings. The *Laws* contains a teaching which claims to be true, i.e. valid for all times. Every serious reader of the *Laws* has to face this claim. Every Muslim reader in the Middle Ages did face it. He could do this in at least three different ways. He could reject Plato's claim by contending that Plato lacked completely the guidance supplied by Revelation. He could use the Platonic standards for judging, or criticizing, specific Islamic institutions, if not for rejecting Islam altogether. He could contend that Islam, and Islam alone, lives up to the true standards set forth by Plato, and on this basis elaborate a purely rational justification of both the content and the origin of Islam."

in the *Political Regime* within a political context much as Plato did in the *Republic* and *Laws*.[62] Hopefully, the preceding analysis of Alfarabi's *Summary* has shown to what extent it is as philosophic as it is political.

The detailed, almost laborious, examination of Alfarabi's novel use of Plato that Strauss initiated sought to explore both what political philosophy entails and how it has been passed on across boundaries erected by time and culture. That approach is resisted within the academic community as much today as when first presented. There are three reasons for that, all rooted in difference of opinion about how to study philosophy and its history.

Most compelling is reluctance to probe for a philosophical interpretation of Alfarabi's writing and insistence on searching for thinkers and trends that might have influenced him, not least because it promises greater certainty through what it adds to, or corrects about, the historical record of what is known about the writings or authors accessible to him. Conviction that Alfarabi's understanding of politics is grounded in a metaphysical teaching he has taken over from Plato or Aristotle is another. A third is the denial that an author intentionally says different things about the same subject, either for political reasons or out of concern about the consequences a particular phrase might have.

Dominic O'Meara and Philippe Vallat best exemplify the first two approaches. Rejection of Alfarabi having anything like an esoteric teaching prompts Vallat first to probe for clues to Alfarabi's putative sources, then to misrepresent the arguments adduced by Strauss and Mahdi. Denying that Alfarabi had access to Plato's *Laws* solely on the authority of Gutas, Vallat derives his political teaching from metaphysical premises stemming from Neoplatonic sources that are based on his logical teaching. For Alfarabi's Neoplatonism, Vallat notes his indebtedness to O'Meara's study of its strands permeating the political thought of authors ranging from Plotinus to Alfarabi. O'Meara considers *al-Madīna al-Fāḍila*, or *Virtuous City*, to be Alfarabi's most important writing, but his novel title for the work—*Best State*—misses both the character of the polity in question and Alfarabi's evaluation of its quality.[63] Cecilia Martini Bonadeo offers a vigorous defense in favor of reading Alfarabi without attention to

62. See Strauss, "Farabi's *Plato*," 358–359.

63. See Philippe Vallat, *Farabi et l'école d'Alexandrie: Des prémisses de la connaissance à la philosophie politique* (Paris: Vrin, 2005), 60, 85–152, 370–371, esp. 151, n. 4; Dominic J. O'Meara, *Platonopolis: Platonic Political Philosophy in Late Antiquity* (Oxford: Clarendon Press, 2003), 185–197.

nuance and insists that any difference in the expression he gives an idea must be due to the sources at his disposal or the way his thought evolved over time, while Charles Genequand grounds his refusal to consider Alfarabi as a philosopher or qualified interpreter of Plato or Aristotle on a dismissal of Strauss's "Farabi's Plato" because it has not been appreciated by most scholars. He then demonstrates that he has either not read it carefully or failed to understand its argument; the alternative reading he proposes ignores the subjects Alfarabi raises in the texts addressed in the *Philosophy of Plato*.[64]

Neither Massimo Campinini nor Ulrich Rudolph resists Strauss or the attempt to explain Alfarabi's teaching in quite the manner of their colleagues. In his attempt to identify the contours of a political theology in Alfarabi, Campinini readily acknowledges that his analysis may be flawed. Rudolph's masterful article on Alfarabi presents an overview of what the sources tell us about the life and works of the "second teacher," a detailed list of his writings, a summary of the teaching set forth in those writings, and an account of the interpretations proposed by the scholars who have written on them. He elucidates these various positions fairly, while suggesting how he understands their merits given his own reading of Alfarabi, and errs only insofar as he reads Alfarabi too literally. That is, he fails to ask how statements that accord with popular opinions can possibly make intelligent sense and takes too seriously Alfarabi's provocative, perhaps even fanciful, assertions about theory guiding practice.[65]

Criticisms notwithstanding, a new era of exchange is dawning. Just as Strauss and Mahdi vigorously opposed the approach of Gabrieli while eschewing ad hominem or other invective, so has such decorum recently been returned to academic discussion about these contested issues.

Helpful as it was to open this analysis of Alfarabi's *Summary* by turning to Avicenna, it may be equally salutary to close it by calling on Averroes

64. See Cecilia Martini Bonadeo, ed. and trans., *al-Fārābī: L'armonia delle opinioni dei due sapienti, il divino Platone e Aristotele* (Pisa: Pisa University Press, 2008), 21–23; Charles Genequand, "Le Platon d'al-Fārābī," in *Lire les dialogues, mais lesquels et dans quel ordre: Définitions du corpus et interprétations de Platon*, ed. Anne Balansard and Isabelle Koch (Bonn: Academia Verlag Sankt Augustin, 2013), 105–106.

65. See Massimo Campinini, "Alfarabi and the Foundation of Political Theology in Islam," in *Islam, the State, and Political Authority: Medieval Issues and Modern Concerns*, ed. Asma Afasaruddin (New York: Palgrave-MacMillan, 2011), 35–52; and Ulrich Rudolph, "Abū Nasr al-Fârâbî," in *Die Philosophie in der islamischen Welt*, Band I: *8.—10. Jahrhundert*, ed. Ulrich Rudolph, with Renate Würsch (Basel: Schwabe, 2012), 363–457, esp. 446–447.

for the guidance he offers concerning the political significance of laws or, more precisely, Laws. Rising to the defense of the philosophers—Alfarabi and Avicenna in particular—against Alghazali's attacks on them in his *Incoherence of the Incoherence*, a lengthy and detailed rebuttal to Alghazali's accusations set forth in the *Incoherence of the Philosophers*, Averroes begins by emphasizing that the philosophers deem Laws central to sound political governance. Indeed, they are

> of the opinion that the Laws direct to the governance of people by means of which a human being exists insofar as he is human and obtains the happiness particularly characteristic of a human being. That is because the Laws are necessary for the existence of the human moral virtues, theoretical virtues, and practical arts.

Averroes goes on to explain the importance of these three things to the philosophers. To obtain the theoretical virtues and the practical arts, humans have need of moral virtue. It is evident that they require practical arts in order to obtain basic goods. The theoretical virtues allow them to understand what they need for their lives to be full and rich. And it is through the teaching of the Laws and the requirements set down in them that human beings obtain the moral virtues. For all these reasons, Averroes insists that the philosophers are great defenders of the Laws:

> In sum, the philosophers are of the opinion that the Laws are the necessary political arts whose principles are taken from the intellect and Legislation, especially those that are common to all the Laws.

Finally, even though the philosophers hold that some individuals are more intelligent and gifted than others, they are aware that the well-being of all citizens is the most important political goal and therefore defend the teaching for all presented in the Laws.[66]

66. These passages are from *Averroès, Tahafot al-Tahafot (L'Incohérence de L'Incohérence)*, 3rd ed., ed. Maurice Bouyges (Beirut: Imprimerie Catholique, 1992), 580:2–5 and 11–13. The translation of them, as well as of the larger passage in which they occur—the concluding pages of Averroes's *Tahāfut* or *Incoherence*—is taken, with minor alterations, from *Averroës, The Book of the Decisive Treatise: Determining the Connection between the Law and Wisdom, and Epistle Dedicatory*, trans., with introduction and notes, by Charles E. Butterworth (Provo, UT: Brigham Young University Press, 2001), 43–46; see appendix B, below, "Averroes's Defense of the Philosophers as Believing in Happiness and Misery in the Hereafter." See also Friedrich Nietzsche, *Beyond Good and Evil*, aphs. 30 and 40.

The Text

[Introduction]

1. The thing by which the human being excels the rest of the animals is the faculty by which he distinguishes among the causes and objects he deals with and observes in order to be cognizant of what among them is useful so as to prefer and attain it while rejecting and avoiding what is useless. It emerges from potentiality into actuality only through experience, namely, reflection on the particular instances of a thing and passing judgment on its universal characteristics from what is found in these particular instances. Therefore, anyone who attains more of these experiences is more virtuous and perfect in being human. However, the one engaging in these experiences may err in what he does and experiences so that he conceives the thing to be in a different state than it truly is.

There are many causes of error, and they have been enumerated by those who discuss the art of sophistry. It is the wise among the rest of the people who are the ones to have attained experiences that are true and sound. Nevertheless, it is natural for all people to pass a universal judgment after observing a few particular instances—"universal," here, meaning what encompasses all the particular instances of the thing as well as their duration in time. So, once it is observed that an individual has done a single thing on a number of occasions, it is judged that he does that thing all the time. For instance, when someone has spoken the truth one, two, or more times, it is natural to judge that he is unqualifiedly truthful and, likewise, when someone lies. Again, when someone is observed to act with courage, cowardice, or any other moral habit a number of times, he is judged to do so wholly and always.

The wise, insofar as they are cognizant of this aspect of people's natures, sometimes repeatedly present themselves as possessing a certain state of character so that people will judge that this is how they always are. Then, afterward, they adopt a different state of character; and that goes unnoticed by people who presume they have the same state of character as they had formerly.

It is related, for example, that a certain abstemious ascetic was reputed for his probity, propriety, asceticism, and piety; and he was well known for this among the people. Having become fearful of the unjust sovereign, he wanted to flee from that city of his. The command of that sovereign having been issued to search for and arrest him wherever he was found, he could not leave from any of the city's gates and became apprehensive lest he fall into the hands of the sovereign's men. So he sought out a garment worn by vagabonds, put it on, took a lute[1] in his hand, and came early at night to the gate of the city, pretending to be drunk and singing to the accompaniment of that lute of his. The gatekeeper said to him: "Who are you?" Jokingly, he said: "I am so and so, the ascetic!" The gatekeeper presumed he was poking fun at him and did not interfere with him. So he saved himself without having lied in what he said. [D 125]

2. Our purpose in making this introduction is this: the wise Plato did not permit himself to present and uncover all kinds of knowledge to all people. Therefore he followed the path of using symbols, riddles, obscurity, and difficulty lest knowledge fall into the hands of those not deserving of it and be deformed or into the hands of someone who is not cognizant of its worth or uses it improperly. In this he was correct. Once he knew and became certain[2] that he had become generally known for that and that it was apparent to people that he expressed everything he intended to say through symbols, he would sometimes turn to the thing he wanted to discuss and declare it openly and clearly; but the one who reads or hears his discussion presumes it is symbolic and that he intends a meaning

1. The term is *ṭanbūr*. See Alfarabi, *Kitāb al-Mūsīqā al-Kabīr*, ed. Ghaṭṭās 'Abd al-Malik Khashaba and Maḥmūd Aḥmad al-Hifnī (Cairo: Dār al-Kitāb al-'Arabī li-al-Ṭibā'a wa al-Nashr, n.d.), 629–771; see also Scheherazade Qassim Hassan, "The Long Necked Lute in Iraq," *Asian Music* 13, no. 2 (1982): 1–18.

2. Reading *istayqan* with the Kabul manuscript, instead of *ustubīn* ("it became clear") with Druart and the Leiden manuscript.

different from what he has openly declared. This notion is one of the secrets of his books.

Moreover, no one can grasp what he declares openly and what he states symbolically or in riddles nor distinguish between the two, unless skilled in the science being discussed. This is how his discussion proceeds in the *Laws*.

In this book, we have resolved on extracting the notions to which he alludes and grouping them together treatise by treatise so that it may be an aid to anyone who wants to be cognizant of that book and sufficient for anyone who cannot bear the hardship of study and reflection. God accommodates to what is correct.

First Treatise

1. [624a] A questioner asked about the cause of setting down laws[3]—"cause" here means the maker, and the one who makes them is the one who sets them down. The interlocutor answered that the one who set them down was Zeus; among the Greeks, Zeus is the father of mankind who is the final cause.

2. [624a–625b] Then he mentioned another setting-down in order to explain that there are many laws and that their multiplicity does not detract from their validity. He supported this by the testimony of generally known and popular poems and accounts in praise of some of the ancient lawgivers.

3. [625a–627b] Then he pointed out that examination of the laws is correct because there are some who detract from their validity and wish to argue that they are foolish. He explained that the laws occupy a very high rank

3. The Arabic term is *nawāmīs* (sing., *nāmūs*), from the Greek *nomoi* (sing., *nomos*); it is used to denote "laws" or "law" in the *Summary of Plato's Laws* and will always be translated as such in what follows. *Sunna* (pl., *sunan*) is the Arabic term that denotes "traditional law" and is translated as such unless otherwise noted. *Sharīʿa* (pl., *sharāʾiʿ*), which occurs only four times here (see 1.9, 2.8, 4.13, 7.2), is translated as "Law" with a capital "L"). The expression *milla*—"religion"—does not occur in the *Summary*, but *dīn*—"creed"—is found at 2.1 below. The Arabic term *wāḍiʿ al-nāmūs*, denoting the one who sets down the law or is in charge of it, is translated as "lawgiver"), while the Arabic terms *ṣāḥib al-nāmūs* and *ahl al-nāmūs* are translated as "legislator" and "legists" respectively. Judges, preachers, governors, and advisers are grouped together under the Arabic term *ḥurrās al-nawāmīs wa al-siyāsāt* at 6.10 below; it is translated as "custodians of the laws and regimes."

and that they are superior to all wise sayings. He examined the particulars of the law that was generally known in his time.

[625b–c] Plato mentioned the cypress trees; he described the path that was being taken by the interlocutor and the questioner and its stations. Most people presume that underlying this there are subtle notions: that by "trees" he meant "men," and similar difficult, forced, and offensive notions that it would take too long to mention. But the case is not as they presume. Rather, he wanted thereby to prolong the discussion and to connect its apparent sense with what resembles it—referring to a notion extraneous to his purpose in order to hide his intention.

4. [625c–e] Then he turned to some of the statutes of that law generally known to them, namely, messing in common and bearing light armor; and he examined them, seeking to determine in what way that law was correct and whether it agreed with what well-directed intellect requires. He explained that such statutes have many advantages, such as promoting camaraderie, mutual aid, protection of one another, and similar things, some of which he mentioned and some he did not. And he explained that they are permitted to carry light armor for yet another reason: because their roads were rugged, most of them were infantrymen rather than cavalrymen. [D 126]

5. [626a–d] Then he explained that, because perpetual war is natural to people in general and to those people in particular, taking up and acquiring appropriate arms, association, and camaraderie are necessary things. He also explained the advantages reaped from war and gave an exhaustive account of the sorts of war, explaining the specific and general sorts.

6. [626d–630d] Then he persevered in speaking about wars to the point of mentioning many aspects of the advantages of the law: among them, a person gaining control over himself, pursuing the ability to suppress evil things (both those in the soul and the external ones), and pursuing what is just. Moreover, he explained in this connection what the virtuous city is and who the virtuous person is. He mentioned that they are the city and the man that conquer by dint of truth and correctness.

He explained also the true need for a judge, the obligation to obey him, and how this promotes common interests. He described who the agreeable judge is, how he ought to conduct himself in suppressing the evil ones and keeping the people from wars through gentleness and good administration, and in beginning with what is foremost—namely, the lowest.

He explained the true need of people for avoiding wars among themselves and the intensity of their inclination to do so insofar as it promotes their well-being. But this is impossible without adhering to the law and applying its statutes. When the law commands waging wars, it does so in the pursuit of peace, not in the pursuit of war—just as what is offensive may be commanded because of its final consequence being desirable.

He also mentioned that it is not sufficient for a person to live in prosperity without security. He supported this by the testimony of a poem by a man well known to them, that is, the poem of Tyrtaeus. He explained further that the courageous person who is praiseworthy is not the one who is first to attack in external wars, but he who, in addition, controls himself and governs to uphold peace and security whenever he can. He supported this statement by poems generally known to them.

7. [630d–631d] Then he explained that the purpose of the lawgiver's forbearance and accomplishment is to aspire to the face of God, Mighty and Majestic, pursue the last reward and abode, and acquire the major virtue that is higher than the four moral virtues. He explained that among the people there may be some who imitate the legislators. These are groups with various purposes who set laws down hastily to achieve their bad aims. In mentioning these groups, he intended only to warn people to guard against being beguiled by the likes of them.

He divided the virtues and explained that some of them are human and others are divine, that the divine are preferable to the human, and that the one who has acquired the divine does not lack the human, whereas the one who has acquired the human may have missed the divine. The human are such as power, beauty, prosperity, knowledge, and others that have been enumerated in the books on ethics. He mentioned that the true legislator is the one who orders these virtues in a manner suitable to lead to the attainment of the divine virtues; for when the human virtues are practiced by the one who possesses them as the law obliges, they become divine.

8. [631d–632c] Then he explained that the legislators are intent on the causes by which the virtues are attained. They command them and urge people to follow them so that through attaining them the virtues will be attained. Examples of these causes are legal marriage, ordering the

appetites and pleasures, and indulging in each only to the extent allowed by the law. The same applies to fear and anger, base and noble objects, and whatever else serves as causes of the virtues. [D 127]

9. [632d–634c] Then he explained that Zeus and Apollo had used all those causes in their two laws. He explained the many advantages of each one of the statutes of their Law—for instance, [those dealing with] hunting, messing in common, war, and so forth.

He explained also that war may take place by necessity or by appetite and preference. He explained which is from preference and seeking pleasure and which is by necessity.

He mentioned obliquely in his discussion that the dispute running between the speaker and the interlocutor may lead to some noble and preferable things being debased and degraded; but what is intended by this is only to examine and ponder them so as to explain their excellence, remove suspicion[4] from them, and ascertain that they are valid and preferable. This is correct. He presented this as an excuse for anyone who argues for condemning any of the statutes of the law, providing his intention is examination and inquiry, not contention or mischief.

10. [634d–635b] Then he started to blame some of the statutes they were cognizant of in those laws. He mentioned that to assent to such statutes, regardless of one's suspicion from the outset that they may be defective, is to act like children and those who are ignorant. It is obligatory for one who is intelligent to examine such statutes in order to overcome his doubt and grasp what is true about them.

11. [636a] Then he explained that to carry out what the law makes obligatory is one of the most difficult things, while to pretend[5] and make unfounded claims is very easy.

12. [636a–637e] Then he mentioned some of the generally known statutes from prior laws, for instance, the ones concerning festivals—how they are extremely correct because they involve pleasure to which all people are naturally inclined and how the [ancient lawgivers] set down a law that

4. Literally, "presumption" (*ẓann*), both here and in the next section.
5. Reading *al-firāya* with the Leiden manuscript, rather than *al-qawl bih* ("speak about it") with Druart and the Kabul manuscript.

renders pleasure divine.[6] He praised it, approved of it, and explained its advantages. Another instance is wine drinking and drunkenness, their advantages when practiced as the law obliges, and what they give rise to when practiced in a different manner.

13. [638a–b] Then he warned against presuming that the conquerors are always correct and that the conquered are always in error. For conquest may be due to large numbers, and they may very well be in the wrong; therefore, human beings should not be deluded by conquest but should reflect on their conditions and the conditions of their laws. If they are in the right, it makes no difference whether they are conquerors or conquered. Nevertheless, in most cases the one who is in the right is the conqueror; if he is conquered, it is only accidentally.

14. [638c–639b] Then he mentioned that not everyone who wishes to become one is a true lawgiver, but only the one whom God creates and equips for setting down laws. The same applies to every master in an art, such as the navigator and others, who is then deserving of the name master both when practicing his art and when kept from practicing it. Just as the one who is kept from practicing an art after being reputed for it is deserving of the name master, so the one who practices an art without being good at it, equipped for it, or proficient in it is not deserving of the name master. [D 128]

15. [639b–640d] Then he explained that the lawgiver ought first to practice his own laws and then command [others to practice] them. For when he does not practice what he commands others and does not require of himself what he requires of others, his command and his argument will not be received well[7] and suitably by the ones whom he commands—just as the leadership of the general who is not himself a hero able to fight wars will not have the suitable effect. He gave an example of this drawn from the drinking party. He said that when their leader and master is also drunk like the rest, he will not govern the party in the correct way. Rather, he ought to be sober and extremely sharp-witted, aware, and vigilant so that it is possible for him to govern a drinking party. What he said is true.

6. Reading *ilāhiyya* with the Kabul manuscript, rather than *al-ilāhiyya* ("[as] the divine [thing]") with Druart and the Leiden manuscript.
7. Literally, "nobly" (*al-jamīl*).

For when the lawgiver is as ignorant as his people, it will not be possible for him to set down the law that benefits them.

16. [641b–d] Then he mentioned that education[8] and training are useful in preserving the laws and that the one who neglects himself or his subordinates will end up in great confusion.

17. [641e–642a] Then he explained that when a person becomes generally known for his ability as a good dialectician and discussant[9] and as a prolix and able speaker, then whenever he is intent on praising and describing something as being excellent, it will be presumed that the thing itself is not as excellent as he describes but [seems to be so] only from his ability as a discussant.

This is a disease that often afflicts the learned. Thus it is obligatory on the one who listens to a discussion to use his intellect to reflect soundly and exhaustively on the thing itself to determine whether the stated descriptions exist in it or whether they are only things the discussant describes because of his ability to discuss and slide over things or because of his love for that thing and the fine opinion he has of it. If he finds the thing venerable in itself and deserving of those descriptions, let him drive from his mind the suspicion[10] we have described. In itself, the law is venerable and excellent; it is more excellent than anything said about it and in it.

18. [643b–d] Then he explained that there is no way to be cognizant of the truth of the laws and their excellence and the truth of all things, except through logic and exercise in it and that it is obligatory for people to exercise and train themselves in it. Although initially their purpose may not be to grasp the truth of the law, this training can be of benefit to them later on. He gave an example of this drawn from the arts; for example, the child who sets up doors and houses for play, whereby he acquires positive dispositions and accomplishments in an art that become useful to him when he wishes to acquire the art seriously.

8. "Education" or "discipline" (*ta'addub*) is to be distinguished from "instruction" (*ta'līm*) in the more formal sense. Other expressions from the same root are *adab* (translated as "upbringing") and the plural form *ādāb* (translated as "character traits").

9. Literally, "goodness in dialectic and discourse" (*jawdat al-jadal wa al-kalām*). The term *kalām* is also used to denote dialectical theology.

10. Literally, "presumption" (*ẓann*); see above, n. 4.

19. [643d–644b] Then he inclined toward the legislator and mentioned that training from childhood in political issues and reflection on what is correct and erroneous with respect to them benefit him when he becomes seriously engaged in them. Then, because of his earlier training and exercise in them, it will be possible for him to restrain himself and face what confronts him with perseverance. [D 129]

20. [644c–645c] Then he began to explain that in the soul of every human being there are two opposing powers, one pulling to attract against the other, so that he finds himself to have sorrow and joy, pleasure and pain, and the other opposites. One of these two powers is discerning and the other bestial. The law operates through the discerning, not through the bestial. He explained that the attraction exercised by the bestial power is strong and hard, while the attraction exercised by the discerning aspect is softer and milder.

It is obligatory on the individual man to reflect on the conditions of his soul with respect to these attractions and to follow the discerning one. And if the inhabitants of the city are not by themselves able to be discerning, they are to accept the truth from their lawgivers, those who follow in their path, those who speak the truth about their laws, those who are good, and those who are righteous.[11]

21. [646b–c] Then he explained that it is true and extremely true that one should bear the toil and discomfort commanded by the legislator because of the ensuing comfort and virtue—just as the pain that comes upon the one who drinks distasteful medications is praiseworthy because, in the end, it leads to the comfort of health.

22. [646e–647c] Then he explained that moral habits follow from and resemble one another and that one ought to distinguish them from their contraries. For example, modesty is praiseworthy; but in excess, it becomes impotence and blameworthy. And having a noble presumption about people is praiseworthy and [an expression of] openheartedness; but if it is of one's enemies, it becomes blameworthy. So, too, caution is praiseworthy; but in excess, it becomes cowardice and inaction and thus is blameworthy. He explained, further, that if a person arrives at a goal he is intent on, even if it is an extremely good and virtuous one, but does so

11. The term is *ṣāliḥ* and denotes those who do what is right and sound.

by pursuing a path that is not praiseworthy, that is then blameworthy. It would be finer for him to arrive at what he is intent on through what is noble and preferable.

23. [647c–649b] Then he mentioned something useful, namely, that it is obligatory for an intelligent person to draw near to evil things and be cognizant of them so that he not fall into them and that he be more cautious about them. He gave an example drawn from drinking [wine] and explained that the sober person ought to draw near those who are drunk and attend their parties so as to be cognizant of the base things that drunkenness engenders and to be cognizant of how to avoid the base and blameworthy things that occur among them. For instance, after drinking a few cups, someone with a weak body may presume himself to be strong although he is nothing of the sort. Because he presumes himself to be strong, he wishes to shout and fight; but his strength fails him. And there are numerous other things that happen to [wine] drinkers.

24. Then he explained that anyone who wishes to acquire one of the virtues ought first to exert himself in driving away the vice that is opposed to it. For virtue is seldom attained until after vice has departed.

25. [650b] Then he explained that every nature has an activity particularly suited to it. Hence it is obligatory for the individual and the legislator to be cognizant of this so as to set down each one of the statutes with what is suitable and appropriate to it so that it is not dissipated. For when a thing is not properly placed, it will be dissipated and no trace of it will be left. [D 130]

Second Treatise

1. [653a] He explained in this treatise that in a human being there are natural things that are the causes of his moral habits and his actions. Therefore the lawgiver ought to be intent on those things, straighten them out, and set down laws that straighten those things out. For when they are straightened out, the moral habits and actions will be straightened out as well. (I presume that by "children" [in this connection] he means all beginners, whether in age, knowledge, or creed.)[12]

12. The term translated as "creed" here is *dīn*.

[653a–654a] He explained that these natural things are based on, and originate from, pleasure and pain. It is by these two that the virtues and the vices—and, later on, intelligence and the sciences—are attained. The straightening out of these two [that is, pleasure and pain] is called educating[13] and training. Had the legislator commanded people to avoid pleasures altogether, his law would not have been rightly established and they would not have followed it because of their natural inclination to pleasures. Instead, he provided for festivals and times during which they could pursue pleasures; in this way these pleasures become divine. This is also the case with the various kinds of music that the legislators have permitted, knowing that people are naturally inclined toward them and in order that taking pleasure in them will be divine. He gave as examples of this things that were generally known among them, such as dancing and flute playing.

[654b–657a] He explained that everything is made up of what is fair and what is base. The fair kind of music is what is suited to the fine natural dispositions and promotes noble and useful moral habits, such as generosity and courage. And the base kind is what promotes contrary moral habits. He gave examples of this drawn from the tunes and the figures that had existed in the temples of Egypt and among its inhabitants and had been instrumental in sustaining the traditional laws; and he explained that they were divine.

[657d–658e] He explained, further, that anyone who is younger in age is more prone to rejoice in those pleasures, while the one who is older is calmer and more staid. The skilled legislator is the one who introduces the law that gracefully draws everyone toward goodness and happiness. Furthermore, every group, every one of the generations, and all the inhabitants of a region have their own natural dispositions that differ from those of others. The skilled [legislator] is the one who introduces the kind of music and other statutes of traditional laws[14] that control those natural dispositions and compel them to accept the law, despite the differences in the natural dispositions and the variety and multiplicity of their moral habits, not the one who introduces certain statutes that control some people and not others; for the latter can be accomplished by the majority of the members of the group who practice it naturally. Moreover, the one

13. The term translated as "educating" here is *taʾdīb*; see above, 1.16 and n. 8.

14. The term is *aḥkām al-sunan* and could therefore also be translated as "traditional statutes."

who introduces a law that compels the obedience of a man who is knowledgeable, sophisticated, and experienced is more excellent than the one who introduces a law that compels the obedience of a group that is neither knowledgeable nor sophisticated: the former is like a singer who excites an old, sophisticated, rugged, and tenacious person.

[659c–e] The legislator and those who establish the law and its burdens ought to restrain the many and different human issues in every respect and in all their details so that none of these issues escapes them or they neglect anything in them; for once [the citizens] become used to neglect on their part, they will find excuses whenever they can. When a thing is neglected once, twice, or more, it is lost sight of and its edges are blunted—just as when it is used once or twice, it becomes an inescapable habit: it is fixed or lost sight of to the extent that it is, respectively, used or neglected. The young in age and children are not cognizant of this; they should be made to accept it and to act accordingly. For if they get used to enjoying themselves, following their appetites, and taking pleasure in what is contrary to the law, it will then be very hard to straighten them out in accordance with the law. Rather, they ought to experience pleasure in [obeying] its regulations;[15] both men and children should be required to be in intimate association with it [the law] and to follow it in practice.

[659d–660a] The legislator ought to address every group of people with what is closer to their understanding and intellects and straighten them out by means of what they are able to do. For sometimes it is difficult for people [D 131] to understand a thing, or they are incapable of doing it. Its difficulty motivates them to reject it and prompts them to abandon and discard it. He gave as an example of this the skilled and gentle physician who offers a sick person the medications that are useful to him in his familiar and appetizing food.

2. [660d–661d] Then he wished to explain that the good is only relative, not absolute. He supported the soundness of his statement by the testimony of an ancient poem in which are mentioned the things—such as health, beauty, and affluence—that some people count as good while others do not. He explained that all these things are good for good people; for the evil and unjust, however, they are not good and do not lead them to happiness either. Indeed, even life is evil for evil people, just as it is good for good people. Therefore it is correct to say that the good is only relative.

15. "Regulations" (*qawānīn*, sing. *qānūn*), from the Greek *kanon*.

This is a notion the legislator and likewise the poets and all those who write down their sayings ought to pay great attention to so that they will not be misunderstood.

3. [661d–663d] Then he explained that the assertion that all good things are immediately pleasant, that everything that is noble and good is pleasant, and that the converse assertion is also sound is not demonstrable. For many pleasant things are not good—namely, everything that is a source of pleasure to those of weak intellects. Upon my life,[16] the good may be pleasant to the one who is cognizant of its outcome, but not to the one who has not ascertained that outcome. The same applies to the assertion concerning the just ways of life and that they are the converse of the good things.

4. [665b–666d] Then he explained further that it is not obligatory for all people to follow the very same statute, but that there are statutes for each group that are not obligatory for others. He gave an example of this drawn from flute playing performed by different age groups and how the conditions that call for flute playing and the use made of it differ among different people, whether they differ in age or in some other conditions that befall them at particular times. For when a thing is not used in its proper place, it will not have the glitter, comeliness, approval, and acclaim[17] that it has when used in the place suitable to it. He gave examples of this, such as it not being suitable for an elderly person to play the flute or to dance; if he does either of these or anything similar at a public gathering, the public will not cheer or approve of it. Likewise, it is extremely repugnant and base for one to play the flute or dance on an occasion when it is not obligatory to do anything like that. This is the case with everything that is done by an unsuitable person, or in a place or time in which it is not approved for such things to be done by such as he, or when it is not obligatory to do them—all this is repulsive, unsuitable, and objectionable. It prompts the onlookers to reject it and to consider it base and repulsive, especially if they happen to lack sophistication.

16. This first oath by Alfarabi mirrors the first oath by the Athenian Stranger; see Plato, *Laws* 2.662c.
17. Literally, "argument" (*al-qawl*).

5. [666d–668a] Then he explained that pleasures also vary with respect to the differences in people, their conditions, natural dispositions, and moral habits. To explain this, he gave examples of courageous persons and the practitioners of the arts. For what is pleasant to the practitioner of one art is different from what is pleasant to the practitioner of another art. The case is the same with what is decent, what is noble, and what is balanced. [D 132]

6. Then he spoke extensively about this subject in order to explain that all these things are primarily noble and base in relation to other things and not noble and base in themselves. He said that if the practitioners of arts were to be asked about this notion, they would undoubtedly confirm it.

7. [668c–669a] Then he explained that anyone who does not know a thing's whatness, essence, or indeedness[18] cannot know whether its parts are well ordered, whether it is commensurate, or what its concomitants and consequences are simply by chasing after it. And if anyone claims he can do so, he is making a false claim. Also, the one who is cognizant of a thing's whatness may not have noticed how fair, fine, bad, or base it is. The one who has perfect cognizance of a thing is the one who is cognizant of the thing's whatness, then of how fair it is, [and] then of how fine or bad and base it is. This is the case with respect to laws and to all arts and sciences.

[669a–670d] Therefore the one who judges their fineness, or deficiency and badness, ought to have acquired about them the three things mentioned above and mastered them very well; only then should he judge them, so that his judgment may be correct and proper. Even more excellent than a judge is the one who constructs and sets down a thing. For the one who constructs it and sets it down, because he has the three kinds of knowledge mentioned above, has the ability to set down what is suitable for each condition. Now how could anyone who lacks one of these three kinds of knowledge and that power be able to set it down and construct

18. Reading *inniyya*, for sense, rather than *āniyya* ("that-ness") with Druart. In the opening lines of *Book of Letters*, Alfarabi says "the philosophers call perfect existence the 'indeedness' of the thing—namely, its very whatness—and they say 'and what is the indeedness of the thing,' meaning what is its most perfect existence, namely, its whatness"; see Alfarabi, *Kitāb al-Ḥurūf*, part 1, chap. 1, sec. 1. See also *Abū Naṣr al-Fārābī, Kitāb al-Alfāẓ al-Musta'mala fī al-Manṭiq*, ed. Muhsin Mahdi (Beirut: Dār al-Mashriq, 1968), sec. 7/1, 45:4–11.

it? Nor is this peculiar to laws alone, but holds for every science and every art. He gave examples of this drawn from poems and their meters and tunes, and from music and those who compose[19] it and play its various modes.

8. [669b–671a, 673a–d] Then he spoke at length, mentioning dancing and flute playing. His entire purpose with these examples is to explain that each of the statutes of the Law and of traditional law ought to be employed in the suitable place and for those who can endure it and that the corruption resulting from transferring and employing a thing in a place unsuitable to it is worse and baser than what results from abandoning it altogether. He described the praise that was bestowed on those who played tunes of which they were cognizant in their proper places and to an appropriate audience; and he mentioned the blame bestowed on those who altered these tunes, tampered with them, and played them at unsuitable times with the result that they stirred up afflictions and evils.

The art of singing occupied a wonderful position among the Greeks, and their legislators paid complete attention to it. In truth, it is very useful, especially because its working penetrates the soul. And since the law is especially concerned with the soul, he spoke effusively about this subject. Now such training as the body needs is only for the sake of the soul; when the body is made fit, it leads to the fitness of the soul.

9. [671a–674c] Then he explained another notion suited to what he was describing, namely, that the same thing may be used in one law and abandoned in another law. This is neither repugnant nor base, because the law is to be in keeping with the exigencies of the situation so that it leads the people to the ultimate good and to obedience to the gods. He gave an example of this drawn from wine and wine drinking: how an ancient group of Greeks used it, while it was shunned by another group even in the case of necessity. The situation that necessarily calls for drinking wine is that in which one needs to be deprived of intellect and cognizance, for instance, in childbirth, cauterization, and the painful doctoring of the body. Similarly, there is the situation in which it is used as a treatment for procuring health when nothing else will procure it. [D 133]

19. Literally, "those who set it down" (*al-wāḍiʿīn lahā*).

Third Treatise

1. [676a–677a] He started to explain that setting down laws, their obliteration, and their restoration are not things that have arisen at this time; rather, they have occurred in ancient times and will occur in times to come. He explained that the corruption and obliteration of the law come about in two ways: the one from the passage of long periods of time and the other from general cataclysms that arise in the world, such as deluges and epidemics that annihilate people.

2. [677a–680a] Then he set about explaining how cultures develop; how the conditions that necessitate regimes and laws arise, giving examples drawn from a deluge that floods all cities, after which a [new] city begins to come together and grow; and how groups and cities, which he named and of which they were cognizant at that time, were ruined and then other cities grew up in their stead. Initially, people had praiseworthy moral habits; but as their numbers increased and they engaged in rivalry, these moral habits changed. For example, at that time—I mean, in the aftermath of the deluge—people regarded each other cheerfully and were on familiar terms with one another. However, when their numbers increased, envy gradually began to spread among them until they hated each other, broke off relations, parted company, and waged war against one another. Moreover, the arts disappeared at that time—I mean, in the aftermath of the deluge—until gradually, and compelled by need, people began to develop them somewhat. Examples of this are mining minerals, harvesting plants, and constructing edifices and houses, and other things not difficult [to figure out] for anyone who looks into the original work on which this book is based and reflects a little on the cognizance it provides him so that he knows that at first the arts are developed only insofar as they are necessary, whereas later on they are for the sake of noble and fair things. For example, [at first] clothes are worn to cover and hide the genitals and to protect against heat and cold; then, later on, they are pursued with an eye to what is fine and fair. The same can be said about all the other arts.

[680e–681e] He explained further that the cities, fortresses, and shelters that people undertook at the outset were only to fortify themselves against beasts, wild animals, and other harmful things; then, later on, after wars gradually developed among them, they began to fortify themselves against each other.

[681a–682e] He explained further with respect to traditional laws how they come about and that they were only the traditional laws sons had [derived] from the ways of life of their fathers. Then, later on, when those traditional laws led to solidarity,[20] need compelled [them] first to a lawgiver of a general law that would unite the different ways of life, the members of numerous households, and the descendants of numerous ancestors with regard to a single thing encompassing their well-being. He supported this by the testimony of a statement from the poet Homer describing the city of Ilium and the issue[21] with respect to it.

3. [682c–e] Then he explained the struggle for domination that stems from solidarity, the hatred, and the [desire for] coercion that the inhabitants of one city have with respect to those of another. And [he explained] that these things do not present any usefulness since they are not in accordance with the law. He gave as an example those cities that the ancient Greeks besieged and conquered, [mentioning] how their situation exemplifies this notion. [D 134]

4. [683c–686c] Then he set about explaining that the ways of life of the people living in a single city who follow the way of life of their king can be corrupted and conquered in two ways only: one way is through the corruption attaching to the people because of themselves and their abandoning the practices that benefit them; the other is through another king conquering them. The latter may come about lawfully. When it is lawful, one, two, or many kings may join together against a single city and compel it to accept the divine law. This is like what he mentioned by means of examples drawn from cities generally known to them at that time. He explained moreover that the inhabitants of some cities may corrupt their traditional law more quickly than the inhabitants of another city because of the bad natural dispositions of the group, as he explained by means of examples.

5. [686c–687e] Then he set about explaining that approval may lead a person to adhere to the law, mentioning that a person may approve of

20. The term "solidarity" (*ʿaṣabiyya*) is central for Ibn Khaldūn; see Muhsin Mahdi, *Ibn Khaldun's Philosophy of History* (Chicago: University of Chicago Press, 1971), 193–204, esp. 196, n. 1.
21. Literally, "cause" (*sabab*).

something not good in itself and how he is to proceed in approving of a law that is perhaps neither good nor conducive to happiness, and mentioning the difficulty in distinguishing such things. He gave as examples someone who sees a wondrous ship, approves of it, and yearns to possess it, or someone who sees and approves of splendid riches and money and so yearns for a setting in which he would possess them, although that may not be unconditionally good. He explained moreover that a child may wish to possess things of which he approves while he is a child; but as he goes beyond the age of a child, he neither wishes for nor approves of them even though the things themselves are the very same and have not changed.

6. Then he demonstrated that the thing approved of that is truly so[22] is better than what receives approval but is not good. Therefore he said: "We, ourselves, see that the father does not approve of the same thing that the child approves of. Rather the father, being intelligent while the child is not intelligent, beseeches God to put an end to the child's approval. The thing that is fair and noble in itself is what intelligent people approve of, whereas what those who are not intelligent—be they a child, adult, or old person—approve of is what ought to be rejected."

7. [688e–689c] Then he explained a fair notion, namely, that what testifies to the truth and goodness of the law and exhorts to it is the intellect. Therefore, it is obligatory on the legislator that he be intent on the things that foster intellect in souls and that he make complete provision for them. For the more secure this is, the more secure and reliable the law[23] will be. Now upbringing is what fosters intellect because anyone who lacks upbringing finds pleasure in evil things, whereas anyone who has upbringing finds no pleasure except in what is good. The law is the path to good things, their fount, and their origin. It is therefore obligatory on the legislator to establish upbringing as firmly as he can.

8. Then he explained that once upbringing is instilled in the natural dispositions of the rulers of cities and their counterparts, it will result in their

22. That is, truly worthy of approval.
23. Literally, "the issue of the law" (*amr al-nāmūs*).

preferring and approving of good things and testifying to their truth. And harmony[24] among the testimonies of those who have upbringing is the wisdom to be preferred.

9. [689e–690c] Then he explained that the city is not complete unless it includes rulers and ruled. Exemplary of the rulers are those who are virtuous, mature, and experienced; while the ruled are those inferior to these such as children, youths, and the ignorant. Whenever this is the case, it is exceedingly correct. [D 135]

10. [690d–691a] Then he set about explaining that, when kings and rulers do not possess upbringing, they and their flocks[25] will become corrupt, as he explained in the examples he gave of Greek kings who did not possess knowledge. Therefore, they corrupted their flocks and themselves[26] to the point where their cities were ruined. Ignorance is more harmful in kings than in the common people.

11. [691c] Then he explained that the inhabitants of the city cannot do without a ruler possessed of upbringing[27] and an agreeable regime to run their affairs properly, just as the body cannot do without nourishment and the ship cannot do without the sail. Likewise the soul cannot do without a regimen[28] or else its affair will become corrupt, as he explained in connection with the Messenians.[29] Just as the sick body can neither bear toil nor function in a fine or useful manner, so the sick soul can neither distinguish nor choose what is finer and more useful. Now sickness of the soul is for it to lack the character traits [promoted by] the divine regime.

24. "Harmony" or "consensus" (*ijtimā'*); Greek, *sumphonia*.
25. Literally, "their affair and that of their flocks" (*amruhum wa amr ri'āyāhim*).
26. Literally, "the affair of their flocks and their own affair" (*amr ri'āyāhim wa amr anfusihim*).
27. The term is *ra'īs adīb;* were it not so awkward, given the immediately preceding "do without," the term could be translated "ruler with up-bringing."
28. Or, more literally, a "regime" (*siyāsa*), as in the preceding sentence.
29. Reading *al-māsināyyūn* for sense, rather than *al-mā'inaliyyūn* with Druart who—presumably inspired by Mahdi's suggestion in "*Editio Princeps*," 20—so deciphers the Leiden manuscript, and rather than *al-mā'ilūn* with the Kabul manuscript. Literally, the clause reads "the affair of the Messenians" (*fī amr al-māsināyyūn*).

12. [691d–693a][30] Then he gave examples of rulers who, presuming themselves to be learned and to be well brought-up[31] while not being so, pursued domination and thereby corrupted the affair [of the city].

13. [693a–696a] Then he explained that the legislator's major concern ought to be the issue of affection and freedom so that the people will be attached to both of them and the laws thus be quickly established and easy to effect.[32] Otherwise, the issue will be hard and difficult for him.

He explained further that a multiplicity of rulers[33] will corrupt the issue and that it is obligatory for the lawgiver to be intent on exclusive rulership. Otherwise, he will not make good headway toward his intention. Once his law appears, it will not endure unless he is intent on being the single, exclusive source of law. Indeed, this is an issue that cannot put up with compromise and compliancy.

He explained moreover that the path of freedom is the most useful and the finest for the legislator to pursue and that a ruler should not be envious; indeed, envy pertains to slavish moral habits, and a slave never achieves complete rulership. If the issue proceeds in accordance with the path of freedom, the compliance and obedience of those who are ruled will be with appetite and cheerfulness and more likely to continue. For these notions and their contraries, he gave examples drawn from the Persians, their kings, and their moral habits. And he spoke extensively about that.

14. [696a–700a] Then he set about explaining the divisions of the virtues and character traits, which of them is prior and which emphatically posterior, which of them stands apart by itself and which does not stand apart from what accompanies it. For example, moderation is not beneficial when it does not go together with justice, and similarly the rest of the virtues and character traits. He mentioned that it is obligatory for the legislator to distinguish these moral habits, to do whatever he ought to do so as to

30. This identification seems appropriate; Druart offers no indication of a corresponding passage in the text of the *Laws*.

31. Or, "to have upbringing," the term being *udabā'*, which is the plural of *adīb*.

32. Reading *al-'illa* with the Leiden manuscript, rather than *al-ghalaba* ("domination") with Druart and the Kabul manuscript.

33. Literally, "a multiplicity of rulerships" (*al-ri'āsāt al-kathīra*), but the exposition in the rest of the section makes it clear that Alfarabi means to speak here of the problems arising from multiple rulers.

order them and exhort others to them, and to compel the people to accept and adhere to them in keeping with freedom and not in keeping with slavery. Indeed, it was the corruption engendered by slavery that he mentioned in the examples he gave of the Persians.

Then there occurred a useful notion in his tales of the Persians, the transferring of authority from their king to his son, and the war they waged at sea—namely, that when something terrifying strikes enemies in one city, they become friends. Thus, it is obligatory for the legislator to examine whether the affection among the followers of his law is of this type or not, so that he structures his governance[34] accordingly with certainty and cognizance lest harm and corruption affect the law in that manner. [D 136]

15. [700a–702b] Then he rushed on to explain the issue of the music provided for by the statutes of those ancient traditional laws. He explained a certain aspect of it he had already mentioned before, namely, the well-being derived from accepting traditional laws in keeping with freedom versus the corruption that occurs from accepting them in keeping with slavery and coercion. He mentioned what is offensive and distasteful about slavery and that when the affair of the city is not based on fundamental[35] affection, thorough[36] upbringing, and perfect intellect, it is destined to destruction and corruption. On the other hand, when these three are present, it is destined to goodness and happiness. The argument about a whole city, a single household, and a single man is the same.

Fourth Treatise

1. [704a–705b] He set about now in this treatise explaining that the city in truth is neither the place that is called "city" nor a gathering of people. Rather, there are stipulations for it, among which are that its inhabitants accept the traditional laws of the regimes, that it have a divine governor, that its inhabitants manifest commendable and praiseworthy moral habits and customs, and that its territory be naturally suited for making it

34. Reading *fa-yudabbir tadbīrah* with all of the manuscripts, instead of *fa-yudabbiruh tadbīrah* ("he structures it, his governance") with Druart. Here, the less literal "he structures his governance" seems preferable to "he governs his governance."
35. Literally, "essential" (*al-dhātiyya*).
36. Or, more literally, "complete" (*al-tāmm*).

possible to bring to it the provisions its inhabitants need and everything else indispensable to them.

2. [705d–707a] Then he explained another notion, namely, that the law set down for the inhabitants of the city is not merely for the purpose of its inhabitants listening and obeying, but rather also for them to come to have praiseworthy moral habits and agreeable customs. He mentioned another notion, namely, that a person whose customs and moral habits are not in accordance with the law, noble, and agreeable will always be deteriorating and regressing; and it is base for a person to regress as he advances in years. He gave as an example courageous persons who disregard exercise to the point where they are forced to take up lowly arts and occupations such as sailing and the like. He gave an example drawn from a poem of Homer that was generally known to them and one about a lion that neglected itself to the point where its courage slipped away and it came to fear mountain goats.

3. [709b–e] Then he began to explain this notion in relation to an entire city. He also explained that it is fine, good fortune for a city if the one who sets down its traditional laws is skilled, cognizant, and well trained with regard to all instances of good fortune connected with prosperity and other things. And [he explained], further, that it is good fortune for the legislator to have the inhabitants of his city be those who listen, obey, and are disposed to accept the traditional laws embodied in regimes.

4. [709e–712b] Then he set about explaining the issue of domination. There may be a need for it when the inhabitants of the city are not good persons with fine natural dispositions. For domination is blamable only when the ruler is dominating by nature and uses it to satisfy his appetites, not when there is a need of it for the sake of the inhabitants of the city. Now when the city is such that the leader cannot dispense with coercing it and so does coerce it and sets down in it traditional laws that are divine, this is very praiseworthy and agreeable. [D 137]

5. [710e–713a] Then he explained that the domination taking place in this manner is more appropriate and easier in many respects than rule by means of choice since, by confronting the inhabitants of the city with domination, it is possible for the one who sets down traditional laws to make the inhabitants upright in the briefest period. In contrast, the one

who does not dominate but proceeds in accordance with the path of freedom, cannot do without gentleness; and gentleness takes more time.

6. Then he explained that just as domination and coercion are exceedingly fine for those who are slaves and evil, domination and coercion are exceedingly bad for those who are free and virtuous. He gave examples of the Knossians[37] and the inhabitants of other cities generally known to them.

7. [713a–714a] Then he explained that whenever the inhabitants of the city are better, their ruler is more divine. Therefore, their ruler is much more excellent than the rulers of a less excellent city. So this situation may evolve to the point where the governor of a city comes to be of the genus of divine beings and has only a little in common with these humans. He gave as an example of this notion the inhabitants of a city generally known to them.

8. [714b] Then he explained that the kinds of regimes correspond numerically to the kinds of traditional laws because regimes follow on traditional laws, draw from them, and are built on them. Moreover, rulerships correspond to them in number and kind as well as in way of life. If the one is fine, then so is the other; if bad, then bad; and if superior, then superior—with this departing only slightly from the truth.

9. [714c–716b] Then he explained that the vain ruler who cherishes his own beauty, money, lineage, or anything pertaining to his virtues is neither praiseworthy nor agreeable since the greatest concern of the ruler ought to be the well-being of the ruled. He who is arrogant is occupied only with himself and his own fate. He thus becomes loathsome to the gods. Anyone who becomes loathsome to them does not have their support. And the one who does not have their support will not pass along a noble and agreeable heritage.

10. [716c–718c] Then he set about describing him[38] and explaining the things he ought to be concerned about. He should begin with the fate of the body, then the fate of the soul, and then external things one after the other.

37. Reading *al-qunūsiyyīn* for sense, rather than *al-qubrusiyyīn* ("Cypriots") with Druart and the Leiden manuscript.

38. Namely, the good ruler.

He gave examples and spoke effusively on this subject because of its great usefulness. He ended up with a discussion of the rights and duties of sons and fathers, how they are to fulfill them, what they are when they start out in life, and what they become when they reach the end of their days.

11. [718d–719a] Then he explained what both the difficulty and the ease of this virtuous path consist in, giving an example drawn from a generally known poem. [D 138]

12. [719b–e] Then he explained that the poet, disputant, and discussant[39] may say both a thing and its contrary, whereas the one who attends to the traditional laws ought to defend only the one thing useful to him.

13.[40] Then he gave an example of that drawn from some of the statutes of Laws—namely, burying and shrouding the dead; what the legislator ought to command with respect to them; and how those others, whom we enumerated,[41] talk about them.

14. [719e–720e] Then he explained how the law should be implanted in the hearts of the people, giving as an example a doctor who treats children with gentleness. He mentioned that doctors have servants who imitate them. Likewise, there are judges who emulate legislators in giving guidance. It is obligatory on them to employ extreme gentleness in restoring traditional laws and preserving them for the people.

15. [720e–722c] Then he explained that the city begins to flourish only as a result of the law concerning marriage and procreation. Therefore that law ought to be extremely refined and precise. He mentioned how wrong it is to disregard things that were generally known in the traditional laws in those times, like fines and punishments.

16. [722c–723b] Then he set about explaining that, for traditional laws to become firmly established in the hearts of the inhabitants of the city,

39. The Arabic term is *mutakallim* and may also be understood as "dialectical theologian"; see also, above, 1.17, and Leo Strauss, "How Fārābī Read Plato's Laws," in *What Is Political Philosophy* (Glencoe, IL: Free Press, 1959), 139, 143.

40. This section is not recognized as a separate one by Druart. Thus, in the translation, the numbering of the subsequent sections in this treatise differs from hers.

41. That is, at the beginning of sec. 12.

preludes must be made prior to setting them down. Of these preludes, some are accidental and due to good luck, others are imposed, and still others are natural. The accidental preludes are like a mishap befalling its inhabitants that corrupts relations among them so that they are compelled to adopt a traditional law that brings them together and binds them in unity and unanimity. Natural preludes are like the corruption that comes about as a result of the passage of long and extended periods of time and the weariness that comes upon people because they are naturally disposed to it. Imposed preludes are like proclamations effected through discussion and clarifications effected by disputations. Thus, if these three [kinds of] preludes take place, the people's desire to follow traditional laws will be genuine and they will be compelled toward them so that, when they find them, they will accept them cheerfully.

Then there is another kind of prelude not belonging to the genus of these three, namely, the praiseworthy and noble moral habits that legislators and judges extol and that the ignorant and children follow so as to become habituated to these moral habits. Once they become states of character for them, these people are more easily led to accept traditional laws and more quickly hasten to adhere to them. For evil people are not led to good things easily, whereas those adhering to the mean are.

17. [724a–b] Then he himself promised to explain later on what is required for the issue of the soul of the inhabitants of the city, their bodies, customs, and characters.

Fifth Treatise

1. [726a–727e] In this treatise, he explains that the issue of the soul is the first thing that ought to be cared for because it is the most venerable of things and has the third rank among divine things. The most fitting type of care that can be bestowed on it is honor, since being contemptuous of the soul is base. He explained that honor is [D 139] among the divine issues and is the most venerable of them; since the soul is venerable, it ought therefore to be honored.

To honor the soul is not to satisfy its appetite. For, were this the case, it would be obligatory on a child as well as on an ignorant person to satisfy the appetites of their souls because they presume that the appetites of their souls are for fine and preferable things. And yet great harm would come about if they were to satisfy those appetites. Rather, honoring the soul consists in disciplining it and satisfying those appetites praised by divine traditional laws. The more the laws condemn them, the more it is an act of honoring the soul to keep it from them, even if this is painful at the moment. Anyone who presumes that the body is more venerable than the soul on the grounds that the soul would not exist were it not for the body has an erroneous presumption; his error will become evident with the slightest effort.

2. [727e–728a] Then he explained how the soul ought to be honored in many of the activities that a human being pursues, such as amassing money and other things.

3. [728a] Then he pointed to how the soul is honored by saying, "they[42] ought to be made to accept instruction from the legislator because this is his issue."

4. [728c–729a] Then he also mentioned that after honoring the soul, it is obligatory to honor the body. He explained that it is not the beautiful, powerful, nimble, sound, or corpulent body that is honorable, but the one that adheres to praiseworthy and agreeable customs and to ways of life that are in agreement with the traditional laws. The way to honor the body is to adhere to moral discipline. He explained this notion by means of an extensive discussion and useful, clear examples.

5. [729a–c] Then he set about explaining that the traditional laws for disciplining children to honor the body are none other than the traditional laws for disciplining middle-aged and old people when they are ignorant.

6. [729c–730b] Then he explained that the traditional laws with respect to honoring the soul apply equally to strangers, kinsmen, and inhabitants of the city, whereas the traditional laws with respect to bodily discipline that hold for strangers ought to be distinct from the ones for kinsmen. Now in the disciplining of bodies, there are punishments for crimes. So if the stranger and the kinsman are on an equal footing in this, that will lead to traditional laws and laws becoming corrupt.

42. That is, the inhabitants of the city; see above, 4.17.

7. [730b–732b] Then he explained the path one ought to move along in acquiring the moral virtues and that spending time is indispensable in this. For a custom is attained only when practiced over a period of time, in every social situation, and together with all groups. Otherwise, it will not become a custom. The path to becoming accustomed to justice, moderation, courage, and other things is the same. Likewise, removing blamable things requires time in which a person accustoms himself to abandoning base things. If a human being is not high-minded or has no natural strong indignation, the training of his soul cannot be at all complete. That is because a human being is naturally disposed to wink at most of the faults of his beloved—and there is no beloved more beloved to a person than his own soul. Since this is so, strong indignation is indispensable so that it is possible for one to restrain one's beloved soul from pleasant appetites. In this situation, anger alone is useful in keeping one from approving of all one's soul does and accustoming it instead to being displeased with such things from the outset. [D 140]

8. [732b–d] Then he explained that it is obligatory for people with upbringing first of all to command their own souls to abandon unbalanced actions, such as perpetual gladness, excessive laughter, intense sadness, excessive grief, and the like. Then after having so commanded their own souls, they are to command it of their subordinates.

9. [732d–734e] Then he mentioned that it is obligatory for them to seek the gods' assistance in connection with all these character traits and their acquisition by beseeching and invoking them and asking their assistance in what they are doing so that it is in accordance with the law, praiseworthy, and divine. A person must also strengthen his hope in the gods so that his existence is more felicitous and his way of life more noble. A noble way of life may be noble according to one group but not to another, or it may be noble in the eyes of the gods. So it is obligatory to consider this and reflect on it thoroughly.

He spoke about this notion extensively and explained the chosen way of life with respect to each moral habit and statute. He enumerated some of them by way of examples until he mentioned moderation. He explained that choosing the pleasurable over the painful is the way of life of compulsion, while choosing the painful over the pleasurable is the way of life of choice.

10. [734d–735a] Then he also mentioned this with respect to health, courage, knowledge, and so on.[43]

He mentioned, moreover, that the affair of the city cannot be complete unless the traditional laws are prepared for by preludes having to do with regimes so that, once these preludes are established, the great and splendid traditional law will perform its function. He gave as an example the warp and the woof of cloth.

11. [735a–c] Then he declared that these regimes are of two kinds. One consists of the rulers of tribes and their regimen[44] over them; the other consists of the traditional laws set down by those who set them down. He mentioned that this notion applies to all beings that are regimented—cattle and people. For each sort of the one and the other has a regimenting officer and a pattern that is other than the regimenting officer and pattern of the other.

12. [735c–e] Then he mentioned another notion useful in this connection, namely, that domination is needed as a prelude to divine traditional law. The need for it comes from two notions: one is for purging—I mean, purging the city of those evil people whose diligence, behavior, art, and zeal form resistance to the rulers—while the other notion is for them to become a lesson and warning to the good people so that they easily and cheerfully accept the traditional law of those who identify themselves with what is divine. He gave examples of that and expounded on all of them eloquently.

13. [735e–736a] Then he explained that, if there is not a genuine and urgent need for something, then the matter will not be executed with the ultimate in precision. He gave as an example migration and poverty that can be made the foundation of a virtuous city on account of the migrants' genuine need to settle and the genuine need of the poor for what assures their livelihood. [D 141]

43. Druart places this sentence at the end of sec. 9.

44. The term is *siyāsa*, heretofore translated as "regime." Here and in the rest of this section, it seems to make more sense to translate *siyāsa* and its cognates as "regimen," "regimented," and "regimenting."

14. [736c–739a] Then he explained that upright distribution is the fundament of the city's affairs lest anything increase to the point of becoming a preoccupation or decrease below what is obligatory so that strife comes about among its inhabitants. He began by enumerating in that regard first land and territories, then companions and brothers, then provisions and nourishments, then farms, then mosques, and then indispensable storehouses. He mentioned that such distribution, although necessary, is a difficult issue. It is for the one who sets down traditional laws to establish statutes in the city on which basis they will build their affair. He gave examples drawn from what was generally known to them. He mentioned various ways that legislators distributed worldly goods among the inhabitants of cities. His intention will not be hidden from anyone who reads those chapters.

15. Then, finally, he said, "This, then, is the city whose existence we wanted from the outset."[45]

16. [739c–741a?] Then he came back to mention how the conditions of the children and youths, and likewise those of the ignorant, ought to be administered.

17. [741a–e?] Then he followed that with the command to honor traditional laws and regimes and to look on them with veneration and exaltation.

18. [742a–744a] Then he set about explaining the details of amassing money from non-lowly occupations. Thus he mentioned that when money is accumulated in praiseworthy ways, it is much more excellent than poverty. However, when it is amassed from occupations that taint a human being with various types of disgrace, then it is better to abstain from earning it. He spoke extensively on this subject and gave examples of praiseworthy ways of amassing money drawn from the occupations of the Greeks that were generally known to them, both praiseworthy and not, such as traveling and commerce. In short, what is earned without harming traditional law and the character traits that constitute preludes to traditional laws or what honors the soul and honors the body is very praiseworthy. But if it is harmful in one of these respects, then it is blameworthy. And it is better

45. This section is not recognized as a separate one by Druart. Thus, in the translation, the numbering of the subsequent sections in this treatise differs from hers.

to be contented than to engage in any of these things because the purpose intended is to keep upbringing and traditional laws alive.

He mentioned that it is obligatory for the one who sets down traditional laws to prohibit all persons of upbringing and intelligence as well as those who comply with these traditional laws from being engaged in such occupations. And [it is obligatory for him] to set down punishments and to explain their meanings and consequences so that people adhere to these traditional laws and do not violate them.

[744a–745b?] The sage[46] spoke extensively on this subject and on it being obligatory for the legislator to care for the poor just as he cares for the rich: he must set up traditional laws to make them upright and to soothe their souls, or else corruption that it is impossible to control or to remove will be engendered.

[746d–747d] It is also obligatory for him to set down traditional laws concerning weights and measures, everything in which the people deal in the city, and trading so as not to disadvantage one group nor allow others to become reckless. And [it is obligatory for him] to proceed similarly with regard to the special positions of each of the inhabitants of the city, rich and poor, so that no class of people remains exempt from a traditional law concerning it; for that would lead to corruption of inestimable proportion and consequence. In short, divine traditional law ought not to contain disparity or disorder—the meaning of "not to contain disparity" here is that all those who have the same status as the one who sets down the divine traditional law and who come after him to look on it approve of it and find no fault with it. [D 142]

Sixth Treatise

1. [751a–c] He had resolved to explain in this treatise that the virtuous city is the one whose rulers and rulership are ordered fairly and naturally—for when the city lacks this element, it will not endure. If the legislator does not order the rulers, judges, and companions naturally, then he will be ridiculed and become a laughingstock at the outset, and his undertaking[47] will subsequently become twisted and his law corrupted. And the corruption of laws entails the corruption of cities.

46. That is, Plato.
47. Literally, "his affair" (*amruh*).

2. [752b–c] Then he set about explaining that, when the inhabitants of this city are ignorant, unsophisticated, and childish, they rarely accept these regimes and that order brought forth by the legislators.

3. [752d–755b] Then he explained a stratagem for gaining their acceptance, pointing out that the city must be either ancient or new. If it is ancient, then the legislator's task is easier due to what has taken place with the previous laws, traces of which still remain in the natural dispositions of the people, thus forming a prelude to the recent law. If the city is new, the task is somewhat more difficult because the legislator is obliged to choose from the city's men those people with natural dispositions ready to accept the laws. He will then come to an agreement with them as to what he wants, establish the traditional laws in their souls, seek their assistance, and strengthen himself against the others. And if he should happen upon groups from the inhabitants of another city who have observed the laws and become cognizant of them, let him seek their assistance against the inhabitants of his city—since they are also descendants of the same race—so that they propagate his law in that city itself with [the help of] another city.

Similarly with regard to the issue of the elders, he is also obliged to seek the assistance of those who are sophisticated and have fine natural dispositions against those who are inferior to them among the childish and ignorant. Thus, if the legislator happens upon the likes of these, let him order them as he deems he ought and as is most fitting and let him entrust each with those traditional laws that he knows it is possible for him to undertake as is required and is able to fulfill.

What we have mentioned is the meaning of what he symbolized in those examples about the inhabitants of Crete and other cities that he mentioned and about tablets, markets, and other things. He went on effusively about this, mentioning such things as how a city is delimited[48] when at the outset it is founded, how to order the people there, how to order their stipends and needs, and how to order their activities in accordance with their ages; for the tasks and activity that the elderly undertake and adequately perform, the youth cannot undertake and adequately perform; and the tasks and activity that the youth undertake and adequately

48. Reading *al-madīna kaifa tuḥaddad* for sense, rather than *al-madīna kaifa tattaḥid* ("how a city is united") with Druart and the Leiden manuscript.

perform, the elderly cannot undertake and adequately perform. He explained this through a lengthy, extensive discussion.

4. [755b–756b] Then he explained that after ordering the inhabitants of the city, it is obligatory to order the warriors, their rulers, and their governors; for wars constitute one of the greatest factors[49] for cities. [D 143]

5. [755c–d?] Then he mentioned another notion with respect to ordering, namely, that the ordering that occurs at the outset may not be entirely correct. Thus if [the legislator] sees that some ruler is not accomplished in or is inadequate for the issue he is to execute and someone more skilled and accomplished in it is found, he should not hesitate to dismiss the first and put the second in his place so that the issue will proceed in as fine and as upright a manner as possible. Being heedful of rights[50] in such a situation is harmful.

6. Then he alluded to it being obligatory for complete care to be given to the issue of ministers, people with experience, advisers, and governors with an eye to times of consultation whether they are at war or in peace. For legislators and the inhabitants of cities cannot do without such people; therefore, ordering them is necessarily obligatory for the well-being of cities. He explained, moreover, that the honors bestowed on those so ordered differ. Among them, there is: a primary honor, such as extolling and glorifying the person himself;[51] a secondary honor, like benefit; a tertiary honor, like a noble promise; and a fourth honor, like appearing to be positively disposed and to hold out hope—without actually saying as much.

[755b–756b] The warriors have beneficial and financial honors that are also ordered according to a scale, and all of these ought to be tended to very well.

[756b–e] He explained, moreover, that it is obligatory for the rulers to present those who are lazy and stubborn with fines instead of honors in order to straighten out the city's affairs, because honors and fines lead to corruption of the law when they are not ordered naturally so that every deserving person receives his due.

49. Literally, "causes" or "reasons" (*asbāb*), here, as well as in 6.9, 6.14, 6.16, and 6.17 below.
50. Literally, "right" (*ḥaqq*).
51. Literally, "extolling and glorifying the [person's] soul" (*al-ʿizz al-nafsānī wa al-ijlāl*).

7. [756e–758a] Then he pointed out a subtle notion in connection with ordering, namely, that equality fosters friendship, both of which are to be preferred. Let no one presume that equality consists in placing those who are slavish and ignoble on the same level as the free and the virtuous in rank and honors. Rather equality consists in assigning each the status each deserves. This is the equality that fosters affection and friendship.

8. [757d–758a] Then he mentioned another useful notion, namely, that something may occur with a group composed of equals in ability and rank that necessitates delegating a particular issue to one of them rather than to another, thereby causing them to quarrel and have a change of heart. In a situation such as this, one should avail oneself of things such as drawing by lots, chance, and what resembles them. It falls to the legislator to take care of this situation completely.

9. Then he explained the issue of generosity and miserliness in connection with expenditures, because handing out stipends to people—given their differences and taking into account [how these affect] their expenditures and their openhandedness—is one of the most difficult factors for a regime. This is because anyone who takes his stipend and does not spend it so as to benefit his subordinates, but amasses it instead for himself, causes great harm. It is up to the rulers to investigate the issue of those who are like this—and the issue of extravagant people as well—and to prevent and obstruct them subtly. He elucidated this notion adequately and explained as well the issue of profligate people who increase their expenditures and stipends because their expenditures and stipends are spent on what begets great, harmful evils in the city and on what is ephemeral and, therefore, of no avail. [D 144]

10. [758a–e] Then he mentioned the issue of the guardians and the custodians. These are of two kinds: one consists of the guardians of the city like soldiers, night watchmen, and warriors; the other consists of the custodians of the laws and regimes like judges, preachers, governors, and advisers. He gave as an example a ship at sea. He mentioned further the usefulness of the institution of messengers and how it embodies alertness and eliminates laxness from issues entrusted to those who are ordered and keeps them at their post. This is an equitable Law, because assigning functions is enormously and completely useful.

11. [759a–b] Then he mentioned the issue of informers and spies who approach the inhabitants of the city and question them on behalf of their enemies. He commanded that this issue be watched closely and that one be wary of them.

12. Then he digressed to mention the substances of men and commanded something useful with respect to that, namely, selecting for important, urgent issues those legislators and also those rulers who are men with some experience in freedom so that, because of their fine natural dispositions, they will be furthest from evils.

13. Then he spoke extensively about natural orderings. ("Natural" means an adequate amount in proportion to the situation, the issue, and the condition: if [things call for] a hundred, then [provision should be made for] a hundred; if ten, then ten; if one, then one.)

14. [776b–778a?] Then he began with the issue of servants, explaining that the issue of servants is one of the important factors for the inhabitants of cities. They are of two sorts: one sort consists of slaves and handmaids; the other sort consists of animals that are needed in the city in peace and in war. It is obligatory for the legislator and the rulers after him to have in mind the issue of servants and their governance by setting down traditional laws for them and concerning them.

15. [761a–c] Then he described the issue of water since there is no way for the inhabitants of the city to settle down unless the governance of their water is extremely correct. It is up to the legislator and the rulers to take complete care of the issue of water and channeling it so that it is distributed equitably and not given abundantly in one place while lacking in another or given to some people while being kept from others.

16. [761a–c] Then he mentioned the issue of benevolent gifts in connection with sources [of water][52] like cisterns and travel facilities[53] for the needy. For that is one of the greatest factors causing cities to exist, flourish, and have lasting renown. It is up to the one who sets down traditional laws

52. The Arabic term *ma'ādin* means "sources" or "mines."

53. Literally, "causes" or "reasons" (*asbāb*), both here and in the last sentence of this section; similarly, the term translated as "factors" in the next sentence is *asbāb*.

and to the judges to be extremely solicitous about the maintenance of these facilities.

17. [761d–762b] Then he digressed to another notion from among the most important factors of the city, namely, the taxes that ought to be levied on the people—such as alms, land taxes, and the poll tax. These taxes are of two types: one is levied for [natural] resources;[54] the other is levied for humiliation—to keep the youth from inclining toward practices other than those of the legists and toward ways of life different from the ways of life and laws of the inhabitants of the cities. [D 145]

18. [761d–762b?] Then he mentioned the issue of crimes and punishments. There are two sorts of crimes: one sort concerns recalcitrance in obeying; the other sort concerns introducing what does not agree with traditional law. If it is committed by one of the ruled, it is up to the ruler to punish him with the punishment that the supreme legislator set down for that crime. If it is committed by a ruler, the other rulers must convene to discipline and reprimand him as the situation requires. For neglect of that will lead to the city's ruin and corruption.

19. Then he began to mention the stipends of the citizens and spoke of it extensively, having previously treated similar issues quite profusely. However, whereas the first one was set forth in a more general vein, this one was in a more specific one.

20. [764a–765d] Then he mentioned what ought to be taken care of with regard to the issue of the rulers of the musicians, because that is also obligatory in every time. However, the care for that was greater in those times. Thus he mentioned that there are two sorts of music: one sort exhorts to combat[55] and the activities of war; the other sort exhorts and conduces to the activities of peace and joyfulness. It is obligatory for the legislator and the rulers to order these [rulers of the musicians] as the laws require.

54. See n. 52.
55. The term is *jihād*.

Seventh Treatise

1. He set about in this treatise explaining the issue of reminders that are indispensable for the legislators to establish so that the reminders will be referred to in their times and after the end of the days of their lives. And, by means of an extensive discussion, he mentioned that this issue is necessary.

2. Then he divided them and said, "some of them are brought forth all at once when they [the legislators] first make their project apparent; some are brought forth one after another; and some are brought forth collectively at the end when they finish legislating their Laws, ordering their statutes, and establishing their traditional laws."

3. Then he mentioned that what is brought forth all at once at the outset is like something counterfeit because of the piecemeal changes and alterations that will be needed as was already mentioned with respect to something similar at some place in this book. That may become a defect in the eyes of the youth and those unsophisticated with respect to traditional laws. What is brought forth gradually, on the other hand, is fair and noble. What is brought forth last is the noblest of all, and the precautions taken in it are most effective.

4. Then he mentioned that what is said in them ought not to belittle the right of anyone who reflects on them and infers their meanings.

5. Then he gave examples drawn from the statements of poets who related the sayings of some ancient legislators and wondered at the rich meanings contained in those few utterances. [D 146]

6. Then he began to explain that these sayings may be innovations that the inhabitants of the cities need to learn and work hard to memorize or they may be innovations based on all that the inhabitants of the cities are already cognizant of. He brought forth examples drawn from ancient books of which they were cognizant.

7. Then he digressed to mention the sorts of things that ought to be set down in those books. He mentioned that the statutes[56] set down by the

56. Reading *fa-dhakar ann al-aḥkām* for sense, rather than the redundant *fa-dhakar ann dhikr al-aḥkām* ("he mentioned that mentioning the statements") with Druart as well as the Leiden and the Kabul manuscripts.

legislator are obviously to be established with the fairest detail and summary possible. Then, [they are to be followed with] exhortations that melt the hearts of the inhabitants of the cities on hearing them, move them to humility and sorrow, and foster in their hearts compassion and humility.

8. Then he brought forth parables with which the inhabitants of the cities will admonish themselves either about bygone peoples whose traces have vanished, leaving only their name, or else about beasts and their conditions, and then about strange matters that leave people perplexed about comprehending them. He described wonderful aspects of the advantages of these strange matters. One is the natural inclination of those who are unsophisticated, as well as the majority of people toward what their intellects find strange even though it is hard for them to perceive its real sense. Another is the wonder they display at some marvelous thing. Yet another is the way it leads to the continued existence of the law due to the people's being continually engaged in extracting the meanings of those strange matters.

9. Then he followed this by mentioning books generally known to the inhabitants of those cities engrossed in discovering their meanings; this became so widespread that poets like Homer and others mention it in their poetry.

10. Then he turned to and explained another notion by means of an extensive speech, namely, that it is obligatory on the legislator to oblige the inhabitants of the cities to preserve and study those sayings; and he is to establish this as one of the most important statutes of his law so that those sayings will not be obliterated.

11. Then he began to mention another notion with regard to the issue of legislators, namely, that none of them ought to repudiate anything that a previous legislator brought forth. When necessity prompts a legislator to change a statute of previous laws, let him repudiate instead the alteration made by the inhabitants of those cities in what was brought forth by their legislators and the distortion of the traditional laws and usages. Then, afterward, he may start[57] to replace [that] with what[58] is more appropriate. He spoke effusively on this subject.

57. Reading *yashra'* for sense, rather than *shara'a* ("he started") with Druart as well as the Leiden and Kabul manuscripts.

58. Reading *bimā* with the Kabul and Escorial manuscripts, rather than *innamā* ("now that") with Druart and the Leiden manuscript.

12. Then he turned to explain the issue of legislators who are brought forth afterward. He mentioned that when a legislator declares that someone else will succeed him, the thoughts and hearts of the inhabitants of the city—especially the unsophisticated ones—become preoccupied with expectation, and this diminishes their desire to adhere to what he himself brings forth. [D 147]

13. Then he himself explained that the legislator ought to be very wary of claiming that he will never have any successor whatsoever. For if that is publicized and then people see someone else appear after him with the passage of time, this will lead them to reject, disown, and discard all laws—his law, the law of his predecessor, and that of his successor. Rather, it is obligatory for him to steer a middle course between denying and confirming it. For example, he is to declare that someone will appear to defend him and his law when these statutes and traditional laws are obliterated as time moves on and people become corrupt. If they ask whether the future legislator will be as excellent as he, let him deny it, since it will not harm him. He brought forth examples drawn from the inhabitants of those cities and their legislators.

14. Then he began after that to explain that there are two sorts of traditional laws. One sort applies particularly to each of the legislators quickly and according to their need at the time as well as to the conditions of their cities. And [the second sort consists of] traditional laws that do not change or alter, namely, the natural ones. He spoke effusively on this subject, bringing forth examples relating to kinsmen, ingratitude for favors, and other things.

Eighth Treatise

1. [828a–c] He had mentioned the issue of festivals in a general way at the beginning of the book. Now, then, he started to mention ordering them. Thus he described a subtle notion that reveals a marvelous advantage of festivals other than the advantage he alluded to at the beginning of the book, namely, exalting the gods and restoring their renown. For exalting and esteeming the gods exalts the traditional laws and the laws. He mentioned that one ought to look into how many gods there are and institute for each one a festival and sacrifices by which the inhabitants seek to gain their favor.

2. [828c–829c] Then he mentioned that there are two sorts of gods, a sort in the heavens that are worshiped and another sort on earth that are esteemed but not worshiped. For each sort, the appropriate sacrifices and activities made obligatory by the law are to be ordered. He described the obligation during these festivals for the young people of the city, after having offered sacrifices, to occupy themselves with exercises that are beneficial to them in combat[59] so that they execute this with cheerfulness.

Let him permit them to sing during these festivals the kinds of songs that contain eulogies and condemnations in order that this lead them to adhere to traditional law with pleasure and cheerfulness. For listening to eulogies and criticisms that come about in an upright manner and as made obligatory by the law instills in the young people's hearts eagerness to acquire the virtues through combat; their eagerness will increase and augment, their hearts grow stronger, and their sense of indignation intensify.

Then, from those exercises performed by the young people at those festivals there come forth activities pertaining to combat demanding great valor that are beneficial to the city. [D 148]

3. [846d–847b] Then he mentioned another of the notions that the rulers of the city ought not to ignore, namely, that those who do the slaughtering for these sacrifices as well as the artisans needed to decorate the festivals are also parts of the city. Since they will be busy with their occupations,[60] they will miss[61] the benefits from attending the festivals. If they miss these [benefits], their consciences become corrupted. Now if their consciences become corrupted and they are numerous, that will lead to corruption in the city. For they are one of the major parts of the city. Therefore, it is obligatory that the rulers not allow a plethora of the city's inhabitants to become practitioners of such arts.

Let him set down for them, then, special permits so that the inhabitants of the city will not be corrupted by this, and let him disclose such base aspects of those arts so that—as a result of those base aspects being disclosed—only people with bad natural dispositions will aspire to them. Otherwise that will lead to weakening the role[62] of traditional laws.

59. The term translated as "combat" here and in the next two paragraphs is *jihād*.
60. Literally, "with their art" (*bi-ṣināʿatihim*).
61. Reading *fātathum* with the Kabul manuscript (Druart reads this as *fa-innahum*), rather than *fa-tuqawwimuhum* ("they will be constituted by") with Druart as well as the Leiden and Escorial manuscripts.
62. Literally, "issue" (*amr*).

4. [829e–834d] Then he came back to mention the exercises that are performed on festival days. He enumerated them and elucidated the issue, enumerating the advantages derived from them—such as various kinds of horsemanship, kinds of practice with weapons, and wrestling in the manner generally known in those days and times and among those groups.

5. [835b–841a] Then he mentioned that these pleasures associated with festivals enter people's hearts as a result of their being occupied with them during the festivals, so that they become overwhelmingly preoccupied with and attached to them on nonfestival days to the point where their preoccupation with them develops into preoccupation with pleasures outside the lawful traditions.[63] Thus, it is up to the legislator to be very mindful of this notion, especially in connection with intercourse and the pleasure associated with it, because it is one of the greatest causes of appetites and pleasures. While these things have a great usefulness, their harmfulness is also great. He spoke a great deal about this notion in particular and this subject, was ample in what he mentioned, and spoke effusively until he proceeded to advance beyond it to mentioning moderation.

6. [841a–c] Then he followed this by speaking about the other virtues and the stages of the young people in regard to them. He mentioned, moreover, how the virtues creep stealthily into the soul along with the display of lawful pleasures while the vices do so along with the display of unlawful pleasures, albeit slightly. That is because this notion is one of the most important issues that the legislator ought to take care of completely.

7. [835d–844d] Then he mentioned the difficulty of this subject and the difficulty of being mindful of and controlling it, because being mindful of and controlling something not distinguishable from its contrary is very difficult. That is because young people and those who are unscrupulous[64] adhere to beautiful appearances that lead them to what they want. As a result, it is hard for rulers to keep them away from what they adhere to. So they lose almost no time before they arrive at their bad appetites, and that ultimately leads to the corruption of the city.

63. Literally, "the lawful traditional laws" (*al-sunan al-nāmūsiyya*).
64. Literally, "companions of bad consciences" (*aṣḥāb al-ḍamāʾir al-radīʾa*).

So it is up to the legislator to take care of each and every one of these issues and, moreover, the issues of the workers, artisans, farmers, and frontier settlers. Let him set down the traditional laws appropriate for making them upright. Then let him devote most of his concern to the issue of temples and esteemed places on earth so that they not change. For changing them will corrupt people's hearts, and corrupting their hearts will, in turn, throw the affair of the city into disorder.

It is up to the legislator [D 149] to teach the administrators[65] and judges how to govern each group of people so that they follow his way and pursue the correct course in that, thereby preventing dissension from arising as a result of badly governing them. He mentioned this notion and gave examples of free people and slaves and of the way people interact with bees in beehives—meaning by this only evil people and vagabonds.

8. Then he mentioned that a single administrator[66] and governor will not be cognizant of the usages, regulations, and customs of the inhabitants of all the regions. Thus one of them may be skilled in administering one group of people and the inhabitants of a particular country. If he is required to administer other groups—even if, for example, they were fewer in number—it will not be possible for him because of their usages, regulations, and customs that escape him and of which he is not cognizant. For this notion he gave examples drawn from administrators at sea and rulers on land. He spoke about this extensively.

9. [844d–845d] Then he started to explain two notions in one, namely, the issue of theft and that of property. He mentioned that it is more fitting not to punish those who, without permission, take property that is insignificant and that is impossible to store, because to dismiss this is manly and gives the inhabitants of the city a good name. But in the case of what can be stored and useful later if it is preserved, it is not base but fair to punish the one who takes it. From this it is clear that anyone who takes the likes of the former things from someone else's possessions is not to be punished like thieves who take things of value. For this notion he gave examples of fruits and other, similar things.

65. Literally, "companions of regimes" (*aṣḥāb al-siyāsāt*).
66. The term is *al-sāʾis*; see preceding note.

10. [846d–847b] Then he digressed to mention the arts and crafts. He explained that it was obligatory for the inhabitants of the city to engage in each of the particular arts for which they are suited. It is obligatory that anyone who would shift[67] from one art to another for fun, diversion, or vanity, without this being called for by necessity, incompetence in the first art, or an obvious excuse or reason, be prevented from doing so by the governor of the city. If punishment is necessary to prevent that, let the person be punished and a fine be imposed on him. For switching from one art to another without an excuse is a powerful cause of confusion and corruption in the [proper] arrangements. He spoke a great deal further about this notion and about fines for it.

11. [847e–848c] Then he himself described the nourishment that is indispensable for the inhabitants of the city. He mentioned that it is obligatory for the administrators[68] of cities to have control over this issue and that those who set down traditional laws should not overlook it. Rather, they should order statutes concerning them to straighten the matter out. These include nourishment for the inhabitants of the city themselves, then nourishment for their slaves, then nourishment for their animals and, finally, what is left over—which they will generously offer to one another.

12. [848c–849a] Then he described the issue of sites in which the gods are worshiped and the issue of places of assembly in which the inhabitants of the city can come together for one or another type of their common interests—like markets. For it is up to the legislator and the rulers of the city to direct their attention to this issue. [D 150]

13. [849a–850c] Then he explained that looking into the issue of sales and purchases so that they will be conducted uprightly is obligatory as well; likewise, the issue of the equipment needed for bodies, sites, mosques, wars, and other things; then the issue of contracts, registrations, deposits, debts, and deeds—for it may be obligatory on the legislator to take care of all of these. He mentioned all these things in a sound discussion at the end of this treatise. The way he meant it will be clear to anyone who reflects on it and is cognizant of the intention of his that we mentioned.

67. Or, more literally, "digress" (*ʿadal*).
68. The term is *suwwās* and is the plural of *sāʾis*; see n. 66.

Ninth Treatise

1. Up to this point he discussed the roots of the laws and what issues it is obligatory on the legislator to care for and not neglect in any way, namely, the regulations and the roots.

2. [854b–c] Then he began now in this treatise to explain things that adorn the law and enhance it and that are the consequences of those roots. He explained that the good inhabitants of this city cannot dispense with practice in adhering to these benevolent actions and consequences, because the free person always obeys voluntarily while the slave must be commanded. It is obligatory for the virtuous legists to take complete care of what adorns traditional laws, establishing them so that the virtuous inhabitants of the city adhere to obeying them voluntarily and come to be good and happy. He gave as examples visiting holy houses, constructing them, and associating with virtuous people.

3. [853a–855c] Then he mentioned what ought to be done with the evil inhabitants in the way of punishment for those crimes of theirs such as not venerating houses of worship as well as not venerating ancestors and rulers. He mentioned that things such as these are entrusted to judges so that criminals are punished as they deserve to be—by being beaten, killed, fined, or something similar.

4. [855a] Then he explained that if the children and relatives of those on whom any of these punishments are inflicted repudiate them and are wary of their company, this is very praiseworthy; and they ought to be honored in the city because it indicates their fine natural disposition. He mentioned that anyone who opposes such beating and punishments and does not approve of them causes great harm to traditional laws and is more harmful to them than a warring enemy.

5. Then he described an aspect of the issue of inheritances, namely, if someone grows up in the city who is more fit for issues previously handled by the aged, let that issue be handed over to him. And if the former dies, the latter will take his place. [D 151]

6. [857a–b] Then he began to expound on the issue of punishments and compensations. He gave as an example theft and other things. If the

thief returns double the amount he took and repents, the punishment of imprisonment and beating will be dismissed. He brought forward other examples.

7. [858c–859b] Then he explained that when the people are good and virtuous, they have no need at all of traditional laws or laws and are very happy. Only those whose moral habits are not valid and upright need laws and traditional laws. He mentioned, moreover, that the reminders the inhabitants of the city find among ancient traditional laws and, similarly, the reminders found in the sayings of the poets, in popular traditional laws, and in famous proverbs benefit them by lessening the need for legislators and by refining the moral habits.

8. [860d–863a] Then he mentioned, moreover, evils done voluntarily and deliberately and those done as a result of natural disposition without deliberation. He mentioned that none of them is in harmony with the traditional laws but instead harm them and corrupt the city's affairs. He mentioned that punishments must be applied to both sorts [of evils]. He spoke extensively about whether injuries that some inhabitants of the city inflict on others are voluntary or involuntary or, rather, out of necessity. He mentioned statutes for them that were generally known to those people. He also explained that notion with respect to justice, injustice, and everything else that takes place in part voluntarily and in part involuntarily.

9. [859c–864c] Then he set about explaining another notion very useful to be cognizant of, namely, that justice is noble. Are, then, all its actions and consequences noble or not? That is, retaliation and punishment for crimes pertain to justice. If one looks into these actions themselves—killing, beating, fining, and similar things—they are, in themselves, perhaps not noble. He gave as an example someone who, having plundered one of the houses of worship, is brought forward and beaten or killed.

He spoke effusively about voluntary and involuntary things, regardless of whether they were noble or base. His purpose in most of this is to explain by what he says whether someone who is born and raised in accordance with the traditional laws, who is not cognizant of any others, and who does nothing other than what is made obligatory by the traditional laws is virtuous and praiseworthy or not. For there continues to be great disagreement among people about this and about whether punishment is obligatory for someone who commits a crime without deliberation on account of his natural disposition, regardless of whether it be an immediate or a future punishment. Upon my life, this notion is exceedingly useful when it is truly expounded.[69]

Amid his statements, he carried on an unconnected discussion in various places. By all of that, he indicates that anyone who has the ability to deliberate and to avoid base things, but neglects himself to the point where he is naturally disposed to commit blameworthy things, will surely incur punishment sooner or later for all he commits.

10. [864d–882c] Then he explained the punishments and divided them according to the kinds of crimes in accordance with what was generally known to them in those times. [D 152]

[Conclusion]

Abū Naṣr al-Fārābī said: "This much of the book has reached us, and we managed to get hold of it. We reflected on it, leafed through it, and extracted those of its notions that dawned on us and that we knew the sage[70] had intended to explain. He perhaps entrusted to his sayings from which we extracted these notions subtleties, details, and useful notions that are several times more than what we mentioned. Nevertheless, he did intend to explain what we brought forth. In bringing it forth, we anticipated recompense and a noble name."

He said: "There remained treatises of this book no copy of which reached us."

He said: "There is disagreement among people as to the number of treatises in this book; some claim there are ten, and some claim there are fourteen. But only those treatises that we discussed have fallen into our hands."

This is the end of the *Laws* by the magnificent, great, and divine Plato, may the most excellent peace be his, expounded on by the Master, the Second Teacher, Abū Naṣr Muḥammad Ibn Muḥammad Ibn Ṭarkhān, may God sanctify his cherished spirit.

Completed in 692 [AH = 1294 CE].

69. Literally, "a true commentary on it is made" (*lukhkhiṣ ḥaqq al-talkhīṣ*).
70. That is, Plato.

Appendix A

Alfarabi, *Enumeration of the Sciences*

Introduction

The book of Abū Naṣr Muḥammad ibn Muḥammad al-Fārābī on the ranks of the sciences.[1]

He said: In this book, we intend to enumerate the well-known sciences, science by science, and to draw awareness to the sum of what each one of them comprises, the parts of each one that has parts, and the sum of what is in each of those parts. We set that down in five chapters: the first is about the science of language and its parts; the second about the science of logic and its parts; the third about the sciences of mathematics, namely, arithmetic, geometry, optics, astronomy, music, measuring, and engineering; the fourth about physical science and its parts, as well as divine science and its parts; and the fifth about political science and its parts, the science of jurisprudence, and the science of dialectical theology.

What is in this book is useful. For when a human being wants to learn one of these sciences and look into it, he will know what to begin with, what to look into, what he will derive by looking into it and what its value is, and what excellence is to be gained from it so that he proceed through the sciences in an aware and insightful manner and not in a blind or confused manner. [44] By means of this book, a human being will be able to compare the sciences so as to know which are more excellent, more useful, more certain, more trustworthy, and more powerful and which are more feeble, more fragile, and weaker.

1. See *Iḥṣā' al-'Ulūm li-al-Fārābī*, edited, with an introduction and notes, by 'Uthmān Amīn (Cairo: Dār al-Fikr al-'Arabī, 1949), 43–44.

It will be of use as well in uncovering someone who claims to have insight into one of these sciences but does not. For when he is asked to give an account of what is in it and to enumerate its parts and the sum of what is in each of its parts and he is not conversant with this, the falseness of his claim will become evident and his deception will be uncovered. By means of it as well, one who has a good grasp of one of the sciences will discern whether he has a good grasp of all of it or of some of its parts and of what extent he has a good grasp.

And it will be useful both to the educated person intent on gaining a summary acquaintance with each science and to the one who would like to resemble scientific people and thus be presumed to be one of them.

Appendix B

Averroes's Defense of the Philosophers as Believing in Happiness and Misery in the Hereafter

[Introduction]

1. When he [al-Ghazālī] finished with these questions, he began to claim that the philosophers deny the resurrection of bodies.[1] This is something for which no statement is found among any one of those who have gone before, although a statement about the resurrection of bodies has been widespread in Laws for at least a thousand years. Yet those from whom philosophy has come to us do not go back that many years. That is because the first to speak about the resurrection of bodies were the prophets of the children of Israel who came after Moses (peace upon him), and that is evident from the Psalms and from many of the writings attributed to the children of Israel. It is also established in the New Testament, and the statement has a tradition going back to Jesus (peace upon him). It is [also] a statement of the Sabaeans, and Abū Muḥammad ibn Ḥazm [581] says that theirs is the oldest of the Laws.[2]

1. Text from Averroes, *Tahāfut al-Tahāfut* (Incoherence of the Incoherence), ed. Maurice Bouyges (Beirut: Imprimerie Catholique, 1930), 580:1–588:6. This translation, with minor alterations, is taken from *Averroës, The Book of the Decisive Treatise: Determining the Connection Between the Law and Wisdom, and Epistle Dedicatory*, trans., with intro. and notes, Charles E. Butterworth (Provo, UT: Brigham Young University Press, 2001), 43–46.

2. Abū Muḥammad 'Alī ibn Aḥmad ibn Sa'īd ibn Ḥazm, a prolific theologian and jurist, was born in Cordoba in 994/384 and died in Manta Lisham, a town near Seville, in 1064/456. The reference is to Ibn Ḥazm's claim about the Sabaeans in his multivolume *Al-Faṣl fī al-Milal wa al-Ahwā' wa al-Niḥal* (Decisive Judgment about Religions, Sects, and Creeds), ed. Muḥammad Ibrāhīm Naṣr and 'Abd al-Raḥmān 'Umayra (Jidda: 'Ukāẓ, 1982), vol. 1, 88:8–89:1.

[The Philosophers' Opinions about Laws]

2. But it appears that the group [of philosophers] is the people who make the most of them and have the most faith in them.[3] The reason for that is their being of the opinion that they [the Laws] direct to the governance of people by means of which a human being exists insofar as he is human and obtains the happiness particularly characteristic of one [sc. a human being]. That is because they [the Laws] are necessary for the existence of the human moral virtues, theoretical virtues, and practical arts. And that is because they [the philosophers] are of the opinion that a human being has no life in this abode but by means of the practical arts and no life in this abode or in the final abode but by means of the theoretical virtues; that neither one of these two is completed or obtained for him but by means of the moral virtues; and that the moral virtues are firmly established only through cognizance of God (may He be exalted) and magnifying Him by means of the devotions set down in the Law for them in each and every religion—such as offerings, prayers, invocations, and similar speeches spoken in praise of God (may He be exalted), the angels, and the prophets. In sum, they [the philosophers] are of the opinion that the Laws are the necessary political arts whose principles are taken from the intellect and Legislation, especially those that are common to all the Laws—even if they [the Laws] do differ about the lesser and the greater with respect to that.

3. They [the philosophers] are of the opinion, moreover, that one ought not to object to their common principles by means of a statement that establishes or rejects—such as whether it is obligatory to worship God [582] or not and, more than that, whether He exists or not. And they are of the same opinion with respect to the rest of the principles—such as the statement about the existence of final happiness and what it is like—because all Laws agree about another existence after death, even if they differ about the description of that existence; just as they agree about His existence, attributes, and actions being cognizable, even if they differ more or less[4] with respect to what they say about the essence of the Principle and His actions. Similarly, they agree about the actions that lead

3. The immediate antecedent of the feminine singular pronoun (*hā*), which may be used to refer to inanimate plural things, must be "Laws" (*sharāʾiʿ*). In the context, it must be understood as the Laws establishing the resurrection of bodies.

4. Literally, "less and more" (*bi-al-aqall wa al-akthar*).

to the happiness of the final abode, even if they differ in the evaluation of these actions.

4. In sum, since they [the Laws] had directed to wisdom by means of a path shared by all, they [the philosophers] held them [the Laws] to be obligatory. For philosophy directs to making only a few intelligent people cognizant of happiness; and it is up to them to learn wisdom, whereas the Laws are intent on teaching the multitude in general. In spite of that, we do not find any one of the Laws that has not been attentive to what particularly characterizes the wise, even though it is concerned with what the multitude share in.

5. Since the select sort of people completes its existence and attains its happiness only through association with the common sort, common education is necessary for the existence of the select sort and for its life both in the moment of its youth and its growing up—and no one doubts that—and as it passes on [583] to what particularly characterizes it. A necessity of the virtue of such a one[5] is not to make light of what he has grown up with; to interpret it in the fairest way; and to know that the intent of that education is what is common, not what is particular. And if he explicitly declares a doubt about the Law-based principles in which he has grown up or an interpretation contradicting the prophets (God's prayers upon them) and turning away from their path, then he is the person who most deserves to have the name of unbelief applied to him and to be judged with the penalty of unbelief in the religion in which he has grown up.

6. In addition, it is obligatory on him to choose the most virtuous one [religion] in his time, even when all of them are true according to him. He is to believe that the most virtuous will be abrogated by one more virtuous. Therefore, the wise men who were teaching the people of Alexandria became Muslim when the Law of Islam reached them. And the wise men who were in the cities of Byzantium became Christian when the Law of Jesus (peace upon him) reached them. And no one doubts that among the children of Israel there were many wise men. This is apparent from the books that are found among the children of Israel attributed to Solomon (peace upon him). Nor has wisdom ever ceased to exist among those with revelation—namely, the prophets (peace upon them). Therefore the truest of all propositions is that every prophet is a wise man, but not every wise

5. That is, someone who is of the select sort.

man a prophet. Rather, they are the learned [584] of whom it is said that they are the heirs of the prophets.

7. If the principles of the demonstrative arts are postulates and fundamentals that are posited, how much more appropriate must that be with respect to the Laws taken from revelation and intellect. Every Law comes about from revelation and has intellect mixed with it. For anyone who holds that it is possible for a Law to come about from intellect alone, it necessarily follows that it is more deficient than the Laws inferred from intellect and revelation. And everyone agrees that the principles of practice must be taken on authority, for there is no way to demonstrate what practice makes obligatory except through the existence of virtues acquired through practical, moral actions.

[The Superiority of the Religion of Islam]

8. Now it has become evident from this statement that wise men in their entirety are of this opinion with respect to the Laws—I mean that the principles of action and the Traditions posited in each religion are to be taken on authority from the prophets. According to them, what is praiseworthy among these necessary principles is what most incites the multitude to virtuous actions, so that those brought up on these are more completely virtuous than those brought up on others—like it is with prayers among us. For there is no doubt that "prayer[6] puts an end to iniquity and transgression," as God (may He be exalted) has said (29:45) and that in the prayer posited in this Law this action [585] is to be found more completely than in the rest of the prayers posited in the rest of the Laws, that is, with respect to what is stipulated as to their number, their times, their calling to mind, and the rest of what is stipulated with respect to them concerning purification and renouncing—I mean, renouncing actions and statements that corrupt them.

9. The matter is the same with respect to the hereafter, for what is said in it urges more to virtuous actions that what is said in the others. Therefore, making an image of the hereafter for them [sc. the people of the religion] by corporeal things is better than making an image of it by

6. Reading *al-ṣalwa*, with the Istanbul Yeni Jāmiʿ manuscript no. 734, to accord with the verse from the Quran, rather than *al-ṣalawāt*, with Bouyges on the basis of the other manuscripts. See *Decisive Treatise*, section 50.

spiritual things, as He (may He be glorified) said: "The likeness of Paradise promised to the pious, from beneath which rivers flow" (13:35).[7] And the Prophet (peace upon him) said: "What is in it, no eye has seen, nor has ear heard, nor has it occurred to the mind of man." And Ibn 'Abbās said: "There is nothing of this world in the world to come but names."[8] He signified that that existence is another growth higher than this existence and another phase better than this phase. That is not to be denied by anyone who believes that we perceive a single existing thing being transformed from one phase to another, like inorganic forms being transformed until they come to perceive their [own] essences—namely, the intelligible forms. Those who doubt these things, object to that, and give expression to it are surely those intent on rejecting the Laws and rejecting the virtues. They are the atheists who are of the opinion that a human being has no end other than the enjoyment of pleasures—this no one doubts. Any of these who is capable of this will undoubtedly be killed by the companions of the Laws [586] and by the wise in their entirety. For the one who is not capable of it, the most complete statements needed are the significations contained in the Precious Book.

10. What this man [al-Ghazālī] said in contending against them is good. And in contending against them, the soul should by all means be posited as immortal—as is signified by the intellectual and the Law-based indications. And it should be posited that what comes back [to life] are bodies like these that were in this abode—not these very ones, because what has perished does not come back as an individual entity. Existence comes back only to a likeness of what has perished, not to what has itself perished, as Abū Ḥāmid [al-Ghazālī] has explained. Therefore, the statement about coming back in the doctrine of the dialectical theologians, who believe that the soul is an accident and that the bodies that come back are those that have perished, is not correct. That is because what perishes, then exists, is one in kind—not one in number. Rather, it is two

7. The rest of the verse reads: "and partaking of it and of its shade is perpetual. That is the outcome of those who are pious, and the outcome of the unbelievers is the fire."

8. 'Abd Allāh ibn 'Abbās ibn 'Abd al-Muṭṭalib was a paternal uncle of the Prophet Muhammad and a recognized authority in the interpretation of the Quran as well as in the traditions about the Prophet's sayings and deeds; he was born in about 535 and died in 32/653. See W. Montgomery Watt, "al-'Abbās b. 'Abd al-Muṭṭalib," in *Encyclopaedia of Islam*, 2nd ed., ed. P. Bearman, T. Bianquis, C. E. Bosworth, E. van Donzel, and W. P. Heinrichs, Brill Online, 2014, http://referenceworks.brillonline.com.proxy-um.researchport.umd.edu/entries/encyclopaedia-of-islam-2/al-abbas-b-abd-al-muttalib-SIM_0017.

in number. And [it is not correct] in particular for those of them who say that accidents do not last during two periods of time. [587]

[Conclusion]

11. This man [sc. al-Ghazālī] accuses the philosophers of unbelief with respect to three questions. One of them is this one, and we have said enough about the opinion of the philosophers with respect to this question and that, according to them, it is one of the theoretical questions. The second question is their saying that He does not know particulars, and we have also said that this is not a statement of theirs. The third is their statement about the eternity of the world, and we have also said that what they mean by this name is not the meaning for which they are accused of unbelief by the dialectical theologians. In this book [sc. *The Incoherence of the Philosophers*], he said that not a single Muslim speaks about spiritual return. Yet in others, he says that the Sufis do speak about it and that, accordingly, there is no consensus for accusing of unbelief those who speak about spiritual but not about sense-perceptible return and that speaking about spiritual return is permitted. In yet another book, moreover, he repeats this accusation of unbelief based on consensus. So, as you see, all of this is confused. God is the one who conduces to what is correct and selects whom He wills for the truth. [588]

12. I came to the opinion I would stop speaking about these things here and would ask to be pardoned for discussing them. Were it not for the necessity of seeking the truth with the one capable of it—and he, as Galen says, is one in a thousand—and resisting discussing it with those not capable of it, I would not have discussed that. God knows every letter, and perhaps God will accept my asking for pardon about that and excuse my stumbling through His grace, nobility, goodness, and superiority. There is no Lord but He!

Glossary A

Arabic–English

	ALIF
atā ʿalā	to bring forward
īthār	preference
akhīr	final
muta'akhkhir	last, posterior
adab	character trait
ta'addub	education, discipline
idhn	permission
ta'līf	composition
i'tilāf	concord, consonance
amr	command, affair, issue
ta'ammala	to reflect
anniyya	thatness
ahl	inhabitant, adept
inna	indeed
inniyya	indeed-ness
ista'hala	to deserve
ayn	where
ayy	which
	BĀ
bukhl	greed
bada'a	to innovate
badhakh	haughtiness
tabdhīr	wastefulness
bara'a	to create
baṣar	vision
baṭala	to be null, void
abṭala	to nullify, deny
ibtagha'a	to aspire
bighḍa	hatred
bughya	appetite
balagha	to obtain
bāl	mind
bālā bi	to care
bunya	structure
bayyin	evident
	TĀ
tabiʿa	to succeed
talā	to follow
	THĀ'
thabāt	firmness
athbata	to affirm
tharwa	affluence
thawāb	reward
	JĪM
jabbār	tyrant
jubn	cowardice
jarbadha	deception
jarīra	outrage
jazā'	requital

jaza'	apprehensiveness
ja'ala	to establish, make
jalāla	majesty
jumūd	hardness
majmū'	aggregate
jamīl	noble
jumhūr	public
tajannub	avoidance
jihād	struggle
tajawwuz	permissiveness, metonymy
jawhar	substance

ḤĀ'

maḥabba	love
ḥathth	exhortation
ḥadatha	to generate, emerge, arise
ḥādhiq	skilled
ḥirṣ	covetousness
ḥarf	letter, particle
inḥirāf	deviation
aḥrā	more deserving
ḥasad	envy
ḥasan	fine
inḥaṣara	to be confined
ḥaṣala	to attain, reach
'alā al-taḥṣīl	definitely, determinately
taḥaffaẓa	to be heedful
ḥaqq	truth
ḥaqīa	true
aḥaqq	more appropriately
ḥikma	wisdom
ḥulm	intelligence
ḥumq	stupidity
ḥunka	sophistication
ḥāza	to embrace
inḥāza	to isolate oneself, be singled out
ḥāl	condition
iḥtawā	to comprise
ḥayā'	modesty

KHĀ

khibb	fraudulence
khubth	deceitfulness
mukhātala	wiliness
istakhraja	to derive
khasīs	vile
khāṣṣa	particular characteristic
khaṭa'	error
khālifa	pronoun
khilāf	difference
ikhtilāf	disagreement
khalq	creature, mankind
khilqa	make-up
khulq	moral habit, temper
khilw min	devoid of
khawf	fear
khair	good
ikhtiyār	choice
takhyīl	imaginative evocation
takhayyul	imagination

DĀL

mudabbir	governor
adraka	to apprehend
dahā'	cunning
dawām	permanence

DHĀL

dhakā'	quick-wittedness, acumen
dhahl	absentmindedness
dhihn	discernment, mind
dhāt	essence
dhātiyya	essential quality

RĀ'

rābiṭa	link
rutba	rank
martaba	ranking
raḥma	compassion
rakhāwa	slackness
radī'	bad
ardafa	to complement

radhīla	vice
rasm	description
irāda	volition
raḍā	to content
riḍan	contentedness
raf'	nominative (case)
taraffuh	luxury
raghba	desire
riqqat al-nafs	delicateness of soul
tarkīb	synthesis, combination
rāma	to wish
rawiyya	deliberation

ZĀ'

za'ir	peevish
zawāl	extinction

SĪN

sabab	cause, reason
sabīl	approach
sakhā'	liberality
sakhiṭa	to annoy
saddada naḥwa	to aim, direct toward
sadīd	valid
sa'ā	to strive
maskan	dwelling
salaka	to pursue
salīm	unimpaired
ism	noun, name (Greek, *onoma*)
ism mutarādif	consignificant noun
ism mushtarak	ambiguous (homonymous) noun
ism mushakkik	equivocal noun
ism mutawāṭi'	synonymous noun
ism muttafiq	ambiguous noun
tasāmaḥa	to be indulgent, lax
sū'	wicked
sā'ir	famous

SHĪN

shajā'a	courage
shadda	to harden, make firm
sharr	evil
sharraḥa	to explain
sharṭ	stipulation
sharīf	venerable
ishtirāk al-ism	homonymity
sharah	avidity
sha'ara bi	to be attentive
shaqā'	misery
shakl	pattern, shape
ishtamala	to comprehend
shani'	repugnant
mashhūr	generally accepted
shahwa	yearning
ishtahā li	to yearn for
mashī'a	will
ashāra bi	to advise
tashawwaqa	to long for
shawq	longing

ṢĀD

ṣaḥīḥṣawāb	sound, healthy, correct
ṣadda 'an	to hinder
ṣidq	veracity
ṣādiq, ṣadīq	veracious
ṣāliḥ	righteous, upright
muṣmat	solid
ṣanf	sort
ṣinā'a	art
ṣawāb	correct, sound, healthy
ṣawt	speech-sound
ṣūra	form

ḌĀD

ḍabiṭ li-nafsih	self-restrained
ḍidd	contrary
ḍarb	type
taḍarru'	entreaty
ḍamīr	breast, mind, conscience

aḍmara	to suppress
taḍammana	to include
iḍāfa	relation
muḍāf	relative
muḍāfān	correlatives

ṬĀʾ

ṭabʿ, ṭabīʿa	nature
ṭarīq	method
ṭalaba	to seek
ṭilba	request
ʿalā al-iṭlāq	unqualifiedly
ṭamiʿa	to become ambitious
ṭāʾifa	faction, party
aṭāfa bi	to encompass
inṭawā	to be enveloped

ẒĀʾ

ẓarf	wittiness
ẓanna	to presume
ẓāhir	apparent

ʿAYN

istiʿdād	disposition
ʿudda	reserve
ʿadāla	justice
iʿtadal	to equilibrate, balance
iʿtidāl	equilibrium, balance
ʿadam	privation
ʿadam al-iḥsās bi-al-ladhdha	insensibility to pleasure
iʿrāb	declension
ʿaraḍ	accident
ʿiffa	moderation
taʿaqqaba	to scrutinize
ʿaql	intellect
maʿqūl	intelligible
ʿāda	custom
ʿāfa	to feel disgust
ʿilla	reason, cause
ʿāmm	ordinary, general
ʿiwaḍ	recompense
ʿāʾiq	impediment
istaʿāna bi	to have recourse to

GHAYN

ghabaṭa	to admire
gharaḍ	purpose
ghaṣb	usurpation
ghaḍab	anger
aghḍā ʿan	to wink at
ghalaṭ	mistake
ghamm	distress
ghamr	simple person
ghāya	end
ghaira	jealousy
ghaiẓ	fury

FĀʾ

faḥwā	tenor
farraqa	to separate, differentiate
mufarriq	separate
faziʿa	to frighten
tafāsud	enmity
fassara	to comment
faṣl	differentia
faṭara	to endow innately, to constitute innately
fiṭra	innate character, innate constitution
fiʿl	action
bi-al-fiʿl	in actuality
infiʿāl	passion
iftaqara ilā	to require
infakka	to detach
fikr	calculation
fahm	understanding
tafāwut	disparity
afāda	to provide
istafāda	to procure
fāza bi	to achieve

QĀF

qabīḥ	base
iqtabasa	to secure
muqābil	opposite
taqtīr	stinginess
qudra	ability
iqdām	boldness
qarana	to bind
qarīḥa	talent
qāsim	coordinating
qasīm	coordinate
anwāʿ qasīma	coordinate species
anwāʿ muqassima	
qaswa	harshness
qaṣd	intention
iqtaṣara	to be limited, limit oneself
iqtiḍāʾ	postulation
qānūn	regulation
iqtanā	to acquire
quwwa	faculty, power
bi-al-quwwa	potentially
qawl	sentence, statement
qawl jāzim	declarative sentence
maqūla	category
qāʾim	conspicuous
qawm	group
qayyada bi	to restrict
qayyim bi-al-nāmūs	custodian of the law

KĀF

kadd	toil
karāha	loathing
iktasaba	to earn
kaff	dissuasion
kalām	discussion
kam	how much
kammiyya	quantity
kamāl	perfection
kais	cleverness
kaif	how
kaifiyya	quantity

LĀM

iltaʾama	to constitute
lāḥiqa (pl. *lawāḥiq*)	appendage
lakhkhaṣa	to expound, break down
alzama	to result, be inevitable
lisān	language, tongue
lugha	idiom, language
iltamasa	to look, search

MĪM

mā	what
matā	when
majūn	impudence
mādda	material, matter
madīna	city
insān madanī	citizen
mizāj	temperament
makr	trickery
tamakkana	to settle firmly
milla	religion
malaka	state (of character)
manʿ	refusal
mihna	craft
māhuwa	what-is
māhiyya	whatness
mayyaza	to distinguish

NŪN

manḥan	aim
nakhwa	arrogance
nidāʾ	direct address
intazaʿa	to select, extract
manzal	household
manzila	station, status
nisba	connection, ratio
tanāsub	proportion
anshaʾa	to originate, construct
naṣb	accusative (case)

naṭaqa	to articulate, pronounce
naṭq	reason, articulation
nāṭiq	reasoning, rational
naqqara	to examine
naqṣ	defect, deficiency
naqīḍ	contradiction, contradictory
nāla	to gain
nahy	prohibition

HĀ

hadaf	goal
harab	fleeing
inhaḍā	to inspire
hal	whether
himma	endeavor
tahawwur	rashness
istihāna	contempt
huwiyya	identity
hawā	to crave
haïa	trait
hayūlā	primordial material, matter

WĀW

wathāqa	sureness
wajada	to exist, find
mawjūd	existent, existing
wujdān	encountering
wujūd	existence
wādi‘	calm
warada	to accrue
ṣifa	attribute
wuṣla	tie
ṣila	kinship
awṣā bi	to counsel
waḍa‘a	to posit, set down
wāḍi‘ al-sharī‘a	lawgiver
wāḍi‘ al-nawāmīs	legislator
tawāḍu‘	respectfulness
waẓāba ‘alā	to persist in
waffara	to augment
waqāḥa	insolence
qiḥḥa	impertinence
waqa‘a ‘alā	to apply to
waqafa ‘alā	to grasp, come upon
awlā	more properly
tawallā	to help
wālī	helper
awma'a ilā	to point out

YĀ

yasār	wealth, prosperity
yasīr	slight, trifling

Glossary B

English–Arabic

ability	*qudra*
absentmindedness	*dhahl*
accident	*ʿaraḍ*
to accrue	*warada*
accusative (case)	*naṣb*
to achieve	*fāza bi*
to acquire	*iqtanā*
action	*fiʿl*
in actuality	*bi-al-fiʿl*
acumen	*dhakāʾ*
adept	*ahl*
to admire	*ghabaṭa*
to advise	*ashāra bi*
affair, command, issue	*amr*
to affirm	*athbata*
affluence	*tharwa*
aggregate	*majmūʿ*
aim	*manḥan*
to aim, direct toward	*saddada naḥwa*
to become ambitious	*ṭamiʿa*
anger	*ghaḍab*
to annoy	*sakhiṭa*
apparent	*ẓāhir*
appendage	*lāḥiqa* (pl. *lawāḥiq*)
appetite	*bughya*
to apply to	*waqaʿa ʿalā*
to apprehend	*adraka*
apprehensiveness	*jazaʿ*
approach	*sabīl*
more appropriately	*aḥaqq*
to arise, generate, emerge	*ḥadatha*
arrogance	*nakhwa*
art	*ṣināʿa*
to articulate, pronounce	*naṭaqa*
articulation, reason	*naṭq*
to aspire	*ibtaghaʾa*
to attain, reach	*ḥaṣala*
to be attentive	*shaʿara bi*
attribute	*ṣifa*
audacity	*iqdām*
to augment	*waffara*
avidity	*sharah*
avoidance	*tajannub*
bad	radīʾ
base	*qabīḥ*
to bind	*qarana*
boldness	*iqdām*
to break down, expound	*lakhkhaṣa*
breast, mind, conscience	*ḍamīr*
to bring forward	*atā ʿalā*

calculation	*fikr*
calm	*wādi'*
to care	*bālā bi*
category	*maqūla*
cause, reason	sabab, *'illa*
character trait	*adab*
state of character	*malaka* (pl. *malakāt*)
choice	*ikhtiyār*
city	*madīna*
citizen	*insān madanī*
cleverness	*kais*
to come upon	*waqafa 'alā*
command, affair, issue	*amr*
to comment	*fassara*
compassion	*raḥma*
to complement	*ardafa*
composition	*ta'līf*
to comprehend	*ishtamala*
to comprise	*iḥtawā*
concord, consonance	*i'tilāf*
condition	*ḥāl*
to be confined	*inḥaṣara*
connection, ratio	*nisba*
conscience, breast, mind	*ḍamīr*
consonance, concord	*i'tilāf*
conspicuous	*qā'im*
to constitute	*ilta'ama*
to constitute innately	*faṭara*
to construct, originate	*ansha'a*
contempt	*istihāna*
to content	*raḍā*
contentedness	*riḍan*
contradiction, contradictory	*naqīḍ*
contrary	*ḍidd*
coordinate	*qasīm*
coordinate species	*anwā' qasīma, anwā' muqassima*
coordinating	*qāsim*
correct, healthy, sound	ṣaḥīḥ, *ṣawāb*
to counsel	*awṣā bi*
courage	*shajā'a*
covetousness	*ḥirṣ*
cowardice	*jubn*
craft *mihna*	
to crave	*hawā*
to create	*bara'a*
creatures, mankind	khalq
cunning	*dahā'*
custodian of the law	*qayyim bi-al-nāmūs*
custom	*'āda*
deceitfulness	*khubth*
declarative sentence	*qawl jāzim*
declension	*i'rāb*
defect, deficiency	*naqṣ*
deliberation	*rawiyya*
delicateness of soul	*riqqat al-nafs*
to deny, nullify	*abṭala*
to derive	*istakhraja*
description	*rasm*
to deserve	*ista'hala*
more deserving	*aḥrā*
desire	*raghba*
to detach	*infakka*
determinately, definitely	*'alā al-taḥṣīl*
deviation	*inḥirāf*
devoid of	*khilw min*
difference	*khilāf*
differentia	*faṣl*
to differentiate, separate	*farraqa*
direct address	*nidā'*
disagreement	*ikhtilāf*
discernment, mind	*dhihn*
discipline, education	*ta'addub*
discussion	*kalām*
to feel disgust	*'āfa*

disparity *tafāwut*
disposition *isti'dād*
dissuasion *kaff*
to distinguish *mayyaza*
distress *ghamm*
dwelling *maskan*

to earn *iktasaba*
education, discipline *ta'addub*
to embrace *ḥāza*
to emerge, generate, arise *ḥadatha*
to encompass *aṭāfa bi*
encountering *wujdān*
end *ghāya*
endeavor *himma*
to endow innately *faṭara*
enmity *tafāsud*
entreaty *taḍarru'*
to be enveloped *inṭawā*
envy *ḥasad*
to equilibrate, balance *i'tadal*
equilibrium, balance *i'tidāl*
error *khaṭa'*
essence *dhāt*
  essential quality *dhātiyya*
to establish, make *ja'ala*
evident *bayyin*
evil *sharr*
to examine *naqqara*
exhortation *ḥathth*
to exist, find *wajada*
existence *wujūd*
existent, existing *mawjūd*
to explain *sharraḥa*
to expound, break down *lakhkhaṣa*
extinction *zawāl*
to extract, select *intaza'a*

faction, party ṭā'ifa
faculty, power *quwwa*
famous *sā'ir*
fear *khawf*
final *akhīr*
fine *ḥasan*
firmness *thabāt*
fleeing *harab*
to follow *talā*
form *ṣūra*
fraudulence *khibb*
to frighten *fazi'a*
fury *ghaiẓ*

to gain *nāla*
general, ordinary *'āmm*
generally accepted *mashhūr*
to generate, emerge, arise *ḥadatha*
goal *hadaf*
good *khair*
governor *mudabbir*
to grasp *waqafa 'alā*
greed *bukhl*
group *ṭā'ifa*

to harden, make firm *shadda*
hardness *jumūd*
harshness *qaswa*
hatred *bighḍa*
haughtiness *badhakh*
healthy, sound, correct *ṣaḥīḥ, ṣawāb*
to be heedful *taḥaffaẓa*
to help *tawallā*
  helper *wālī*
to hinder *ṣadda 'an*
homonymity *ishtirāk al-ism*
household *manzal*
how *kaif*
how much *kam*

identity *huwiyya*
idiom, language *lugha*
imagination *takhayyul*
  imaginative evocation *takhyīl*
impediment *'ā'iq*
impertinence *qiḥḥa*

impudence	*majūn*
to include	*taḍammana*
indeed	*inna*
indeedness	*inniyya*
to be indulgent, lax	*tasāmaḥa*
inhabitant	*ahl*
innate character, constitution	*fiṭra*
to innovate	*bada'a*
insensibility to pleasure	*'adam al-iḥsās bi-al-ladhdha*
insolence	*waqāḥa*
to inspire	*inhaḍā*
intellect	*'aql*
intelligence	*ḥulm*
intelligible	*ma'qūl*
intention	*qaṣd*
to be invalid, null	*baṭala*
to isolate oneself, be singled out	*inḥāza*
issue, command, affair	*amr*
jealousy	*ghaira*
justice	*'adāla*
kinship	*ṣila*
language, tongue, idiom	lisān, lugha
last	*muta'akhkhir*
law (convention or nomos)	*nāmūs*
divine law	*sharī'a*
lawgiver	*wāḍi' al-sharī'a*
legislator	*wāḍi' al-nawāmīs*
to be lax, indulgent	tasāmaḥa
letter	*ḥarf*
level*manzila*	
liberality	*sakhā'*
to be limited, limit oneself	*iqtaṣara*
link	*rābiṭa*
loathing	*karāha*
to long for	*tashawwaqa*
longing	*shawq*
love	*maḥabba*
luxury	*taraffuh*
majesty	*jalāla*
to make, establish	*ja'ala*
make-up	*khilqa*
mankind, creatures	*khalq*
material, matter	*mādda*
primordial material, matter	*hayūlā*
method	*ṭarīq*
metonymy, permissiveness	*tajawwuz*
mind	bāl, *dhihn, ḍamīr*
misery	*shaqā'*
mistake	*ghalaṭ*
moderation	*'iffa*
modesty	*ḥayā'*
moral habit	*khulq*
name, noun (Greek, *onoma*)	*ism*
ambiguous (homonymous) noun	*ism mushtarak*
ambiguous noun	*ism muttafiq*
consignificant noun	*ism mutarādif*
equivocal noun	*ism mushakkik*
synonymous noun	*ism mutawāṭi'*
nature	*ṭab', ṭabī'a*
noble	*jamīl*
nominative (case)	*raf'*
to be null, invalid	*baṭala*
to nullify, deny	*abṭala*
to obtain	*balagha*
opposite	*muqābil*
ordinary, general	*'āmm*

to originate, construct	*ansha'a*
outrage	*jarīra*
particle, letter	*ḥarf*
particular characteristic	*khāṣṣa*
party, faction	ṭā'ifa
passion	*infi'āl*
pattern, shape	*shakl*
peevish	*za'ir*
perfection	*kamāl*
permanence	*dawām*
permission	*idhn*
permissiveness, metonymy	*tajawwuz*
to persist in	*waẓāba 'alā*
to point out	*awma'a ilā*
to posit, set down	*waḍa'a*
posterior	*muta'akhkhir*
postulation	*iqtiḍā'*
potentially	*bi-al-quwwa*
power, faculty	*quwwa*
preference	*īthār*
to presume	*ẓanna*
privation	*'adam*
to procure	*istafāda*
prohibition	*nahy*
pronoun	*khālifa*
to pronounce, articulate	*naṭaqa*
more properly	*awlā*
proportion	*tanāsub*
prosperity	*yasār*
to provide	*afāda*
public	*jumhūr*
purpose	*gharaḍ*
to pursue	*salaka*
quality	*kaifiyya*
quantity	*kammiyya*
quick-wittedness	*dhakā'*
rank	*rutba*
ranking	*martaba*
rashness	*tahawwur*
ratio, connection	*nisba*
reason, articulation	*naṭq*
reasoning, rational	*nāṭiq*
reason, cause	*'illa, sabab*
reception	*jarbadha*
recompense	*'iwaḍ*
to have recourse to	*ista'āna bi*
to reflect	*ta'ammala*
refusal	*man'*
regulation	*qānūn*
relation	*iḍāfa*
relative	*muḍāf*
correlatives	*muḍāfān*
religion	*milla*
repugnant	*shani'*
request	*ṭilba*
to require	*iftaqara ilā*
requital	*jazā'*
reserve	*'udda*
respectfulness	*tawāḍu'*
to restrict	*qayyada bi*
reward	*thawāb*
righteous, upright	*ṣāliḥ*
to scrutinize	*ta'aqqaba*
to search, look	*iltamasa*
to secure	*iqtabasa*
to seek	*ṭalaba*
to select, extract	*intaza'a*
self-restrained	*ḍabiṭ li-nafsih*
sentence, statement	*qawl*
to separate, differentiate	*farraqa*
separate	*mufarriq*
to set down, posit	*waḍa'a*
to settle firmly	*tamakkana*
shape, pattern	*shakl*
simple person	*ghamr*
to be singled out, isolate oneself	*inḥāza*
skilled	*ḥādhiq*
slackness	*rakhāwa*
slight, trifling	*yasīr*
solid	*muṣmat*
sophistication	*ḥunka*

sort	*ṣanf*
sound, healthy, correct	*ṣaḥīḥ, ṣawāb*
speech-sound	*ṣawt*
state (of character)	*malaka*
station, status	*manzila*
stinginess	*taqtīr*
stipulation	*sharṭ*
to strive	*sa'ā*
structure	*bunya*
struggle	*jihād*
stupidity	*ḥumq*
substance	*jawhar*
to succeed	*tabi'a*
to suppress	*aḍmara*
sureness	*wathāqa*
synthesis, combination	*tarkīb*
talent	*qarīḥa*
temper, moral habit	*khulq*
temperament	*mizāj*
tenor	*faḥwā*
thatness	*anniyya*
tie	*wuṣla*
toil	*kadd*
tongue, language	*lisān*
trait	*hai'a*
trickery	*makr*
truth	*ḥaqq*
true	*ḥaqīq*
type	*ḍarb*
tyrant	*jabbār*
understanding	*fahm*
unimpaired	*salīm*
unqualifiedly	*'alā al-iṭlāq*
upright, righteous	*ṣāliḥ*
usurpation	*ghaṣb*
valid	*sadīd*
venerable	*sharīf*
veracity	*ṣidq*
veracious	*ṣādiq, ṣadīq*
vice	*radhīla*
vile	*khasīs*
vision	*baṣar*
volition	*irāda*
wastefulness	*tabdhīr*
wealth	*yasār*
what	*mā*
what-is	*māhuwa*
whatness	*māhiyya*
when	*matā*
where	*ayn*
whether	*hal*
which	*ayy*
wicked	*sū'*
wiliness	*mukhātala*
will	*mashī'a*
to wink at	*aghḍā 'an*
wisdom	*ḥikma*
to wish	*rāma*
wittiness	*ẓarf*
to yearn for	*ishtahā li*
yearning	*shahwa*

Bibliography

Adamson, Peter. *The Arabic Plotinus: A Philosophical Study of the "Theology of Aristotle."* London: Duckworth, 2002.

Alexander of Aphrodisias. *On the Soul.*

Aouad, Maroun. "Les lois selon les *Didascalia in* Rethoricam (*sic*) *Aristotelis ex glosa Alpharabii.*" In *Mélanges de l'Université Saint-Joseph* 61 (2008), *Actes du Colloque International, Les doctrines de la loi dans la philosophie de langue arabe et leurs contextes grecs et musulmans*, 452–470. Edited by Maroun Aouad.

Aristotle. *Metaphysics.*

——. *Meteorology.*

——. *On Coming to Be and Passing Away.*

——. *On the Heavens.*

——. *On the Soul.*

Arnaldez, Roger. "Ibn Ḥazm." In *Encyclopaedia of Islam*. 2nd ed. Edited by P. Bearman, T. Bianquis, C. E. Bosworth, E. van Donzel, and W. P. Heinrichs. Brill Online, 2014. http://referenceworks.brillonline.com.proxy-um.researchport.umd.edu/entries/encyclopaedia-of-islam-2/ibn-hazm-COM_0325.

Asín Palacios, Miguel. *Abenházam de Córdoba y su historia crítica de las ideas religiosas.* 5 vols. Madrid: Tipografía de la "Revista de archivos," 1927–1932.

Averroes. *See* Ibn Rushd, Abū al-Walīd Muḥammad Ibn Aḥmad.

Avicenna. *See* Ibn Sīnā, Abū ʿAlī al-Ḥusayn.

Benardete, Seth. *Plato's "Laws."* Chicago: University of Chicago Press, 2000.

Blitz, Mark. "Strauss's *Laws.*" *Political Science Reviewer* 20 (1991): 186–222.

Butterworth, Charles E. "Alfarabi's Goal: Political Philosophy, Not Political Theology." In *Islam, the State, and Political Authority: Medieval Issues and Modern Concerns*, edited by Asma Afasaruddin, 53–74. New York: Palgrave-MacMillan, 2011.

——. "What Might We Learn from al-Fārābī about Plato and Aristotle with Respect to Law-Giving?" In *Mélanges de l'Université Saint-Joseph* 61 (2008), *Actes du Colloque International, Les doctrines de la loi dans la philosophie de langue arabe et leurs contextes grecs et musulmans*, 471–489. Edited by Maroun Aouad.

Campinini, Massimo. "Alfarabi and the Foundation of Political Theology in Islam." In *Islam, the State, and Political Authority: Medieval Issues and Modern Concerns*, edited by Asma Afasaruddin, 35–52. New York: Palgrave-MacMillan, 2011.

Colmo, Christopher A. *Breaking with Athens: Alfarabi as Founder*. Lanham: Lexington Books, 2005.

Crone, Patricia. "Al-Fārābī's Imperfect Constitutions." In *Mélanges de l'Université Saint-Joseph* 57 (2004), *The Greek Strand in Islamic Political Thought: Proceedings of the Conference Held at the Institute for Advanced Study, Princeton, 16–27 June 2003*, 191–228. Edited by Emma Gannagé, Patricia Crone, Maroun Aouad, Dimitri Gutas, and Eckart Schütrumpf.

D'Ancona, Cristina. "Greek into Arabic: Neoplatonism in Translation." In *The Cambridge Companion to Arabic Philosophy*, edited by Richard C. Taylor and Peter A. Adamson, 10–31. Cambridge: Cambridge University Press, 2005.

Dozy, R. *Supplément aux dictionnaires arabes*. Beirut: Librairie du Liban, 1968.

Druart, Thérèse-Anne. "Un sommaire du sommaire Farabien des *Lois* de Platon." *Bulletin de Philosophie Médiévale* 19 (1977): 43–45.

Fārābī, Abū Naṣr al-(Alfarabi). "Book of Letters." Translated by Charles E. Butterworth. Unpublished manuscript.

——. *Abū Naṣr al-Fārābī: Épître sur l'intellect*. Translated by Philippe Vallat. Paris: Les Belles Lettres, 2012.

——. *Abū Naṣr al-Fārābī: Le régime politique*. Translated by Philippe Vallat. Paris: Les Belles Lettres, 2012.

——. *Abû Nasr al-Fârâbî: La politique civile ou les principes des existants*. Translated by Amor Cherni. Paris: al-Bouraq, 2012.

——. *Abû Nasr al-Fârâbî: La religion, al-Milla*. Translated by Amor Cherni. Paris: al-Bouraq, 2012.

——. *Abû Nasr al-Fârâbî: Opinions des habitants de la cité vertueuse*. Translated by Amor Cherni. Paris: al-Bouraq, 2011.

——. "Alfarabi: The Political Regime" [Part 2]. Translated by Charles E. Butterworth. In Parens and Macfarland, *Medieval Political Philosophy*, 36–55.

——. Alfarabi, *Plato's Laws* (Introduction). Translated by Muhsin Mahdi. In Parens and Macfarland, *Medieval Political Philosophy*, 72–73.

——. *Abū Naṣr Al-Fārābī, Die Prinzipien der Ansichten der Bewohner der vortrefflichen Stadt, Mabādi' ārā' ahl al-madīna al-fāḍila*. Translated by Cleophea Ferrari. Stuttgart: Reclam, 2009.

——. *al-Fārābī. L'armonia delle opinioni dei due sapienti, il divino Platone e Aristotele*. Edited and translated, with introduction and commentary, by Cecilia Martini Bonadeo. Preface by Gerhard Endress. Pisa: Pisa University Press, 2008.

——. *The Principles of Existing Things*. In *Classical Arabic Philosophy: An Anthology of Sources*, 81–104. Translated by Jon McGinnis and David C. Reisman. Indianapolis: Hackett, 2007.

——. Al-Fārābī, *Directing Attention to the Way to Happiness*. In *Classical Arabic Philosophy: An Anthology of Sources*, translated by Jon McGinnis and David C. Reisman, 104–120. Indianapolis: Hackett, 2007.

——. *Le compendium des Lois de Platon*. Translated by Stéphane Diebler. Introduction by Pauline Koetschet. In *Al-Fārābī: Philosopher à Baghdad au Xe siécle*. Edited by Ali Benmakhlouf and Pauline Koetschet. Paris: Éditions du Seuil, 2007. 130–191.

——. *Le livre de la religion* and *Textes complémentaires d'al-Fārābī*. Arabic text and translation by Stéphane Diebler. In *Al-Fārābī: Philosopher à Baghdad au Xe siécle*, edited by Ali Benmakhlouf and Pauline Koetschet, 42–93 and 95–129. Paris: Éditions du Seuil, 2007.

——. *Al-Fārābī: Aphorismes choisis*. Translated by Soumaya Mestiri and Guillaume Dye. Paris: Fayard, 2003.

——. *Al-Fārābī: La philosophie de Platon*. Translated by Olivier Seyden. Paris: Allia, 2002.

——. *Alfarabi: Philosophy of Plato and Aristotle*. Translated by Muhsin Mahdi. Ithaca, NY: Cornell University Press, 2001.

——. *Alfarabi: The Political Writings: "Selected Aphorisms" and Other Texts*. Translated by Charles E. Butterworth. Ithaca, NY: Cornell University Press, 2001.

——. *Abû Naṣr al-Fârâbî: Épître sur l'intellect, al-Risâla fi-l-ʿaql*. Translated by Dyala Hamzah. Preface by Jean Jolivet. Postface by Rémi Brague. Paris: L'Harmattan, 2001.

——. "Le sommaire du livre des 'Lois' de Platon (*Ǧawāmiʿ Kitāb al-Nawāmīs li-Aflāṭūn*) par Abū Naṣr al-Fārābī." Edited by Thérèse-Anne Druart. In *Bulletin d'Études Orientales* 50 (1998): 109–155.

——. *"El libro de la política."* In *Al-Fārābī: Obras filosóficas y políticas*, 1–70. Translated by Rafael Ramón Guerrero. Madrid: Debate, CSIC, 1992

——. *Al-Fārābī, Kitāb al-Tanbīh ʿalā Sabīl al-Saʿāda*. 2nd ed. Edited by Jaʿfar Āl Yāsīn. Beirut: Dār al-Manāhil li-al-Ṭibāʿa wa al-Nashr wa al-Tawzīʿ, 1987.

——. *Al-Farabi on the Perfect State, Abū Naṣr al-Fārābī's Mabādiʾ Ārāʾ Ahl al-Madīna al-Fāḍila*. Revised text with introduction, translation, and commentary by Richard Walzer. Oxford: Clarendon Press, 1985.

——. *Al-Fārābī. Risāla fī al-ʿAql*. 2nd ed. Ed. Maurice Bouyges. Beirut: Dār al-Mashriq, 1983.

——. *Al-Fārābī: The Political Regime (Al-Siyāsa al-Madaniyya), also known as the Treatise on the Principles of Beings*. Translated by Thérèse-Anne Druart. Translation Clearing House, Department of Philosophy, Oklahoma State University, 1981. Ref. no. A-30-50d.

——. *Abû Naṣr al-Fārābī, Fuṣūl Muntazaʿa* (Selected Aphorisms). Edited by Fauzi M. Najjar. Beirut: Dār al-Mashriq, 1971.

——. *Abū Naṣr al-Fārābī, Kitāb al-Ḥurūf*. Edited by Muhsin Mahdi. Beirut: Dār al-Mashriq, 1969.

——. *Abū Naṣr al-Fārābī, Kitāb al-Alfāẓ al-Mustaʿmala fī al-Manṭiq*. Edited by Muhsin Mahdi. Beirut: Dār al-Mashriq, 1968.

——. *Abū Naṣr al-Fārābī, Kitāb al-Milla wa Nuṣūṣ Ukhrā*. Edited by Muhsin Mahdi. Beirut: Dār al-Mashriq, 1968. 41–66.

——. *Abū Naṣr al-Fārābī, Kitāb al-Siyāsa al-Madaniyya, al-Mulaqqab bi-Mabādiʾ al-Mawjūdāt*. Edited by Fauzi M. Najjar. Beirut: al-Maṭbaʿa al-Kāthūlīkiyya, 1964.

——. *Risāla fī Ārāʾ Ahl al-Madīna al-Fāḍila*. Edited by Friedrich Dieterici. Leiden: E. J. Brill, 1895; reprint 1964.

——. "Alfarabi: The Political Regime" [part 2]. Translated by Fauzi M. Najjar. In Lerner and Mahdi, *Medieval Political Philosophy*, 31–57.

——. *Summary of Plato's Laws* (introduction plus first treatise and second treatise). Translated by Muhsin Mahdi. In Lerner and Mahdi, *Medieval Political Philosophy*, 83–94.

——. *Falsafat Arisṭūṭālīs*. Edited by Muhsin Mahdi. Beirut: Dār Majallat Shiʾr, 1961.

——. *Alfarabius: Compendium Legum Platonis*. Edited and translated by Francesco Gabrieli. Plato Arabus, vol. 3. London: Warburg Institute, 1952.

——. *Kitāb al-Siyāsa al-Madaniyya*. Ḥaidar Ābād al-Dukn: Maṭba'a Majlis Dā'irat al-Ma'ārif al-'Ūthmāniyya, 1346 AH [1927].

——. *Alfarabi: The Political Regime I*. Translated by Miriam Galston. N.d.

——. Alfarabi: *Kitāb al-Mūsīqā al-Kabīr*. Edited by Ghaṭṭās 'Abd al-Malik Khashaba and Maḥmūd Aḥmad al-Hifnī. Cairo: Dār al-Kitāb al-'Arabī li-al-Ṭibā'a wa al-Nashr. N.d.

Genequand, Charles. "Le Platon d'al-Fārābī." In *Lire les dialogues, mais lesquels et dans quel ordre: Définitions du corpus et interprétations de Platon*. Edited by Anne Balansard and Isabelle Koch, 105–115. Bonn: Academia Verlag Sankt Augustin, 2013.

——. "Loi morale, loi politique: al-Fārābī et Ibn Bāǧǧa." In *Mélanges de l'Université Saint-Joseph* 61 (2008), *Actes du Colloque International, Les doctrines de la loi dans la philosophie de langue arabe et leurs contextes grecs et musulmans*, edited by Maroun Aouad, 491–514.

Glasse, Cyril. *Nāmūs*. *Concise Encyclopaedia of Islam*. San Francisco: Harper & Row, 1989.

Gutas, Dimitri. "The Meaning of *madanī* in al-Fārābī's 'Political' Philosophy." In *Mélanges de l'Université Saint-Joseph* 57 (2004), *The Greek Strand in Islamic Political Thought: Proceedings of the Conference held at the Institute for Advanced Study, Princeton, 16–27 June 2003*. Edited by Emma Gannagé, Patricia Crone, Maroun Aouad, Dimitri Gutas, and Eckart Schütrumpf, 259–282.

——. "Fārābī i. Biography," *Encyclopaedia Iranica* 9/2, 208–213; updated version online at http://www.iranicaonline.org/articles/farabi-i.

——. "Fārābī's Knowledge of Plato's *Laws*." *International Journal of the Classical Tradition* 4, no. 3 (1998): 405–411.

——. "Galen's *Synopsis* of Plato's *Laws* and Fārābī's *Talkhīṣ*." In *The Ancient Tradition in Christian and Islamic Hellenism: Studies on the Transmission of Greek Philosophy and Sciences, Dedicated to H. J. Drossaart Lulofs on His Ninetieth Birthday*, edited by Gerhard Endress and Remke Kruk, 101–119. Leiden: Research School CNWS, 1997.

Harvey, Steven. "Can a Tenth-Century Islamic Aristotelian Help Us Understand Plato's *Laws*?" In *Plato's Laws: From Theory to Practice, Proceedings of the VI Symposium Platonicum, Selected Papers*, edited by S. Scolnicov and L. Brisson, 320–330. Sankt Augustin: Academia Verlag, 2003.

——. "Did Alfarabi Read Plato's *Laws*?" In *Medioevo: Rivista di storia della filosofia medievale* 28 (2003): 51–68.

Hassan, Scheherazade Qassim. "The Long Necked Lute in Iraq." *Asian Music* 13, no. 2 (1982): 1–18.

Ibn al-Nadīm. *Kitāb al-Fihrist*. Edited by Gustav Flügel. Beirut: Maktabat Khayyāṭ, 1964. Reprint of Leipzig, 1871.

Ibn Ḥazm, 'Alī ibn Aḥmad. *Al-Faṣl fī al-Milal wa al-Ahwā' wa al-Niḥal*. Edited by Muḥammad Ibrāhīm Naṣr and 'Abd al-Raḥmān 'Umayra. Jidda: 'Ukāẓ, 1982.

Ibn Rushd, Abū al-Walīd Muḥammad Ibn Aḥmad. *Averroës: The Book of the Decisive Treatise: Determining the Connection between the Law and Wisdom, and Epistle Dedicatory*. Translated by Charles E. Butterworth, with introduction and notes. Provo, UT: Brigham Young University Press, 2001.

——. *Averroes on Plato's "Republic."* Translated by Ralph Lerner. Ithaca, NY: Cornell University Press, 1974.

Ibn Sīnā, Abū ʿAlī al-Ḥusayn (Avicenna). "On the Division of the Rational Sciences." Translated by Muhsin Mahdi. In Parens and Macfarland, *Medieval Political Philosophy*, 75–76.

——. *Lettre au Vizir Abū Sa'd*. Translated and edited by Yahya Michot. Beirut: al-Bouraq, 2001.

——. "On the Division of the Rational Sciences." Translated by Muhsin Mahdi. In Lerner and Mahdi, *Medieval Political Philosophy*, 95–97.

——. *Fī Aqsām al-ʿUlūm al-ʿAqliyya*. In *Tisʿ Rasāʾil*, 104–118. Cairo, 1908.

Kraemer, Joel L. *Maimonides: The Life and World of One of Civilization's Greatest Minds*. New York: Doubleday, 2008.

Lahoud, Nelly. "Al-Fārābī: On Religion and Philosophy." In *Mélanges de l'Université Saint-Joseph* 57 (2004), *The Greek Strand in Islamic Political Thought: Proceedings of the Conference held at the Institute for Advanced Study, Princeton, 16–27 June 2003*, edited by Emma Gannagé, Patricia Crone, Maroun Aouad, Dimitri Gutas, and Eckart Schütrumpf, 283–301.

Lerner, Ralph, and Muhsin Mahdi, eds. *Medieval Political Philosophy: A Sourcebook*. 1st ed. New York: Free Press of Glencoe, 1963.

Lings, Martin. *Muhammad: His Life Based on the Earliest Sources*. New York: Inner Traditions International, 1983.

Mahdi, Muhsin S. "Al-Fārābī." In *Dictionary of Scientific Biography*, edited by C. C. Gillispie, 4:523–526. New York: Charles Scribner's, 1971.

——. *Alfarabi and the Foundations of Islamic Political Philosophy*. Chicago: University of Chicago Press, 2001.

——. "Al-Fārābī's Imperfect State." *Journal of the American Oriental Society* 110, no. 4 (1990): 712–713.

——. "The *Editio Princeps* of Farabi's *Compendium Legum*." *Journal of Near Eastern Studies* 20, no. 1 (1961): 1–24.

——. *Ibn Khaldun's Philosophy of History*. Chicago: University of Chicago Press, 1971.

——. "Philosophy and Political Thought: Reflections and Comparisons." In *Arabic Sciences and Philosophy* 1, no. 1 (1991): 9–29.

Morrow, Glenn R. *Plato's Cretan City*. Foreword by Charles H. Kahn. Princeton, NJ: Princeton University Press, 1993.

O'Meara, Dominic J. *Platonopolis: Platonic Political Philosophy in Late Antiquity*. Oxford: Clarendon Press, 2003.

Pangle, Thomas. "Interpretive Essay." In *The Laws of Plato*, translated by Thomas Pangle, 375–510. New York: Basic Books, 1980.

Parens, Joshua. *Metaphysics as Rhetoric: Alfarabi's Summary of Plato's "Laws."* Albany: SUNY Press, 1995.

Parens, Joshua, and Joseph C. Macfarland, eds. *Medieval Political Philosophy: A Sourcebook*. 2nd ed. Ithaca, NY: Cornell University Press, 2011.

Plotinus. *The Enneads*. 4th ed. Translated by Stephen MacKenna. Revised by B. S. Page. London: Faber and Faber, 1969.

Rudolph, Ulrich. "Abû Nasr al-Fârâbî." In *Die Philosophie in der islamischen Welt*, vol. 1, *8.–10. Jahrhundert*, edited by Ulrich Rudolph, with Renate Würsch, 363–457. Basel: Schwabe, 2012.

——. *Islamische Philosophie: Von den Anfängen bis zur Gegenwart*. 3rd ed. Munich: C. H. Beck, 2013.

Strauss, Leo. *The Argument and the Action of Plato's Laws*. Chicago: University of Chicago Press, 1975.

——. "Farabi's *Plato*." In *Louis Ginzberg Jubilee Volume*, 357–393. New York: American Academy for Jewish Research, 1945.

——. "How Fārābī Read Plato's *Laws*." In *What Is Political Philosophy?*, 134–154. Glencoe, IL: Free Press, 1959. Reprinted from *Mélanges Louis Massignon*, 3:319–344. Damascus: Institut Français de Damas, 1957.

——. "Introduction." In *Persecution and the Art of Writing*, 7–21. Glencoe, IL: Free Press, 1952. Adaptation of "Farabi's *Plato*."

——. "Quelques remarques sur la science politique de Maïmonide et de Fârâbî." In *Revue des études juives* 197 (1935): 1–37. Reprinted in Leo Strauss, *Gesammelte Schriften: Philosophie und Gesetz: Frühe Schriften*, edited by Heinrich Meier, 125–166. Stuttgart: Verlag J. B. Metzler, 1997.

——. *Thoughts on Machiavelli*. Glencoe, IL: Free Press, 1958.

Streetman, W. Craig. "'If it were God who sent them . . .': Aristotle and al-Fārābī on Prophetic Vision." *Arabic Sciences and Philosophy* 18, no. 2 (2008): 211–246.

Vallat, Philippe. *Farabi et l'école d'Alexandrie: Des prémisses de la connaissance à la philosophie politique*. Paris: Vrin, 2004.

Veccia Vaglieri, L. "'Abd Allāh b. al-'Abbās." *Encyclopaedia of Islam*. 2nd ed. Edited by P. Bearman, T. Bianquis, C. E. Bosworth, E. van Donzel, and W. P. Heinrichs. Brill Online, 2014. http://referenceworks.brillonline.com.proxy-um.researchport.umd.edu/entries/encyclopaedia-of-islam-2/abd-allah-b-al-abbas-SIM_0035.

Wallis, R. T. *Neoplatonism*. London: Duckworth, 1972.

Walzer, Richard. "Platonism in Islamic Philosophy." In *Greek into Arabic: Essays on Islamic Philosophy*, 236–252. Cambridge, MA: Harvard University Press, 1962. Reprinted from *Entretiens*, 3:203–224. Vandoeuvres-Geneva: Fondation Hardt, 1957.

Watt, W. Montgomery. "al-'Abbās b. 'Abd al-Muṭṭalib." In *Encyclopaedia of Islam*. 2nd ed. Edited by P. Bearman, T. Bianquis, C. E. Bosworth, E. van Donzel, and W. P. Heinrichs. Brill Online, 2014. http://referenceworks.brillonline.com.proxy-um.researchport.umd.edu/entries/encyclopaedia-of-islam-2/al-abbas-b-abd-al-muttalib-SIM_0017.

Index

active intellect, 10, 12, 30–33, 37, 46–49, 62–67
administrators, 169
adornments of law, 171
affection, 114, 148
Alfarabi, ix–x
  access to Plato's *Laws*, 100–107
  Attainment of Happiness, xi, 108
  Book of Letters, xii
  Book of Religion, xi, xii, 26, 108
  editorial comments, 121–23
  Enumeration of the Sciences, x, xii, 175–76
  Harmonization of the Two Opinions of the Two Sages, xii
  influences on, 125
  Philosophy of Aristotle, xi–xii, 107
  Philosophy of Plato, xi–xii, 101–2, 107, 126
  Political Regime, xi–xiv, 7–8, 108, 124–25
  Selected Aphorisms, xi, xii, 25–26
  Summary of Plato's Laws, xi, xii, xiii, xiv, 99–100
  Virtuous City, xi–xii, 108, 125
Alghazali, 177–82
  Incoherence of the Philosophers, 127, 182
amicability, 114
ancestry, distinguished, 79
Apollo, 110, 112, 134
approval of law, 145–46
Aristotle, *On the Soul*, 69
arts, 66–67, 170
ascetic, story of, 108–9, 130
assembly, places of, 170
associations, 15, 60–61
Averroës, 106–7, 124, 126–27, 177–82
  Book of the Decisive Treatise, xiv
  Incoherence of the Incoherence, 127
Avicenna, 99–100, 99n7, 102, 110
  On the Division of the Rational Sciences, 99

bad actions, 72
beauty, 41–42
being, realms of, 54–60
bestial people, 76
bodies
  kinds of, 8, 29
  possible, 56–58
body, honoring, 154
Bonadeo, Cecilia Martini, 125–26

calamities, 118
Campinini, Massimo, 126
  character, innate, 65–66
Cherni, Amor, 5–6
choice, 63
city
  ancient and new, 159
  contrary to virtuous city, 76
  democratic, 19–21, 86–88
  of domination, 19, 81–86
  errant, 19–20
  founding of, 117–18
  hedonistic, 77–78
  ignorant, 19, 76
  immoral, 19–20
  necessary, 19–20, 77
  of play and jesting, 85
  plutocratic, 77
  rankings of inhabitants, 72–73

CPSIA information can be obtained
at www.ICGtesting.com
Printed in the USA
LVHW100503120123
736863LV00004B/507

9 781501 746796